MW01032227

daily focus

daily

focus

Daily Readings for Integrating Faith in the Workplace

THOMAS G. ADDINGTON AND STEPHEN R. GRAVES

W PUBLISHING GROUP™

www.wpublishinggroup.com

A Division of Thomas Nelson, Inc.
www.ThomasNelson.com

Daily Focus

Copyright © 2001 Cornerstone Companies

Published by W Publishing Group, a division of Thomas Nelson, Inc., P.O. Box 141000, Nashville, Tennessee 37214, in association with the literary agency of Alive Communications, Inc., 7680 Goddard Street, Suite 200, Colorado Springs, Colorado 80920.

All rights reserved. No portion of this book may be reproduced, stored in a retrieval system, or transmitted in any form or by any means—electronic, mechanical, photocopy, recording, or any other—except for brief quotation in printed reviews, without the prior permission of the publisher.

Unless otherwise indicated, Scripture quotations used in this book are from the *Holy Bible, New International Version* (NIV). Copyright © 1973, 1978, 1984, International Bible Society. Used by permission of Zondervan Bible Publishers.

Other Scripture references are from:

The King James Version (KJV)

The *Holy Bible,* New Living Translation (NLT), copyright © 1996. Used by permission of Tyndale House Publishers, Inc., Wheaton, Illinois 60189.

ISBN 0-8499-1714-X

Printed in the United States of America

0 1 2 3 4 BVG 9 8 7 6 5 4 3 2 1

To five men who taught us how to love
and study the Scriptures:

Dr. Gordon Addington,

Dr. Bill Baker,

Dr. Howard Hendricks,

Dr. Walter C. Kaiser Jr.,

and Dr. James Shields

Contents

Acknowledgments

It takes a team effort to produce this type of book, and we are extremely grateful to the players who came together to make Daily Focus happen.

We have the privilege of working with many wonderful people, but every once in a while we come across someone who not only makes an impact on our lives, but also does a magnificent job and is fun to work with. Lois Flowers is one of those unusual people. She has contributed to this project in her usual manner—with great competence, clarity of thought, flexibility, and real insight, theological and otherwise. For us, Lois challenges the statement "nobody is irreplaceable"—we certainly couldn't have completed this book without her. And although we would prefer not to do any other books without her, her future priorities require her to leave Life@Work to focus on other endeavors. We will forever be asking Lois to help us with writing projects, but until the next one, we wish her the best as she concentrates on writing her own material and building her family.

Two other individuals played a significant role in the completion of this project. We have always humorously referred to Sean Womack as our younger, better-looking, and more gifted partner. He is our in-house renaissance man, a fact that he demonstrated once again as he shouldered a considerable portion of the writing load for this book. As devotionals often do, his writing provides a window into his heart and into his passion as a follower of Jesus. We appreciate him for applying his skills and his depth to this project.

Stephen Caldwell has tracked with us in the faith-at-work category since the very beginning of *The Life@Work Journal.* He was our founding editor and was an essential contributor and collaborator on this project. One of the things we appreciate about many of the people with whom we've been privileged to work is that they have a maturing, growing relationship with Jesus Christ. Stephen certainly falls in that category, and his devotionals evidence the thinking that accompanies that kind of spiritual progress.

We're extremely grateful to Rosemary Walch, Dianna Stockdale, Steve Griffith, Marcia Ford, Kristi Reimer, and Jennifer Stair for joining us at various stages of this project to help us concept, organize, transcribe, write, or edit the material in this book.

We also appreciate our agent, Chip MacGregor of Alive Communications, for his interest in and dedication to the world of work. We're thankful for the advice and help he gives us as we navigate the often-complicated process of taking a book project from conception to publication.

Finally, thanks to W Publishing Group representatives Mark Sweeney and Ami McConnell, two people with whom we are building a genuine friendship after eight projects. Ami, in particular, brings a real sense of focus to every project we've done with W—she has seen them all through to the finish line.

Introduction to Wisdom Literature

All the books in Scripture contain wisdom—that almost goes without saying. There are, however, certain books in the Bible that are identified specifically as wisdom literature, including Job, Psalms, Proverbs, Ecclesiastes, and Song of Solomon in the Old Testament and the Book of James in the New Testament.

You may be wondering why The Life@Work Co., an organization that seeks to help people integrate their faith and their work, would choose to produce a daily devotional book on the wisdom literature. That's a good question. Any book of the Bible could be used as the foundation for a set of devotionals, given the fact that all Scripture is inspired by God and "useful for teaching, rebuking, correcting and training in righteousness" (2 Timothy 3:16). But the wisdom literature is particularly helpful for people who work because it focuses specifically on us as individuals and on the normal everyday situations of life that confront us as we roll through our days, our weeks, and our months on the job. (Because the Song of Solomon does not have obvious application to the world of work, we chose to concentrate on the wisdom literature books that clearly do have relevance to the workplace.)

The historic and the prophetic books of the Old Testament deal corporately with God and the nation of Israel, while the wisdom literature is far more personal. In the prophetic and the historic books, the emphasis is on the collective group; in the wisdom books, the emphasis is on individuals and their personal relationships with God.

This personal emphasis in the wisdom books comes into focus in a number of ways. In Job, it comes in the form of questions. From every possible angle, the main character—who was really a philosopher at heart—examines the primary question, "If God is really in charge, why do righteous people suffer?" Job was in the middle of an intense, painful experience, and he was earnestly trying to figure out how to make sense of what was going on within the boundaries of a firm conviction that God is caring, just, and has the freedom to do whatever He chooses. Job's book explores these issues in the form of a philosophical dialogue.

Psalms takes a different approach. While Job primarily is a conversation between a man in distress and his friends, Psalms is a conversation between people and their God. The entire Book of Psalms is, in essence, a dialogue between the psalmists and the Lord. It consists of songs and prayers that emphasize the two-way nature of genuine biblical communication.

The Book of Proverbs contains short, succinct tidbits of wisdom that make us stop and think about the practical, daily issues of life. Most of the proverbs are written in a two-phrase format, and they represent statements that are generally true, but not guaranteed.

Ecclesiastes represents the teaching notes of a professor who is conducting a class for up-and-coming young professionals. This twelve-chapter book is a distilled set of realities. It focuses on the nagging inconsistencies of life that face young leaders as they attempt to live their lives in alignment with God and also as they attempt to make sense out of the things that go on around them that they wish they could control but really cannot.

James is the New Testament book most closely associated with the wisdom literature of the Old Testament. It most closely resembles the Book of Proverbs, although rather than using two-phrase snippets, James features short discourses on specific subjects such as the tongue, how a person handles riches and relates to people who don't have great wealth, and endurance.

So again, we return to the question of why we decided to camp on these five books for this volume of devotionals. The answer is simple. Charles Swindoll once said that the problem with life is that it is so daily. We certainly could revise that to say that the problem with work is that it is so daily. Work is very immediate. Issues must be resolved, decisions must be made, projects must be finished, strategies must be written, people must be dealt with, and the future must be predicted—and it all must be done *now*. On top of all that, we must face the fact that there are some things we can control and some things we can't, regardless of the level and span of our authority. So the question we are faced with countless times in a day and innumerable times in a career is, "What do we do about *this?*"

When we ask that question at work, we need a concrete answer. And, in a very practical sense, the wisdom literature points us in the right direction, no matter what the situation involves. Because the wisdom books are both personal and practical, they provide direction for our work lives that is easy to apply *today*.

A word of warning is in order. The answers that we receive from Scripture to the questions we ask in an everyday context aren't always what we expect, and some even may be disturbing. But if our goal is to think about life the way God thinks about life, then it is absolutely essential that we understand the wisdom literature. And a devotional approach is an effective way to increase our understanding, because the essence of devotional thought is that we pause, take a time-out, and reflect on what we're reading. When everything in our work world is so fast, a devotional time during the day needs to be slower and characterized by thinking, considering, and reflecting. All of this should, ultimately, bring our words, actions, and thought patterns into alignment with Jesus and His teaching.

We've tried to make the process as easy as possible. For each book of wisdom literature, we've included an expanded introduction and a series of devotionals. The devotionals are arranged in a daily format, one for each day of the workweek and one for the weekend. The books are arranged according to how they appear in the Bible, but feel free to read them in any order you find most helpful. If you read one each workday and one per weekend, you will complete the book in one year. We've also included a Vacation Appendix, a short guide to help you get the most out of an intentional time away from work.

It is our prayer that reading through these devotionals will give you a better understanding of Who God is, who you are, and how you can use your life at work to honor and glorify Him.

THOMAS G. ADDINGTON and STEPHEN R. GRAVES
Cofounders, The Life@Work Co.

1

Job

Responding When Life Gets Dark and Lonely

Introduction to Job

The Book of Job contains what could be thought of as the most complete psychoanalysis of any individual in the Bible. As Job sat in the ash heap, overwhelmed with pain unlike any of us have known, his friends put his life under the microscope and brutally examined its most intimate details. They left no stone unturned as they tried to figure out why Job was suffering so much.

It's as if Job went in for a counseling session, only to have four psychiatrists examine him relentlessly, for days at a time. And if that weren't bad enough, when they were done, they released their observations for the whole world to read. Talk about full disclosure. Job's was a life examined in the most heightened way.

Many scholars trace the Book of Job back to the patriarchal period of 1900 to 1700 B.C., which would make it the oldest book in the Bible. Some argue that Job is a mythical figure, but the fact that other biblical writers hold him up as a man of righteousness and endurance (Ezekiel 14:14, 20; James 5:11) indicates that he was a real person who actually experienced everything his book describes.

The popular theme of the Book of Job revolves around two probing questions: *Why do the righteous suffer?* and *How could a loving God allow good people to endure such suffering?* Another theme looks beyond such theological mysteries and focuses on our personal relationships with God. It asks the question, *What is the nature of our faith and how does it correspond to the nature of our relationships with God?*

Because James, the writer of the New Testament book by the same name, refers to Job as a man of perseverance, we can also include endurance as a theme of this book. Job endured a heavy load of difficult circumstances, and he emerged as someone with an incredible depth of personal faith and an intimate relationship with the God of the universe. He was tested and tried; yet his faith allowed him not only to survive, but also to thrive.

From a literary standpoint, Job is a poetic book that contains a rich variety of literary styles—adventure, romance, mystery, narrative, legal argument, and lament. Structurally, the book can be divided into three parts. The stage for the book is set in the first two chapters. We learn about Job, his life, his family, his business, and his faith, and we also meet God and Satan—two other primary characters in the book. The bulk of the book, chapters 4 through 37, is comprised of the dialogue between Job and his four friends, Eliphaz, Bildad, Zophar, and Elihu. Finally, in the last five chapters, God engages in a private conversation with Job. He humbles Job, and then He restores honor to his life and blesses him.

The Book of Job holds tremendous application to the world of work. Our jobs test our endurance as much as anything else in life. At work, we encounter circumstances we cannot control. We deal with people who might mean well but offer very little wisdom or guidance. We face perplexing situations that are beyond our ability to comprehend, much less to solve. We experience downturns and setbacks that rock us to the core. All of these prompt us to ask that quiet, secret nagging question that has been echoed down through the ages: *Why?*

We don't find many answers in the Book of Job. But we do find someone who experienced horrendous grief yet refused to relinquish his faith. By following Job's example, we, too, can have the strength to say, "Though he slay me, yet will I hope in him" (Job 13:15).

Multidimensional, Multiseasonal Success

In the land of Uz there lived a man whose name was Job. This man was blameless and upright; he feared God and shunned evil. He had seven sons and three daughters, and he owned seven thousand sheep, three thousand camels, five hundred yoke of oxen and five hundred donkeys, and had a large number of servants. He was the greatest man among all the people of the East. JOB 1:1–3

In our culture, it's easy to find a one-dimensional success story—a person who is exceptionally skilled in her career, an individual with a wonderful family, or someone who has a great deal of spiritual passion. It's a bit more difficult to find someone who has all three at once.

Job was just such a person. He aggressively and successfully engaged in commercial efforts, family priorities, and spiritual passion. He was a successful businessman, his family loved him, he was a well-respected member of his community, and he had an authentic, vibrant relationship with God. He scored well in all the key areas of life.

Some people prefer to concentrate on one area of life at a time. "I'm going to focus on my career now," one says. "Then when that's going great, I'll start spending more time at home." "I'm going to devote myself to my family right now," another says. "Then when the kids are grown, I'll get back into church."

Unfortunately, such trade-offs rarely work. There are ebbs and flows in various areas of life, to be sure. We may not be at the top of our game in every area simultaneously. But we need to make sure we're not scoring ourselves against just one dimension of life. We can't be satisfied to get top grades at work when our families are falling apart and our spiritual lives are failing. On the flip side, we can't settle for mediocrity at work just because our families are doing well and we're walking closely with God. As Job so aptly demonstrates, a successful life is an *integrated* life.

Which dimensions of success are you measuring, and how are you doing in each of them?

No Substitute for a Peer

In the land of Uz there lived a man whose name was Job. JOB 1:1

Few Bible characters provide a better example of how to live than Job. He successfully managed his family, spiritual life, and career. Realizing how little control he had over life, he simply tried to do it right today and let tomorrow take care of itself. He also struggled with deep questions about himself, God, his friends, and his life. Because of all this, we can easily identify with him. In short, he is a peer.

God never intended us to live life alone. He intended us to live in the context of relationships and, more specifically, in the context of relationships with people who are our peers. Only a peer can provide the iron-on-iron type of connection that the writer of Proverbs recommends so highly (Proverbs 27:17). If we want to change significant patterns in our hearts or lives, we can't do it by ourselves. We need truth and accountability. And peers provide the greatest access to both of those.

If you put a surgeon in a room with an entrepreneur and the pastor of a megachurch, all three might have seemingly valid excuses for not doing what they're supposed to be doing. They can safely play the trump card of "You don't really understand my world" to explain away their behavior. But put a surgeon in the room with another surgeon, and the excuses evaporate. One cannot tell the other, "You don't know what it's like to deal with life-and-death issues every day," because that's simply not true.

That's the value of a peer. We all have a penchant for excusing our actions and ourselves, and only a peer can bring to the table the sharp edge of accountability that says, "I understand your world, and there is no excuse for your behavior."

Do you have a peer who can proclaim truth in your life and hold you accountable for your attitudes and actions?

Preconditioned for Blessing

"Does Job fear God for nothing?" Satan replied. "Have you not put a hedge around him and his household and everything he has?" JOB 1:9–10

From start to finish, the story of Job uncovers the fact that, deep inside, most of us are preconditioned to think that every downturn has an upturn, that every stormy day is followed by weeks of sunshine, and that every flood eventually subsides.

In other words, we are preconditioned to believe that although we will experience difficulty from time to time, we *will* be blessed again. Much of our thinking is built around an "if/then" philosophy. *If I live a righteous life, then my life will be trouble-free. If I make right ethical decisions, I won't lose my job. If I tithe, I will recover from this financial disaster. If I have enough faith, I will be healed. If I pray hard enough, God will answer my prayer the way I want Him to.* And on it goes.

Unfortunately for us, the Book of Job blows the "if/then" theory right out of the water. The text reiterates several times that Job did nothing to deserve the trials that came his way. Job lived a righteous life, and a significant portion of his life was anything but trouble-free.

Although correct attitudes, habits, and actions often do result in blessing, such blessing is not guaranteed. The storm may never blow over. The sun may stay behind the clouds for a very long time.

This doesn't mean we shouldn't have hope in the midst of trouble. Nor does it mean that God doesn't hear our prayers or that we shouldn't trust Him. It simply means that we shouldn't expect to receive blessings from God in exchange for good living. He owes us nothing.

Satan expected Job to crumble in the face of adversity, because he thought the ancient patriarch was faithful only because God had placed a hedge of protection around him and everything he had. He quickly found out Job's faith was much deeper than that.

"Shall we accept good from God, and not trouble?" Job asked his wife (Job 2:10). It's a question we would all do well to ask ourselves when a stormy day comes or when we're in the middle of a downturn.

No Explanation

While he was still speaking, yet another messenger came and said, "Your sons and daughters were feasting and drinking wine at the oldest brother's house, when suddenly a mighty wind swept in from the desert and struck the four corners of the house. It collapsed on them and they are dead, and I am the only one who has escaped to tell you!" JOB 1:18–19

In a book called *Affliction*, Edith Schaeffer calls the first two chapters of Job "a look behind heaven's curtain." It's a fitting description. But did you ever stop to think about the fact that Job was not privy to such a peek? He had no clue his life was the key agenda item at a heavenly summit between God and Satan. He had no idea that God granted Satan permission to rock his life to its very foundation.

From Job's perspective, one day his life was going great; the next day, the bottom fell out of his world. He had no warning whatsoever.

Now fast-forward to the end of the book. After all was said and done, we're told, "The LORD blessed the latter part of Job's life more than the first" (Job 42:12). But we never find out *why* God allowed Satan to attack Job in the first place. Did He just feel like it? Did He want to prove a point to Satan? Was He trying to teach Job a lesson? We are given no explanation.

This is a rather difficult scenario for most of us to handle. Whenever something goes wrong, particularly at work, we automatically look for a discernable explanation. What did we do wrong? Is there something going on in the economy? Did someone make a bad business decision? Is a client upset with us? What's going on?

As we learn from Job's life, however, some things remain a mystery. Job never found out why he lost his first family, his business holdings, his home, and his health. And we may never find out why certain bad things happen to us.

Are you experiencing a trial in your life? Take comfort in knowing that God knows why. And even if that is the all comfort we have, that is comfort enough.

Stripped Down to Nothing

"Naked I came from my mother's womb, and naked I will depart." JOB 1:21

We are all layered with self-sufficiency. The Book of Job gives us an incredibly graphic picture of God removing those layers one by one.

First, Job lost all his business holdings. In one tragic event, all his livestock and employees were gone. Then he received news that all his sons and daughters had been killed. And some time later, he became so sick that all he could do was sit in an ash heap and scrape with a piece of broken pottery the painful sores that covered his body.

Many of us would have folded at that first blow. All we'd have to do is lose our financial security, and we'd find ourselves running away from God, kicking and screaming. But not Job. As layer after layer was stripped away, he remained faithful. He didn't turn away from God when he lost his wealth, his family, or his health. And as each layer was removed, it revealed more of the deep-rooted faith and inner strength that made Job the righteous man that he was.

Life has a way of stripping us down to our true selves. We can go into a trial displaying a certain depth of character, but only when we hit rock bottom do we find what we're really made of. And only when we're stripped down to nothing do we discover how little all that stuff we thought was so important is really worth.

Amazingly, Job was able to keep a godly perspective on his losses. After he learned all his children were dead, he fell to the ground and worshiped God, proclaiming, "Naked I came from my mother's womb, and naked I will depart" (Job 1:21).

What kind of character would be exposed if God were to strip away all the layers of your life?

Measuring Success Correctly

"The LORD gave and the LORD has taken away; may the name of the LORD be praised." JOB 1:21

It's often difficult to tell who is successful and who's not. Our culture holds up a standard of success that centers on money, prestige, and power, and it's easy for followers of Christ to get sucked into using that same standard. If someone has a good job, drives a trendy car, lives in an upscale neighborhood, and has a well-dressed wife and kids, he must be a success, right?

Not necessarily.

If success is built on anything besides a person's relationship with Jesus Christ, it will not hold up when life goes sour and one thing after another is taken from him.

At the beginning of the Book of Job, the main character was considered hugely successful. He easily could have based his success on the fact that he was a good husband and father, an expert businessman, a pillar of the community, or a wise philosopher. But then when all that was ripped away, he would have found himself wallowing in the depths of failure.

Instead, Job defined his success on his intimate relationship with God. This, and this alone, was what enabled him to utter those amazing words in Job 1:21: "The LORD gave, and the LORD has taken away; may the name of the LORD be praised."

Life has a way of giving things to us and taking things away from us—things that outside observers would list as the trappings of success. But developing a huge stock portfolio doesn't bring us joy. Working in the corner office doesn't bring peace. Having healthy families won't satisfy our deepest need for fulfillment.

It was Job's unwavering belief in God that made him successful—at the beginning of the book, in the midst of his suffering, and at the end when all God's blessings returned to him.

What is your standard of success? Perhaps it's time to reevaluate to see whether it's based on something temporary or Someone eternal.

Not without Permission (Part One)

The LORD said to Satan, "Very well, then, everything he has is in your hands, but on the man himself do not lay a finger." JOB 1:12

If God is not in control of everything—both the good and the bad—then we're in big trouble. Thankfully, the Book of Job helps us understand that the forces of evil are not running about in reckless abandon, wreaking whatever havoc they want on our world. That may seem like what is happening, but it's not so.

Satan is still under the thumb of a sovereign God. That is clear from the exchange the two had in the opening chapters of Job. Satan had to receive permission from God to unleash his onslaught of tests and temptations on Job, and he had to operate within the boundaries that God gave him. In round one, God said Satan could destroy all of Job's possessions, but he could not touch his health (Job 1:12). In round two, God allowed Satan to do whatever he wanted to Job physically, except take his life.

When terrible things happen around us—when mothers murder their children in cold blood, when ruthless dictators massacre thousands of innocent people, when a godly friend fights a losing battle with cancer, when we are overwhelmed by circumstances at work that we did not create—it's tempting to wonder if God is really in charge of the universe. While the rest of Scripture is clear that He is, it's still difficult to understand how a loving God could allow the forces of evil to pervade our world.

That's where faith comes in. We don't have all the answers. Until we get to heaven, we will never understand why bad things happen to good people. Satan and his demons definitely are at work among us, and their influence cannot be taken lightly. But rather than wring our hands and blame everything bad that happens to us on the devil, we can rest in the knowledge that God knows *exactly* what's going on down here on earth. He *is* in control. Satan may seem to win a skirmish every now and then—probably more frequently than we'd like—but his ultimate doom is sure.

When something bad happens to you, do you automatically chalk it up to spiritual warfare, or do you stop to acknowledge that God may have allowed it to happen for a very specific reason?

Not without Permission (Part Two)

The LORD said to Satan, "Very well, then, he is in your hands; but you must spare his life." JOB 2:6

It might seem like a radical idea, but knowing that Satan must get God's permission before he tempts or tries us in any way can be a great source of comfort to a believer who is in the midst of suffering. No matter what pain we bear, no matter how much we hurt, no matter how disappointed we are, no matter how misunderstood or maligned we are, absolutely nothing happens to us that does not first filter through God's sovereign hands.

This concept can be rather jarring because it might not fit into our narrow concept of Who God is. It may force us to reexamine our entire theological framework and come to grips with the fact that the God we thought we were worshiping is far more incomprehensible than we imagined. As He declares through the prophet Isaiah, "My thoughts *are* not your thoughts, neither *are* your ways my ways" (Isaiah 55:8 KJV).

The comfort lies in the understanding that God loves us and knows exactly what we can bear. As Paul wrote to the believers in Corinth, "No temptation has seized you except what is common to man. And God is faithful; he will not let you be tempted beyond what you can bear. But when you are tempted, he will also provide a way out so that you can stand up under it" (1 Corinthians 10:13).

The amazing thing is that when we rely on Jesus for our strength, we can bear a lot more than we think. And if we see the trial through to the end, hanging on to God and His promises for dear life, our lives are usually much fuller, our communion with Christ much sweeter, and our influence on others much greater because of it.

How might the knowledge that everything that happens to you first filters through God's hands affect how you view the trial you're experiencing today?

An Easy Target

[Job's] wife said to him, "Are you still holding on to your integrity? Curse God and die!" He replied, "You are talking like a foolish woman. Shall we accept good from God, and not trouble?" In all this, Job did not sin in what he said. JOB 2:9–10

Of all the people who surrounded Job as he endured his suffering, his wife is a prime target for condemnation. How could a loving wife give such terrible advice? Why wasn't she more supportive of her husband? How could a righteous man like Job have a shrew like her for a wife?

All those seem like perfectly reasonable questions, at least on the surface. But look a little closer. Put yourself in her shoes. Everything he experienced, save the physical suffering, she experienced, too. Those were her ten grown children who died, too. Those were her livestock that were destroyed, too. It was her livelihood that went down the drain, too. When Job lost everything, she lost everything, too.

On top of that, her husband, once known as the greatest man in the entire region, had been reduced to an oozing shell of a person. Her mate was in terrible pain, and she could do nothing to help him. Her security was gone. Her life was shattered.

It's easy to be hard on Mrs. Job, but be honest. How would you have responded to similar circumstances? It's entirely likely that your faith, like hers, might have caved under the weight of such tremendous suffering.

Thankfully, however, her husband's faith stood strong. "You are talking like a foolish woman," Job chided her. "Shall we accept good from God, and not trouble?" (Job 2:10). In the midst of his wife's despair and foolish advice, Job consistently modeled what it meant to follow God. Mrs. Job wouldn't have won an award for being a model wife, but even in the face of adversity, Job continued to exemplify what it meant to be the spiritual leader of his family.

Next time you're tempted to judge someone for her lack of support in a difficult situation, whether it be at home, at work, or somewhere else, put yourself in her shoes. Her response may be weak, immature, or even totally unbiblical. But rather than criticize her, pray that she will have a Job in her life who will come alongside her and model what it means to follow Jesus in the midst of suffering.

Quiet Time

Then [Job's friends] sat on the ground with him for seven days and seven nights. No one said a word to him, because they saw how great his suffering was. JOB 2:13

Mrs. Job is not the only one who gets a bad rap for an incorrect response to Job's suffering. Eliphaz the Temanite, Bildad the Shuhite, and Zophar the Naamathite score equally as bad on the supportiveness scale. But even though their theology was wrong, their approach was flawed, and their sensitivity levels left much to be desired, they actually had the right idea at the beginning.

As soon as they heard about Job's troubles, they left their homes and went at once to comfort him (Job 2:11). When they got there and realized how great his suffering was, Job's three friends simply sat by his side for seven days and seven nights. They didn't have to say a word; their very presence was a comfort to Job.

As they demonstrated when those seven days and nights were over, it is extremely difficult to sit quietly with someone who is going through a hard time. It is our nature to want to fix things, to attempt to encourage, to try to help. But spouting off Bible verses, pat spiritual answers, well-intentioned advice, or stories about the time when we faced something similar can be like pouring salt in a person's wounds. As hard as it may be, many times caring silence is the best thing we can give hurting friends or coworkers.

If your friend wants to talk, mentally tape your mouth shut and just listen. If he doesn't want to talk, just sit there with him and pray quietly. Don't plan out what you're going to say when he asks for your advice; just be quiet. You would hope for the same if you were in his shoes.

Handling the Inexplicable Hardships of Life
(Part One)

Then Job replied: "If only my anguish could be weighed and all my misery be placed on the scales!" JOB 6:1–2

Many times, life does not work out as we think it should. Situations and circumstances are complicated, confusing, and difficult. We sometimes feel as if we are main characters in a mystery that is never solved.

The Book of Job shows us that it is clearly OK to ask why such things happen. In fact, asking such questions is a part of what it means to be human. The psalmist asked why. The prophets asked why. The disciples asked why.

It's OK to ask why. But it's not OK to slam our fists down on the table and arrogantly proclaim, "I demand an answer."

Sometimes we do get answers, although they don't always fit into the boxes we have prepared. Remember the reaction Jesus' disciples had when they saw a man who had been born blind? "Who sinned, this man or his parents that he was born blind?" they asked Jesus (John 9:2). His response was totally unexpected: "Neither this man nor his parents sinned . . . but this happened so that the work of God might be displayed in his life" (v. 3).

It's easy to see how the work of God could be displayed in the blind man's life—all Jesus had to do was heal him (which He did). But what about the inexplicable hardships we face today? Jesus doesn't work in the cubicle next to us; He's not likely to appear in person and perform a miracle in front of everyone.

But that doesn't mean His work can't be displayed in our lives. It's displayed when we give God credit for the peace we're feeling as we walk through a valley. It's displayed when our coworkers ask how we can remain so calm when our world is falling apart and we tell them. It's displayed when, due to a tragedy or trial in our lives, we experience great spiritual growth.

We may never know why, but if we let Him, God will use the troubles and tests He allows in our lives to draw us closer to Him and make us more like Him. And shouldn't that be our ultimate goal?

Handling the Inexplicable Hardships of Life
(Part Two)

Then Job replied: "If only my anguish could be weighed and all my misery be placed on the scales!" JOB 6:1–2

It's comforting to know that God will use the hardships we experience to draw us closer to Him. But how do we deal with them on a day-to-day basis?

The first step is to verbalize our questions and concerns to God. Job did not mince words when he did this: "I loathe my very life; therefore I will give free rein to my complaint and speak out in the bitterness of my soul," he said. "I will say to God: Do not condemn me, but tell me what charges you have against me" (Job 10:1–2). Job didn't have the energy to sugarcoat it; he was in trouble, and he wanted to know why. His brutal honesty might make us a little uncomfortable, but he had nothing to hide.

Next, we have to acknowledge the difference between verbalizing a question and demanding an answer. God does not have to tell us why. He might, but He's not bound to. So we have to resign ourselves to depositing the mysteries and hardships of life on His shoulders, recognizing that we're not enduring life alone.

Finally, there comes a time when we just have to let it go. We've tried to fix the problem long enough. We've fretted about the cause long enough. We've agonized and pondered and cried long enough. Eventually, we just have to accept the fact that the hardship could very well be here to stay and learn to live with it.

Letting go doesn't mean our faith is weak or that we don't believe God can answer prayers. It simply means that it's time to devote our energies to something else. Our friends, family members, and coworkers may think we're giving up—that we're throwing in the towel—but as Job's life proves, it usually doesn't matter what other people think.

Are you experiencing a trial that doesn't seem to go away, no matter how many times you have asked God to take it from you? Then do what your faith walk with Jesus calls you to do; that is, to cast your burdens on Him, for He will never stop caring for you (1 Peter 5:7).

The Mediator

[God] is not a man like me that I might answer him, that we might confront each other in court. If only there were someone to arbitrate between us, to lay his hand upon us both, someone to remove God's rod from me, so that his terror would frighten me no more. Then I would speak up without fear of him, but as it now stands with me, I cannot. JOB 9:32–35

All of us are in a continual search for someone to mediate life for us—someone to connect us to God, to serve as a bridge between heaven and earth.

We desperately want to have a relationship with the transcendent God, but we know that there's no way we can live up to His standard. That leaves us in the very uncomfortable position of wanting something that, no matter how badly we yearn for it, we can never achieve. Job articulated this desire better than any other Old Testament writer. In this passage, he was crying out for that mediator—the Messiah, the Savior Who was first promised in Genesis 3:15 and finally arrived in Matthew 1:1.

The Book of Job, and these verses in particular, makes it abundantly clear how important the role of Jesus is in our lives. No mere man is strong enough or wise enough to serve as that bridge between heaven and earth. There is no person capable of satisfying the demands of God and the needs of man simultaneously—no person except Jesus, that is. When He died on the cross, He stepped into that unbridgeable gap. With one hand on your shoulder and one hand on God's shoulder, He brought together two parties who otherwise could have never met.

So what difference does this make in our lives at work? The answer is simple. Our coworkers, employees, and colleagues are all searching for the same divine connection we longed for before we met Christ. By our words and deeds, we have the wonderful opportunity to introduce them to the only One Who can bridge the gap for them.

Anybody Can Be a Consultant

Then Bildad the Shuhite replied: "When will you end these speeches? Be sensible, and then we can talk." JOB 18:1–2

It's amazing how quickly the fixer-uppers of the world show up when we find ourselves overcome with trauma, misery, and trouble. They love to play the role of the white knight, and the deeper the trouble, the more dramatic the rescue.

Although Job's friends provided some comfort at the beginning, they couldn't resist putting on their helper hats. They had lots of good theories about why he was suffering. They peered into the deepest recesses of his life, informing Job of all the things that were wrong and what he should do about them. As armchair quarterbacks who had never played the game, they gave him the best advice they could.

At best, however, Job's friends were simply consultants who did not realize that the most obvious explanation is not always the right one. They couldn't comprehend the depths of his experience and the pain of his life, and they certainly didn't understand the theology of what they were discussing.

Every one of his friends thought Job was suffering because he had done something wrong. That made their argument easy. It sounded so logical, so fair, so reasonable, and so spiritual. The only problem was that they were wrong. So instead of helping Job, they lambasted him with thirty-four chapters of baseless blabbing.

We won't adopt their theology, but we can learn a thing or two from Job's friends. Their example teaches us that we should be careful about floating out solutions and answers to people who are facing difficulty. To give conclusive advice without really understanding the situation is foolhardy, perhaps even dangerous. We also should be careful about buying into answers from others too quickly. If Job had begun to agree with his friends at any point along the way, he would have been in a heap of trouble by the time God showed up at the end of the book.

How quick are you to offer advice to people who are hurting? Are you a true friend or merely a consultant?

The Final Analysis

I know that my Redeemer lives, and that in the end he will stand upon the earth.
JOB 19:25

The discussion was well underway. Eliphaz, Bildad, and Zophar had all stated their case, some more than once. Job had tried no fewer than four times to get them to see things his way, to no avail.

It was in the middle of one of these pleas that Job utters one of the most wonderful statements of faith in all of Scripture—a statement that, perhaps more than anything else he said, revealed the depth of his faith and trust in Almighty God. His suffering had not let up; in fact, the misguided advice of his friends had probably made it worse. But he refused to budge from his core beliefs: "Oh that my words were recorded, that they were written on a scroll, that they were inscribed with an iron tool on lead, or engraved in rock forever! *I know that my Redeemer lives, and that in the end he will stand upon the earth*" (Job 19:23–25, emphasis added).

Job wanted to go on the record. He didn't want anyone to miss his meaning. Despite all the suffering he was going through, despite all the losses he had experienced, despite the fact that nobody understood him, Job's faith in God remained unshaken. His words were emphatic: "I *know* that my Redeemer lives, and that in the end he will stand upon the earth" (emphasis added). No uncertainty, no doubt, no wavering, no hesitation. "I *know* that my Redeemer lives!"

It's a statement that should boost our confidence and strengthen our faith when life throws us a curve, when the road gets rocky, and when the bottom falls out of our world. If Job could say it and mean it in the midst of all his suffering, surely we can say it when we experience financial hardship, when we come down with a terminal illness, when a friend or coworker betrays us, when a spouse leaves, when we get laid off, or when we can't figure out what's going on. "I *know* that my Redeemer lives!"

Holding on to Personal Integrity

[T]ill I die, I will not deny my integrity. JOB 27:5

There are many things in life over which we have absolutely no control. But we do have sole responsibility for our personal integrity.

Job was assaulted from many different directions. He was challenged throughout his suffering to throw in the towel. Perhaps the greatest assault came from his own home when his wife said, "Are you still holding on to your integrity? Curse God and die!" (Job 2:9).

Having integrity, or wholeness, meant that the faith Job professed early in the book—the faith that he displayed around his children at family reunions, the faith that he evidenced in town meetings, the faith he lived at work—was authentic. When stripped of every material thing that a man could have—his wealth, his job, his family, his possessions, his friends, even his spouse—Job remained whole on the inside. His faith was not simply a false storefront; it had substance.

Job lost it all, but he would not deny his integrity.

Sometimes it seems as if life would be much easier if we just took the advice of Job's wife and turned our backs on our faith. But if we did that, we would lose two things—our righteousness and our clear conscience. Denying our integrity, letting go of our righteousness, and living with a guilty conscience might give some temporary relief, but it really is only temporary. It's only an illusion.

Over the course of a career, no matter where we work, there are going to be times when it will be more comfortable to shade the truth, to tell a lie, or to leave a perception that we know is untrue even though we haven't actually verbalized something untrue. We might even get rewarded for that. But Job makes it clear that integrity is worth hanging on to for dear life, and that after all is said and done, the gift of a clear conscience is worth whatever pain we have to go through in order to sleep well at night.

How is your integrity? Have you been tempted to give in to practices that only leave you with a guilty conscience? Ask God to give you the strength to resist those temptations and maintain your integrity in all circumstances.

Learning to Hear God

God's voice thunders in marvelous ways. JOB 37:5

It's never too early or too late to learn the skill and discipline of hearing the whisper of God's voice. All of life cannot come down to "rock-paper-scissors" decision-making. That's the game children play when they find themselves unable to make a choice about something. And although few adults would admit to practicing that decision-making method, we have our own grown-up version that includes budgets, calendars, and informal polls.

As men and women of faith in the marketplace, however, we must learn to look for, identify clearly, and follow God's direction. We must look for His fingerprints in our lives. If Job had followed the guidance of his friends or the whispers of his circumstances, he would have been in big trouble. He would have missed the intimate communion with God that happens at the end of the book, and he would have made a wrong analysis.

Incorrect analysis will always deliver incorrect prescription. Had Job listened to his friends when they said he was suffering because of his own sin, he would have been trying to fix a problem that did not exist. Many people get carried away with attributing messages to God that did not originate with Him. In other words, they confidently say, "God told me to do this" or "God said this about you," when what they're really doing is putting their own words in His mouth. We must be careful to avoid this dangerous tendency. However, when we can sort out the voices around us, the voices within us, and the noises that are continually clattering about in our culture and instead detect the voice of God, we are preparing ourselves for a life of adventure and deep fulfillment.

Much of life comes down to making decisions. The rest of life comes down to standing strong on the decisions we've already made or being open to adjusting those decisions. Being able to hear God's voice and know His thoughts on those matters is critical.

Job was able to do that. Are you?

The Greatness of God (Part One)

Where were you when I laid the earth's foundation? JOB 38:4

God was the silent, unseen witness at the lengthy consulting session between Job and his friends. He heard Eliphaz proclaim, "[D]o not despise the discipline of the Almighty" (Job 5:17). He listened as Bildad announced, "Surely God does not reject a blameless man or strengthen the hands of evildoers" (Job 8:20). He stood by as Elihu declared, "Oh, that Job might be tested to the utmost for answering like a wicked man! To his sin he adds rebellion; scornfully he claps his hands among us and multiplies his words against God" (Job 34:36–37). He watched as, time and time again, Job disputed their arguments and stated his own case.

When He'd had enough of the friends' misguided theology, God called Job to attention: "Brace yourself like a man; I will question you; and you shall answer me" (Job 38:3). He then proceeded to give Job one of the most amazing illustrations of His omniscience, omnipresence, and omnipotence ever recorded. "Where were you when I laid the earth's foundation?" (v. 4). "Have you ever given orders to the morning, or shown the dawn its place?" (v. 12) "Have you journeyed to the springs of the sea or walked in the recesses of the deep? Have the gates of death been shown to you?" (vv. 16–17). "Do you send the lightning bolts on their way?" (v. 35). "Do you give the horse his strength or clothe his neck with a flowing mane?" (39:19). "Does the eagle soar at your command and build his nest on high?" (v. 27). "Who has a claim against me that I must pay?" (41:11).

As God barraged Job with these penetrating questions, His message was clear: "Job, who do you think you are?" And it didn't take Job long to come up with a response: "I am unworthy—how can I reply to you? I put my hand over my mouth. I spoke once, but I have no answer—twice, but I will say no more" (40:4–5).

Face to face with God's greatness, Job stopped trying to understand his situation. He responded in the only way possible—with humility and repentance. "My ears had heard of you but now my eyes have seen you," he said. "Therefore I despise myself and repent in dust and ashes" (42:5–6).

How do you respond when you're confronted with God's greatness?

The Greatness of God (Part Two)

Then Job answered the LORD: "I am unworthy—how can I reply to you?" JOB 40:3–4

Job may have considered himself to be a righteous man, especially when he measured himself against the other people in his world. But that approach is fundamentally flawed—it's like comparing one crooked stick to an even more crooked stick.

Unfortunately, it's very easy to practice a crooked-stick theology at work. We're surrounded by people who seem more righteous or less righteous than we are. We deal with people every day who have more or less power, intelligence, influence, or wealth than we do. When we compare ourselves to people who have less than we do, we feel better about ourselves. And when we compare ourselves to those who are better than we are, we feel worse about ourselves. It's a natural response. The only problem is that in the grand scheme of things, such comparisons are meaningless.

God is the only true measuring stick. If we measure ourselves against any of the questions God asked Job, we always come out looking very small. If we measure anyone else—no matter how powerful, intelligent, or influential he or she may be—against the questions God asked Job, that person will come out looking very insignificant, too.

It was only when Job was finally confronted with the greatness of God that he realized how inadequate he actually was. The same applies to us today. If we continually compare ourselves to people who are a little bit worse than we are, we will never experience the greatness of God. It's only when we turn our attention away from others and focus on God that we can truly understand how great our God really is.

Have you been comparing your righteousness to others? If so, delve into Scripture passages that proclaim His glory (Job 38–42, Isaiah 6, among others) to remind yourself of God's greatness.

The Finish Line

The LORD blessed the latter part of Job's life more than the first. JOB 42:12

God intends for us to enjoy more blessings from Him at the end of our lives than at the beginning.

That might sound like a rather brash statement, but that is only if you have preconceived notions of what those blessings should be. We're not saying that our lives will get easier or that we'll have larger bank accounts, bigger families, and fancier homes when we're older. What we are saying is that the longer we walk with Christ, the more spiritual blessings we will receive. At the finish line of life, we should find that our relationships with Jesus are significantly deeper, fuller, and more mature than they were when we first believed.

Many of the spiritual blessings we accumulate as we grow older come in the form of memories of His goodness to us. The memories of times when He showed up in our lives—when we had a financial need, when we were facing a difficult situation at work, or when we just needed a touch of His peace—are worth more than all the stock options in the world. The longer we walk with Christ, the more apt we are to recognize these blessings for what they really are—riches beyond compare.

It's easy to look at Job's story and conclude that life always has a happy ending. It certainly did in Job's case—his livestock holdings doubled, his wife had ten more children (the same number he had before), and he lived for 140 more years—long enough to enjoy several more generations of grandchildren. But it's critical that we don't attach spiritual performance formulas to this discussion. The text is clear. It doesn't say that God blessed Job because he was righteous or because he endured; rather, He blessed him out of His own sovereign plan.

If we start thinking that Job's behavior or attitude had anything to do with the blessings he received in the second half of his life, then we cycle all the way back to the first chapter of the book, where Satan claims that the only reason Job walked with God was that He had given him so much. If we do that, we miss the whole point of the book. Our walks with Jesus are not based on our performance. We don't practice horizontal-first Christianity. Rather, we must remember that it's our vertical relationships with God that results in horizontal expression of our faith.

2

Psalms

Heartfelt Conversations with a Loving God

Introduction to the Psalms

Theologian Harry A. Ironside once addressed his Chicago congregation with a word of caution about the Book of Psalms. To Jews and followers of Jesus, he acknowledged, it is likely that "no portion of Holy Scripture" has carried more meaning throughout the centuries than this book of praise and worship. But Ironside pointed out that the Psalter must be kept in the proper context; we should note that the psalms were written before "this present dispensation of the grace of God."[1] In other words, they were written pre-Jesus. So, for instance, when David prays, "Do not . . . take your Holy Spirit from me" (Psalm 51:11), the informed disciple of Christ understands that the Holy Spirit, thanks to redemption through Christ, now abides in us forever.[2]

Such caveats aside, there is no disputing the impact and the importance of the psalms on those who seek to worship and walk with God. As Ironside put it, "We find a great deal that is precious and a great deal that is wonderfully helpful to feed the soul and uplift the spirit" in the Book of Psalms.[3]

This gripping collection of Hebrew poetry connects man to God and God to man on a variety of levels because it is both so divine and so human. The messages in the verses are universal in their portrayal of human need and divine response. "There are times when we cannot repress the wish to know more of the circumstances which called them forth, of the feelings, the views, the hopes, with which they were written," writes one Bible commentator. "But if we could do this, if the picture of those circumstances were clear and well defined, we might lose more than we should gain. For the very excellence of the Psalms is their universality. . . . Hence they express the sorrows, the joys, the aspirations, the struggles, the victories, not of one man, but of all."[4]

There are 150 psalms divided into five books [Psalm 1–41; 42–72; 73–89; 90–106; 107–150], which many believe is based on the pattern found in the Pentateuch. While each ends with an appropriate doxology, the fact that Psalm 1–2 serve as an opening and Psalm 146–150 serve as a conclusion indicate that the five books should be thought of as a whole unit.

Scholars have identified as many as twelve classifications of psalms, although some boil it down to as few as five:

1. distress of an individual who asks to be saved from a predicament,

2. thanks for redemption from a predicament,

3. distress/calamity involving the community as a whole,

4. communal psalms of thanksgiving, and

5. hymns that praise God, a king, Zion, or the law.[5]

In addition to David (who wrote as many as seventy-three of them), the psalmists include David's singers (the sons of Korah, Asaph, and Ethan), Solomon, and Moses. Forty-nine of the psalms are anonymous.

The Psalter is not considered a prophetic book, yet it contains several prophetic passages. Psalm 22 foretells the pain and suffering Jesus would endure on the cross; it is the first part of verse 1—"My God, my God, why have you forsaken me?"— that Christ quotes as He nears the end of His life on earth (Matthew 27:46). Other prophetic psalms include Psalm 110 (Christ as a perpetual Priest), Psalm 16 (Christ's resurrection), and Psalm 72 (the coming millennial kingdom). Jesus Himself, according to Luke 24:44, notes that the prophecies written about Him in "the Law of Moses, the Prophets and the Psalms" would be fulfilled. So while Ironside is correct that the psalms were written without a full understanding of grace, it is clear that they were written in anticipation of a coming new covenant between God and mankind.

This leaves us back where we started—with a deep appreciation for the multiple levels upon which the psalms satisfy the needs of the human condition. By divine appointment, they are as important to modern readers as they were to their ancient writers. They touch us—our pain and our joys—in deep and personal ways, because they assist in our communication with God. Such an opportunity should inspire us to break out the trumpets, harps, tambourines, stringed instruments, woodwinds, and cymbals. It should inspire us, as the psalmist was inspired, to give an unmistakable display of thanks, or, as he put it in the book's conclusion, to "let everything that has breath praise the LORD. Praise the LORD." (Psalm 150:6).

Where Are You Taking God?

Blessed is the man who does not walk in the counsel of the wicked or stand in the way of sinners or sit in the seat of mockers. PSALM 1:1

A friend met regularly for a Bible study with a small group of high-school boys, some of whom were more committed than others to their walks with Christ. Before they met one week, my friend learned that some of his protégés had become regular participants in the high-school party scene.

As it happened, that week's discussion was on the Holy Spirit. Rather than confront the boys directly, my friend asked a series of leading questions. Who is the Holy Spirit? *One-third of the Trinity. He is God.* And if you have given your life to Christ, what role does the Holy Spirit play? *He is there to guide us.* Where is He? *Well, He lives in our hearts.* So wherever you go, the Holy Spirit is there with you? *Yes.* OK, so if the Holy Spirit is God living within your heart and He goes wherever you go, here's the real question: Where have you been taking Him lately?

The Book of Psalms opens by contrasting the righteous and the wicked. The psalmist describes a righteous person as someone who doesn't follow the lead of people who mock God by living in habitual sin and someone who delights in and meditates on God's laws.

Because we live in a world filled with sin, most of us end up working with or around people who don't know Jesus. Not only are they sinners—as we are—but also they sin without regret or remorse. That's just how they live. And they see no reason that we shouldn't join them. Why not cut corners? Why not gossip? Why not enjoy a one-night stand while on a business trip?

Just before Jesus was arrested, He went off to pray. He took Peter, James, and John with Him and instructed them to stand, watch, and pray. He came back three times, each time finding them asleep. And what did He say to them? "Watch and pray so that you will not fall into temptation" (Mark 14:38).

It's when we let our guards down, neglecting prayer and God's Word, that we drift into the "counsel of the wicked." So the question is, Where have you been taking the Holy Spirit lately?

Sleep Tight

I lie down and sleep; I wake again, because the LORD sustains me. PSALM 3:5

There are several reasons that a person might not be able to sleep. Some people have trouble breathing, so their bodies instinctively wake up throughout the night. Or perhaps the muscles in their legs twitch or another physical problem interrupts their sleep. In any event, such sleep disorders keep many people from experiencing genuine rest even though they most likely never recall waking up during the night.

Before sending a patient to a sleep disorder center for tests, however, most doctors first explore another possible cause of the problem: stress. How are things at work? How are things at home? Very often, we have so much going on in our lives that our minds can't totally turn everything off at night. Or maybe we are regularly indulging in sin, and the guilt tugs the sheets right off our backs, leaving us cold and awake.

In 2 Samuel 15–18, we find Absalom, the son of King David, conspiring to take charge of the kingdom. He plots and schemes for four years, deceiving the people to win their trust so he can overthrow his father. Finally, David has to flee his palace, fearing for his life.

Imagine the stress that David was experiencing. His own son, whom he loved, had turned against him and wanted to kill him. David's power base had evaporated. And yet he said, "I will not fear the tens of thousands drawn up against me on every side" (Psalm 3:6).

How could David say that? Because he was in a no-lose situation. He trusted that the Lord would sustain him. He trusted Him so much that he slept through the night.

Can you turn off the world around you—or more accurately, can you turn the world around you over to God? Can you trust in Him so completely that even when the world seems to be crashing down around you, you can sleep peacefully through the night, wrapped tightly in the Comforter Who sustains you?

Putting Your Anger to Sleep

In your anger do not sin; when you are on your beds, search your hearts and be silent. PSALM 4:4

What is it that really ticks you off?

Maybe a coworker speaks with a condescending and arrogant tone of voice. Maybe a team member always arrives five minutes late for meetings and is never prepared. Maybe a subordinate consistently underperforms, leaving you to pick up the pieces. Maybe your boss preaches ethics and values at staff meetings and sleeps with the wife of his best friend on the weekends. Maybe a competitor is lying about the quality of her products to squeeze you out of the market. Maybe the guy across the hall is an atheist who mocks God at every opportunity.

Anger, by itself, isn't sinful. In fact, righteous anger is part of God's nature. We often read about God's becoming angry with His people—and acting on that anger. Jesus, God in human form, was consumed with zeal for His house, and it showed when, in righteous anger, He chased the moneychangers out of the temple.

Just because you accept Christ doesn't mean you lose your emotions. And, unlike God, we aren't perfect, and therefore we don't always manage emotions such as anger and jealousy in a just and godly manner. So how are you managing those emotions? How do you deal with your anger when, as it inevitably will, it comes over you?

David, in Psalm 4:4, says, in effect, to cool your jets. "When you are on your beds, search your hearts and be silent." The apostle Paul, in his letter to the Ephesians, put it this way: "Do not let the sun go down while you are still angry, and do not give the devil a foothold" (Ephesians 4:26–27).

The picture here is of someone who doesn't act rashly and doesn't allow anger to control his or her actions. In other words, you should turn the issue over to God. "Offer right sacrifices and trust in the LORD" (Psalm 4:5).

Once you have done that, then you can act, all the while asking yourself, *Are my actions honoring God?* If they aren't, then whom are they honoring—and what are you going to do about it?

Divine Nyquil

Many are asking, "Who can show us any good?" Let the light of your face shine upon us, O LORD. You have filled my heart with greater joy than when their grain and new wine abound. I will lie down and sleep in peace, for you alone, O LORD, make me dwell in safety. PSALM 4:6–8

David was in trouble. We don't exactly know what his problem was—maybe it was personal, maybe it was work-related, or maybe it was relational. We only know that the trouble had gotten so bad that other people in his life were asking, "Where's the good?"

That was not, however, a question that David was asking—at least not at this point in his life. He could say, with total honesty, that God had filled his heart with greater joy than when "grain and new wine abound." In other words, God had given him greater joy in the bad times than he had experienced when times were good.

If David's words don't convince you, his sleeping habits should. Instead of pacing the floor, tossing fitfully, or lying awake staring at the ceiling during his time of crisis, David slept like a baby. Why? Because he understood that in God, he dwelled in safety.

Scripture makes it clear that each day will carry its own dose of trouble (Matthew 6:34). But sandwiched between those trouble-filled days, we can sleep in peace, knowing that God is protecting us. It *is* possible to be surrounded by chaos, pressure, and trauma and still enjoy a good night's rest.

How do you sleep at night? Do you spend your nighttime hours stewing over the previous day's failures and worrying about the next day's challenges? Break the pattern tonight. What's done is done, and tomorrow's troubles will come whether you worry about them or not. Sleep in peace.

Turning off the Tears

All night long I flood my bed with weeping and drench my couch with tears.
PSALM 6:6

What does it mean to live in complete dependence upon God? It often seems that such dependence only follows brokenness. Most followers of Jesus will tell you that there has been a time, or there have been times, when they felt totally broken—void of the ability to do anything further on their own. Perhaps you have been there. Perhaps you are there right now. Perhaps your circumstances or personal sins are so overwhelming that you can't even pretend to make another move on your own. You are totally broken, totally dependent upon God.

What does that mean?

The totally broken person is totally humble. Her first request to God isn't for help; it's for mercy. "O LORD, do not rebuke me in your anger or discipline me in your wrath. Be merciful to me, LORD, for I am faint" (Psalm 6:1–2). She knows she doesn't deserve the help she is requesting. There is absolutely zero sense of entitlement.

From this humbleness, the totally broken person has a clear view of her condition. Her bones are in "agony" (v. 2); her soul is in "anguish" (v. 3). She is "worn out" (v. 6) and "weak with sorrow" (v. 7).

But in this humbleness, the totally broken person can embrace the hope that is found only in a loving God. In prayer and confession, the totally broken person gives the circumstances and the sin to the Lord and immediately finds comfort. Evil loses its grip. Depression dissipates. Tears dry up. Strength and power, gifts from God, return. "Away from me, all you who do evil, for the LORD has heard my weeping. The LORD has heard my cry for mercy; the LORD accepts my prayer" (vv. 8–9).

In your lowest moments, how long do you wallow in self-pity, waiting for an entitlement before you finally admit your brokenness and turn it over to God?

Opening Your Closet to God

Judge me, O LORD, according to my righteousness, according to my integrity, O Most High. PSALM 7:8

It should go without saying that God, being God, knows everything there is to know about us. Some might argue that He doesn't care, but they would be wrong. God not only knows every detail about our lives, but He is also intensely interested in things we can't even see. So when we do something wrong, He knows. When we think something inappropriate, He knows. In fact, He knows before it happens.

Remember when Moses is about to turn over the leadership reins to Joshua? Before the people of Israel cross the Jordan River to take possession of the Promised Land—which had to be an exciting and joyful time for that wandering nation— God instructs Moses to write a poem forecasting the sins of the people. "I know what they are disposed to do, even before I bring them into the land I promised them on oath" (Deuteronomy 31:21).

So God knows.

But how many of us are willing to invite God to take a detailed look at our actions and our motives and our thoughts? It's a sobering idea to ask Him to judge us. David does this in his cry for justice (Psalm 7:8), apparently in a Joblike attempt to defend his honor against the slander of a Benjamite named Cush. Whatever it is that David was accused of doing, he proclaims his innocence in the strongest of terms—by laying the matter before God.

Take a quick mental inventory of your relationships at work. Think about your performance on the job. Consider your decisions, your actions, and your nonactions. Like David, you no doubt experience times when you feel you need to fall on your knees and seek forgiveness.

So before you claim innocence in a dispute, search yourself. If you ask God to judge you according to your righteousness and your integrity, He surely will. Are you prepared for that?

Crime Doesn't Pay

He who is pregnant with evil and conceives trouble gives birth to disillusionment. PSALM 7:14

There is a common perception that getting ahead in the marketplace often requires compromise of character. Fudge the numbers. Shade the truth. Hide the facts. Ethics give way to self-interest or corporate interests—or both. And reality tells us that such methods often produce results: a promotion, a deal with a new client, or a windfall of opportunity for the company.

The Scriptures teach that there is a price to pay for such shortcuts, of course—if not here, then in eternity. David speaks of it in Psalm 7 when he says, "He who digs a hole and scoops it out falls into the pit he has made. The trouble he causes recoils on himself; his violence comes down on his own head" (vv. 15–16). That's a pretty clear picture of the old expression "What goes around, comes around."

The scary thing, though, is that it isn't only nonbelievers who walk into this trap. Followers of Jesus are no strangers to temptation. And while Jesus paid the ultimate price for our sins, we know we must answer for our actions. Furthermore, we know that when we are walking in sin, we are walking out of fellowship with Christ. That's why Jesus has us pray that God would "lead us not into temptation." He wants us to avoid the trap.

David describes the trap in Psalm 7:14. First, you are "pregnant with evil" (ungodly desires); second, you "conceive trouble" (you act on those desires in a sinful way); and third, you give "birth to disillusionment" (you die to your sins). James uses the same analogy in James 1:13–15, explaining that although temptations are inevitable, they are not from God and can be resisted with God's help.

Have you been resisting temptation lately? Your effectiveness as a steward of all God has given you depends on how well you manage to stay out of the trap.

Are You Standing in Awe?

What is man that you are mindful of him? PSALM 8:4

Unlike some places in Scripture (Psalm 144:3, Job 7:17; 25:6), there isn't a hint of pessimism or sarcasm when David asks, "What is man that you are mindful of him?" Instead, this question is a heartfelt expression of David's thanks for all that God is and for the favor God has bestowed on man.

You can just see David staring up at a black-velvet sky filled with glowing stars and a picturesque moon, the sounds of the desert night singing in the background as he shouts into the air, "O LORD, our Lord, how majestic is your name in all the earth!" (Psalm 8:1, 9). David is standing in awe of his God, as well he should.

David knew that God gave him the gifts to be a shepherd, a soldier, a musician, and a king, just as we should know that God gave us the gifts to be a plumber or an accountant or a CEO or a painter or whatever. Without God, there is no man. Without God's blessing, not one single piece of technology, ancient or modern, would exist.

Reading Psalm 8 should be a daily requirement, especially during those times when we are feeling really good about life. When life is good—when our families are happy, when our careers are doing well, when our cups overflow—we tend to do one of two things, and this song of worship is appropriate for either of them. Sometimes we allow arrogance and human pride to seep into our minds, and we need this psalm to remind us of our place in the universe. At other times, our hearts are truly grateful to the Lord, and we can read this psalm as an expression of that gratitude.

How often do you look around at God's creation and genuinely marvel at the fact that He created the moon and the stars and all that is in the universe? How frequently do you consider the complexity of His grand design and His sense of order amid the chaos? And how often do you silently whisper the question "What is man that you are mindful of him?" into the gentle night breeze? Do it right now. Not later. Right now.

Forget You!

You have blotted out their name for ever and ever . . . even the memory of them has perished. PSALM 9:5–6

Think for a moment about everything you need to accomplish today. How long is your to-do list? What commitments do you have? What tasks are critical to your work world? Who is depending on you to keep the work moving, to make the deals happen?

Now roll it out for the week. What has to be done? What about for the next two weeks? For the next month?

Overwhelmed yet?

Everything on your list is urgent. It all needs to be done today. This week. This month.

Clearly, God gives us work to do, but work is about more than merely crossing items off a to-do list; it's about honoring God. We honor God with the quality of our work, as defined by God and not by man, rather than the quantity of our work. We honor God with our skill, with our productivity, with our attitude, and with our creativity. We honor God when we work for Him.

Those who don't work for God work against Him. And those who work against God won't leave much of a legacy. They might be remembered for a few days, a few years, perhaps even decades or centuries. But in eternity, their names are "blotted out . . . for ever and ever" and "the memory of them has perished."

How will your work be remembered in heaven?

Do You Know Me?

Those who know your name will trust in you, for you, LORD, have never for-saken those who seek you. PSALM 9:10

Surveys consistently indicate that more than 90 percent of the people in the United States say they believe in God. But how many trust God? How many know God? How many seek God?

Perhaps because God is more complex than any of us can understand, people seem to take for granted the simplicity of God's plan for our lives. They're like the people who shy away from new technology because they don't understand it or who reject innovative business ideas or management techniques because they can't fully grasp how they will work.

What if you rejected the idea of refrigeration because you didn't understand electricity? Or computers because you couldn't comprehend the microchip? Or the automobile because you were overwhelmed by the design of an engine?

Once people embrace a great idea, however, they long for more of what they've found. They seek to learn more about it. And the more they learn, the more they come to trust the idea—if it really works. And if it really works, the idea takes them places they never could have gone on their own.

This is God's simple promise for us. If we seek Him, He won't forsake us. If we get to know Him, we will trust Him. The more we show that we trust Him, the more we show that we know Him.

Do your actions show a genuine trust in God? Do you really know Him—not in the superficial sense professed by the masses, but with an intense intimacy? If you don't know Him, or if you long to know Him more intimately, what will you do today to seek such a relationship?

Alert the Media

Proclaim among the nations what he has done. PSALM 9:11

Human beings are no strangers to proclamations. It's one of the things that we've done best through the ages and something we seem to have perfected in the last century.

Heads of state—especially kings and would-be kings—have a long history of proclaiming their authority and their directives. Governing bodies, from city councils to Congress, proclaim certain days as special or certain citizens as worthy of honor. Associations honor their members. The military honors its heroes. And business honors its products and services.

Marketing and advertising have been developed into an art form. Companies proclaim both the practical and superficial advantages of their products. Individuals have learned to market their personal skills and talents. John Doe can be as much of a brand as Coca-Cola is.

The Scriptures don't issue a ban on advertisements or promotions, but they remind us, over and over, that nothing is more worthy of praise than the God Who has chosen to redeem a fallen world. Talk about a message that deserves a billboard on the busiest highway!

Psalm 9 opens with a phrase common in the Psalter: "I will praise you." Praise, as it is described in the psalms, was rarely a private display of adoration. Praise didn't just involve a man on his knees and God in His heaven. It often took place at the Temple during a very public celebration.

Are you proclaiming God's name in His Temple? Are you proclaiming His name to the assemblies of your life? Are you creatively, compassionately, and respectfully telling others what God has done in your life? Or do you think praise is something just between you and God?

Did You See That, God?

Why, O LORD, do you stand far off? Why do you hide yourself in times of trouble?
PSALM 10:1

For such a personal God, a God who allows us into an intimate relationship with Him, God sometimes can seem extremely distant.

In describing the wicked man, David tells us, "His ways are always prosperous" (Psalm 10:5), which hardly seems fair. But reality tells us that his assertion is valid. We look around at wicked people, and we see that they prosper. They make money. They have power and control and influence. They climb to positions of authority. They fill their lives with pleasures.

This leaves many people to draw one of two conclusions: Either God doesn't care about what happens in the lives of human beings, or God really isn't there. After all, they reason, how could a loving God allow all of this evil?

And yet, He does.

In setting up this portrait of wickedness, David openly wondered why God would allow the wicked to prosper. It's a question he asks many times in Scripture. It's a question others ask in Scripture as well. That's because evil has had a foothold on humanity since the Fall.

But remember, David was crying out for salvation. We live with the promise of salvation. We are blessed to live in the post-Christ era, a time when God's plan for redemption has been unveiled. We should have a greater sense of what eternity will look like, both for believers in Jesus and for the wicked. We know God isn't hiding, that He isn't ignoring the wicked, that He will deliver on David's pleas for relief and justice.

The question, then, is this: What are we doing with that knowledge?

Testing for Wickedness

Why does the wicked man revile God? Why does he say to himself, "He won't call me to account"? PSALM 10:13

It's always important to know the competition. If you know your enemies, you know when to avoid them, when to engage them, and how to defeat them. And, perhaps of equal importance, if you know your enemies, you know how not to become one of them.

In Psalm 10, David paints a vivid portrait of wickedness as it manifests itself in mankind. Here's what it shows: The wicked are arrogant (v. 2). The wicked prey on the weak (v. 2). The wicked devise evil schemes (v. 2, vv. 8–9). The wicked are boastful about the things they desire (v. 3). The wicked reward greed (v. 3). The wicked have too much pride to acknowledge God for Who He is (v. 4). The wicked believe bad things will never happen to them (v. 6). The wicked curse people, lie to people, and threaten people (v. 7). And the wicked ignore God's laws (v. 5) and mock God's sovereignty (v. 11).

Does that sound like the man in the office next to yours? Does it describe the woman who works for a competitor? Does it paint a picture of the world around you? Does it reveal the person you see each time you look in a mirror?

Because we live in a fallen world, we can't totally avoid wickedness. We can work hard to stay away from it, as well we should. But in a fallen world, wickedness will find us. Will you be ready? How are you dealing with the wickedness that surrounds you? And how are you working to make sure you don't succumb to it?

Are You Listening?

*You hear, O LORD, the desire of the afflicted; you encourage them, and you lis-
ten to their cry.* PSALM 10:17

Because the world is filled with wickedness, it also is filled with the afflicted.
People are hurting. People are poor, financially and in spirit. As long as there
are people who abuse, there will be people who suffer abuse.

Often this suffering is obvious. We see orphaned children in Romania. We see
the hungry in Africa. We see families displaced from their homes by disease or natural disaster. We see mothers and fathers crying in the courthouse because the person who murdered their child was set free on a technicality. We only need to read
the newspaper or watch the evening newscast to see obvious suffering.

But what about the suffering that is all around us, suffering that might be hard
to spot or, if we recognize it, easy to avoid? Think about the number of people you
come in contact with on a daily basis. How many of them are in pain? In the busyness of your day, how eager are you to reach out to them? Are you willing to stop
what you're doing—trusting that God will be there for you so that you can be there
for someone else?

God's example is clear: He listens to the cry of the afflicted, and He encourages
them. Sometimes He provides practical and noticeable relief. At other times, He
says, as He told Paul, "My grace is sufficient for you" (2 Corinthians 12:9). If we
are to follow His example, then we have no excuse for turning away from people
who need us. Even if we can't directly solve their problems, we can listen, and we
can encourage. And if they see Christ in that listening and in that encouragement,
then perhaps they will embrace His grace.

Bad Words and Good Words

Everyone lies to his neighbor; their flattering lips speak with deception. . . . And the words of the LORD are flawless, like silver refined in a furnace of clay, purified seven times. PSALM 12:2, 6

Psalm 12 is all about communication. It contrasts the unbelievable deception that continually rolls off the lips and tongues of wicked men with the flawless words of the Lord.

Our world is full of talk. We hear it on the radio, on TV, around the dinner table, at the grocery store, over the telephone, at the ballgame, at the office, and in our cars. Wherever there are people, there is talk.

Unfortunately, much of the talk we hear falls under the category of "harmful words." Boasting, flattery, lies—there's no end to the barrage. Psalm 12:4 indicates that it's even possible for people to win battles with their words—"We will triumph with our tongues," they say. "We own our lips—who is our master?"

They're wrong, of course. They don't own their lips; they're owned by the God Who created them, Who can hear every word that comes out of them. God is like a giant listening station—His antenna is up, and He intercepts and filters every word ever uttered.

He doesn't just listen, however. This passage indicates that He does two things: He protects the righteous from those who malign them (v. 5), and He speaks words that are flawless, pure, and refined (v. 6). This suggests that we ought to have our radars up for dishonest words and that we ought to have our eyes trained on God, because we can be assured that His words contain truth and carry weight.

It's sometimes easy to think that God's Word—the Bible—is reserved for Sundays. But the deceptive speech that goes on all around us isn't reserved for Sunday; in fact, it mostly happens from Monday through Friday. As a result, our need to be connected to God's Word is an everyday need. If we fail to meet that need, we're setting ourselves up to be deceived and maligned.

Are you spending time in God's Word every day?

Measuring Your Words

May the LORD cut off all flattering lips and every boastful tongue. PSALM 12:3

There's no questioning the importance God puts on the spoken word. After all, He spoke into existence the universe and everything in it (Genesis 1). And "the Word" is one of the names God uses for Himself (John 1:1).

We see examples every day of the power words carry—the power to motivate, the power to influence, the power to justify, the power to hurt, and the power to heal.

King David went through a time when he felt that everyone around him was lying, to him and to each other (Psalm 12:2). They said nice things, but their words were lies. They were trying to deceive for their own gain. They flattered others and boasted about their own value, but they had ulterior, selfish motives. David saw through this deception in the people of his day, just as God sees through it in us.

We have to ask ourselves: Are we sincere in the things we say to people, or are we merely trying to impress them or butter them up so they can help us improve our stations in life? That type of talk leads to self-centeredness. It leads us to say, or at least to think, "We will triumph with our tongues; we own our lips—who is our master?" (Psalm 12:4).

What if God did your talking for you? How would that sound? "And the words of the LORD are flawless, like silver refined in a furnace of clay, purified seven times" (v. 6).

Who is doing the talking in your life—you or God?

It's What's inside That Counts

LORD, who may dwell in your sanctuary? Who may live on your holy hill?
PSALM 15:1

God is extremely interested in the contents of our hearts. He certainly observes our external performance, but measuring and evaluating what's in our hearts is His chief concern. It was so for Saul, it was so for David, and it is so for us.

In this passage, the psalmist asks a poignant question: Who can be approved for entry into God's innermost courts? Who is allowed to climb His holy hill and spend time in intimate communion with Him? The answer is simple: a person who has a heart that is fully devoted to God.

This person's ways are blameless and righteous, he tells the truth, he doesn't speak slanderous words, he treats his neighbors and coworkers well, he hates evildoers, he honors others who fear God, he keeps his word even when it hurts, he lends money without charging interest, and he doesn't accept bribes (Psalm 15:2–5).

But all these attitudes and behaviors are merely external indicators of what's inside. At his core, this person has a deep desire to honor God and a healthy fear of Who He is. That and that alone is the motivating force behind his righteous behavior and honest words.

As followers of Jesus, it is our job to bring to the workplace hearts that are set on Christ, that fear God, and that desire for Him to be honored by our conduct and wholehearted devotion to Him. It is that kind of internal posture that will lead to the ethical behavior that can sustain a business enterprise for the long haul. And as Psalm 15:5 says, "He who does these things will never be shaken."

If God answered the question the psalmist asked in Psalm 15:1, would your name be on the list of qualified sanctuary dwellers?

Read My Lips

. . . who keeps his oath even when it hurts. PSALM 15:4

When promises are made today, it often seems there is an unspoken but fully understood rider attached to the contract. This rider says that the promise counts only if it's convenient. So breaking promises—be they wedding vows or project deadlines—is OK if it would hurt to keep them.

Your marriage hits some rough spots? No problem: Get a divorce. Your experience isn't quite good enough to land you the big client? No problem: Falsify your credentials. You aren't going to make those quarterly goals? No problem: Move the goalposts.

In some industries, lies and broken promises are almost expected. In others, they are tolerated. In most, however, consistently failing to live up to your word will cost you credibility—with your clients, with your vendors, and with your coworkers. They may allow you to invoke the "something-came-up" rider to your promise, but your relationship will be damaged. Trust, which requires total faith that you will keep your commitment, erodes with every broken promise.

For many people in today's marketplace, that's just fine. It's a cost of doing business. If clients, vendors, or coworkers don't understand why you couldn't keep a promise, that's their problem.

But God places a high importance on keeping your word. Deuteronomy 23:21–23 warns us not to be slow in fulfilling a vow to the Lord. To break such a vow is a sin and as the writer of Ecclesiastes says, something done only by a fool (Ecclesiastes 5:4). In fact, the writer of Ecclesiastes sums it up pretty well when he continues, "It is better not to vow than to make a vow and not fulfill it" (v. 5).

Perhaps that's why the psalmist includes keeping our word—"even when it hurts"—in a list of things we must do to dwell in God's "sanctuary" and live on God's "holy hill" (Psalm 15:1). God, Who is unfailing in His promises to us, expects us to keep our promises, to Him and to each other—even when it hurts.

I Will Not Be Moved

I have set the LORD always before me. Because he is at my right hand, I will not be shaken. PSALM 16:8

If you are in a position to supervise others, then you have an idea of the qualities you want to find in those workers. (Even if you aren't a supervisor, chances are you still know.) The ideal worker, among other things, is reliable, dependable, and trustworthy. *Your* performance often depends on *her* performance, so you want her to deliver.

In football, the running back who consistently fumbles soon finds himself out of a job—even if he runs with record-breaking speed. In business, the employee who cracks under pressure soon finds himself handling the most menial tasks, provided he isn't fired.

How well do you handle pressure? How dependable are you in the clutch? Are you easily shaken?

God, our Rock, clearly wants us to be unshakable in our devotion to Him, which spills over into the way we handle every aspect of our lives and work. But what does that mean? The biblical root *mowt* is used for words that translate into such ideas as to shake, to slip, to totter, to be moved, to be overthrown, to dislodge, to let fall, and to drop—not exactly ideal qualities in a worker or in a follower of Jesus.

Perhaps that's why the Bible reinforces the idea of doing the things that will keep us from being shaken—following God's law, trusting in God. Eight times the psalmist uses the word *shaken* as something to be avoided and lends advice for not being shaken (Psalm 15:5; 16:8; 21:7; 30:6; 62:2; 62:6; 112:6; and 125:1).

What are you doing to assure that the Lord is before you in all that you do—that your life will not be shaken?

Finding the Good in Life

I said to the LORD, "You are my Lord; apart from you I have no good thing."
PSALM 16:2

Time to make a list. Take a pen and paper, and write down all the good things in your life. Include things from your spiritual life. Include things from your family life. Include things from your social life. Include things from your work life. Include things from any other life you might categorize for yourself.

Now, think about which items on your list you may treat as more important than God. Anything that fits that description is, in fact, a false god—an idol. It's something you worship that you shouldn't worship.

Whether or not a "thing" is good often depends on how you use it. God may grant you special opportunities. He might bless you with certain material possessions. He might give you talents and skills. All of these things start off as good. They become corrupt when they are separated from God.

David figured out that he had "good" things in life whether he was hiding in a cave from King Saul or living in Jerusalem as king of Israel. Even though there were times in his life when he sinned, when David was walking closely with the Lord he saw clearly the danger of following other gods and the importance of focusing on the one true God. As his experiences confirmed, nothing good would come of anything he gained apart from God.

This is true for us, too. If you got your promotion by undercutting a coworker who deserved it more than you did, then you got it apart from God. If you won a sales competition by fudging your numbers, then you got it apart from God. If you cut corners on quality to make an early tee time, then your work was done apart from God. If you hired a new employee based on his or her looks rather than skills, then you did so apart from God.

Only by walking closely with the Lord and focusing on the one true God can we have the genuinely good things in life.

Keep Me and Hide Me

Keep me as the apple of your eye; hide me in the shadow of your wings from the wicked who assail me, from my mortal enemies who surround me. PSALM 17:8–9

Security is a big deal to most people. We can get by in almost any situation if we don't feel as if we're all alone on a rough sea with the wind howling around us and only a thousand feet separating us from the bottom of the ocean floor. When we feel as if we're all alone in a situation at work or in any other part of life, it leaves us feeling frantic and unsettled.

In this passage, David uses two phrases that indicate his deep need for God to do something in his life. He didn't need God to search his heart and find his sin. He didn't need God to make him prosper. He didn't need God to protect him from his enemies. In this case, he desperately needed God to *keep him* as the apple of His eye (or as one who is favored or precious) and to *hide him* in the shadow of His wings (just as a mother bird would protect her babies from attack).

In other words, David was asking God to remain his friend and prevent him from being exposed in such a way that he could be harmed. David goes on to describe what he was facing—wicked people were assailing him and mortal enemies were surrounding him. Pretty rough stuff, to be sure, but David knew he could handle even a hostile situation like that as long as God favored him and was protecting him.

When we get to heaven, nobody will assail us and no wicked people will surround us. Here on earth—and especially at work—we face a starker reality. We will be assailed by people who don't like us and surrounded by people who don't want us around. Like David, however, we can persevere, knowing that if we trust in Him, God will keep us as the apple of His eye and hide us in the shadow of His wings.

Responding in Kind

The LORD has dealt with me according to my righteousness. PSALM 18:20

In the midst of his long song of praise to God for delivering him from Saul, David recognized that he was experiencing what some believers don't experience until they reach eternity—a reward for his righteousness.

He knew that he had "kept the ways of the LORD" (v. 21) and that he had "not turned away from his decrees" (v. 22). He knew that he had been "blameless" before God and that he had kept himself "from sin" (v. 23).

David wasn't bragging. He was rejoicing.

He recognized that God always shows Himself faithful to the faithful (v. 25), blameless to the blameless (v. 25), pure to the pure (v. 26), and shrewd to the crooked (v. 26).

What will you do today to keep the ways of the Lord? What will you do today to keep His decrees? What will you do to avoid sin and to stay pure?

When the day ends, if you find yourself standing before God, waiting for Him to deal with you according to your righteousness, what can you expect?

For one thing, be thankful—very thankful—for the redemptive grace that came with the death and resurrection of Jesus. But don't let that stop you from honoring Him through your actions. As the apostle Paul wrote in his letter to the Romans, we all are spiritual slaves, either to sin or to righteousness (Romans 6:15–23). Which will you be today?

Finding God (Part One)

The heavens declare the glory of God; the skies proclaim the work of his hands.
PSALM 19:1

It can be easy to look at this section of Scripture and wonder why so many people "just don't get it."

In Psalm 19:1–6, the writer paints a wonderful picture of what's been labeled the "general revelation" of God to mankind. That is to say, knowing that God is real is as simple as looking around. Who but God could have made this complex planet with its complex life forms, not to mention the unfathomable universe that surrounds it all?

It's a reality that's open to everyone. Psalm 19:3–4 says, "There is no speech or language where their voice is not heard. Their voice goes out into all the earth, their words to the ends of the world." And Paul confirms this in his letter to the Romans: "For since the creation of the world God's invisible qualities—his eternal power and divine nature—have been clearly seen, being understood from what has been made, so that men are without excuse" (Romans 1:20).

So why don't more people get it?

If you aren't a believer, then that certainly is a fair question. But for the disciple of Jesus, there's a bigger question: Do we get it?

Sure, we understand that God is real. But do we get it? Do we take the time, as David did, to look at our surroundings and marvel at the opportunity we have to see God revealed to us? For David, it was the starry skies. It could just as easily be a palm tree or the waves of the ocean or a piece of art or the attitude of the person who works down the hall.

Acknowledging and embracing God's general revelation to us through our everyday surroundings shapes our daily attitudes. It can fill us with awe and thanksgiving and hope, carrying us through the good times and the bad. No matter our circumstances or our surroundings, we can look around and say, "Wow! God is real!"

Finding God (Part Two)

The law of the LORD is perfect, reviving the soul. PSALM 19:7

What does God's law tell us about God?

Answering this helps us understand where we are putting our faith each morning as we pack up our briefcases and head into our work worlds. The second section of Psalm 19 reveals not only what God's law tells us about God, but also what we can expect if we live within that law.

God's law is perfect, trustworthy, right, radiant, pure, enduring forever, sure, altogether righteous, precious, and sweet. Therefore, God is perfect, trustworthy, right, radiant, pure, enduring forever, sure, altogether righteous, precious, and sweet. And what good does all of that do us as we face each day? It revives the soul, gives wisdom to the simple, gives joy to the heart, and gives light to our eyes (Psalm 19:7–10).

Read back over those descriptions and promises, and ask yourself anew the value of putting your faith in and aligning your actions with God's law. This isn't to suggest a legalistic approach to life. It's to suggest the high measure of respect—of unsuppressed awe—that should come with understanding what is revealed about God through His law.

The psalmist sums it up well and leaves us with a challenge that offers hope for the moment, hope for the day, and hope for eternity: "By them is your servant warned; in keeping them there is great reward" (v. 11).

Make My Life a Sacrifice

May the words of my mouth and the meditation of my heart be pleasing in your sight, O LORD, my Rock and my Redeemer. PSALM 19:14

Life is filled with choices, and every choice can be measured against the ultimate motivation: Are we living for God or for something else?

As followers of Jesus, we claim to live for Him. We have acknowledged and accepted that He died as a sacrifice for our sins, showering us with a grace that secures our place in eternity with the living God. And some sacrifice it was. Retrace the story of the crucifixion, and try to fathom even a small piece of the pain Christ suffered for a sinful world.

Is it too much to ask that our lives be a sacrifice back to God?

When David asked that his words and meditations be "pleasing" to God, he used a word that most often appears in the sacrificial contexts. David wanted his words and even his thoughts to be a sacrifice back to God. And in this instance he did not address God as the ultimate Judge on his life, but as his Rock and his Redeemer—his Refuge and his Champion, his Strength and his Freedom.

What better way to start each morning, to open each meeting, to begin each conversation, to launch each new project than by offering this simple but powerful prayer: "May the words of my mouth and the meditation of my heart be pleasing in your sight, O LORD, my Rock and my Redeemer"?

The Plans of Our Hearts

May he give you the desire of your heart and make all your plans succeed. PSALM 20:4

It's become a well-worn axiom for business managers: Plan the work and work the plan. This statement challenges us to commit significant thought and energy to the details that must be taken care of in order to meet an objective. We have to map out the processes. We have to consider the implications. We need a strategy. We need a plan. And then we need to execute it. We need to stick to it, adjusting only in the face of hard, new evidence and not on a whim.

But who's making this plan? And who is responsible for its success or failure when it is implemented?

The Hebrew word translated "plans" in Psalm 20:4 is sometimes translated as "counsel" or "strategy" (Isaiah 11:2; 36:5). There is an implied understanding of the limitations of human planning. As the king is about to go into battle, his people are praying not only that his plans succeed, but also that God's plan for him succeeds.

- "May the LORD answer you when you are in distress; may the name of the God of Jacob protect you" (v. 1).

- "Now I know that the LORD saves his anointed; he answers him from his holy heaven with the saving power of his right hand. Some trust in chariots and some in horses, but we trust in the name of the LORD our God" (vv. 6–7).

When we're walking with God—when we're joining Him in the things that He is doing—our plans are inseparable from God's plans. We can confidently ask Him to make our plans succeed because those plans are in line with His plans.

Whether it is a king going into battle, a manager planning a sales strategy, or a CEO planning a corporate merger, there are limitations to human planning. Today, take comfort in knowing that God is there to help you plan the work and work the plan.

A Question of Trust

Some trust in chariots and some in horses, but we trust in the name of the
LORD our God. They are brought to their knees and fall, but we rise up and
stand firm. PSALM 20:7–8

It is so difficult to trust in the right thing. We see people; we want to trust
them. We see the stock market; we want to trust it. We see money; we want to
trust it.

We desperately want to trust something tangible because we are visual beings.
It's very difficult for us to trust someone or something we can't see. But as believers, that's exactly what we're called to do. If we trust in people, in the stock market,
in money, or, as these verses state, in chariots and horses, we do so at our own risk.
We're only safe when we trust in the name of the Lord our God.

Understanding that God is the only One in Whom we can safely put our trust
has both long-term and immediate implications. Long-term, we can rest in the
knowledge that although we cannot see Jesus now, we have the hope that we will
see Him in heaven someday. But the psalmist isn't talking about that; he's talking
about today. He's looking over the hill at an army with state-of-the-art chariots and
well-trained horses. Humanly speaking, there's no doubt who's going to win the
battle. But the psalmist doesn't trust in human strength; he trusts in God. And as a
result, he is able to say with confidence that his enemies will be brought to their
knees, and he will stand firm.

On whom do we rely for our promotions—our bosses or God? On whom do we
depend for our paychecks—our companies or God? Who decides whether the big
deal goes through—the decision-maker or God? Who vindicates us when we've
been wronged—our lawyers or God?

When we're preparing for a big meeting, when we have to make an important
decision, or when we're waiting for someone to call us with the big news, we can
anxiously pace around the room, or we can take our concerns to Jesus. After all,
He's the One Who's ultimately in control of what's going on.

The Follower's Prayer

O LORD, save the king! Answer us when we call! PSALM 20:9

In times of high stress or crisis, we often ask God for His guiding hand. We ask Him to show us the way. We ask Him to give us peace and to calm our personal storms.

But our prayers don't end there. We also pray for others. And we pray particularly for those in leadership positions.

This is drastically different from worshiping those in leadership positions. It's one thing to respect and admire a leader and yet another to blindly trust in that leader. Great leaders often find themselves the object of hero worship, and it is their responsibility to set their followers straight, just as it is the responsibility of the followers to understand the human limitations of any leader.

In Psalm 20, the people sing the praises of and offer prayers for their earthly king as he prepares for what appears to be a difficult battle. But they don't confuse their earthly king with the heavenly King. They lift up the one to the other.

Regardless of whether we like the leaders around us, we are obligated to lift them up before God. We ask that they know Him. We ask that they seek Him. We ask that His will be done through them. In what better hands could we place the hearts of the people we're directed to follow?

The Gain from His Pain

My God, my God, why have you forsaken me? PSALM 22:1

Somewhere around the ninth hour of his crucifixion, Jesus hung on a wooden cross and cried out in a loud voice, *"Eloi, Eloi, lama sabachthani?"* (Matthew 27:46; Mark 15:34). He was quoting the prophecy of his death that is found in Psalm 22, which begins with those very words: *Eloi, Eloi, lama sabachthani?* Translation: "My God, my God, why have you forsaken me?" (Psalm 22:1).

Psalm 22 is nothing less than a description of an execution—Christ's execution. There is no other written account to support the suggestion that King David at any time in his life faced an execution of this type. He was persecuted. He was threatened with stoning. But this scene is altogether different. We can walk through it almost line by line and mark the parallels to Christ's death. How could we, as followers of Jesus, read lines such as "they have pierced my hands and my feet" (v. 16) or "they divide my garments among them and cast lots for my clothing" (v. 18) and not get the connection?

Christ's pain and suffering on the cross are more than evident.

But this is more than a psalm of one man's pain. It's a psalm of hope for all mankind. Despite the pain and the suffering, the prophecy goes on to outline the promise of Christ's coming kingdom.

As followers of Jesus, this psalm reminds us of why we work and why we live—for the coming of Christ's kingdom here on earth. We've learned of His pain and suffering in brutal detail, so our challenge is to honor that sacrifice in every detail of our lives while we await His return.

The Working Relationship

The LORD is my shepherd. PSALM 23:1

Take a moment and read this verse five times, each time emphasizing a different word.

In those five words, we learn that there is one all-powerful God Who is committed to a present-tense, personal relationship with each of us in which He embraces the role of a loving, caring owner. There's also the understanding that we, the creation of this God, willingly and gratefully fulfill an obligation to recognize Him for all that He is and all that He does for us.

All of this in five words.

This practical, working relationship between human beings and God works perfectly, doesn't it? The psalmist goes on to show how God, the Good Shepherd, takes care of His sheep, feeding them, keeping them watered, moving them from pasture to pasture depending on the seasons, protecting them from predators and parasites and even from their own stubbornness and ignorance.

He also explains that the good sheep trusts unfailingly in his shepherd, fears no evil, and embraces the rewards of living under the assurance that "goodness and love will follow me all the days of my life, and I will dwell in the house of the LORD forever" (v. 6).

Take another moment and picture a working relationship with a bad shepherd. He doesn't care, so his sheep are fearful and neglected. They're skinny, sickly, and easy targets for bugs and carnivores alike. They live in fear. And they have little hope in the future.

As followers of Christ, we can look across the field to the other ranch where the sheep are untended, and we can say with total gratitude, "The Lord is my shepherd." What difference does that realization make in your life today?

Knowing God at Work

Who may ascend the hill of the LORD? Who may stand in his holy place?
PSALM 24:3

If the mission statement for your career and the mission statement for your life aren't closely aligned, then you might lack a complete view of how your faith plays out in your work. For instance, a staple of every believer's personal mission statement should be to "know God" more intimately. So what does "knowing God" have to do with work?

The psalmist asks, "Who may ascend the hill of the LORD? Who may stand in His holy place?" (Psalm 24:3). In other words, who has the honor of knowing God?

The psalmist's answer gives us a quick but profound guideline for how to approach our work: "He who has clean hands and a pure heart, who does not lift up his soul to an idol or swear by what is false" (v. 4).

That response highlights three foundational components for an appropriate view of faith in the workplace: that we have honorable actions (clean hands), that we have honorable motives (a pure heart), and that we honor the one, true Lord for Who He is (don't lift up your "soul" to an idol).

In the work force, that translates into a person who doesn't steal from the company, who doesn't gossip about others, who plans—but doesn't plot—for a promotion, and who doesn't turn such things as money, power, and position into items of worship.

Taking this approach produces rewards that are both immediate and eternal. "He will receive blessing from the LORD and vindication from God his Savior" (v. 5). The immediate rewards may or may not come in material forms; more importantly, of course, this approach to our work provides the transport so that we might "ascend the hill of the LORD" and "stand in His holy place." Thus, by merely legitimately living our faith at work, the reward is nothing short of knowing God.

Waiting on God

To you, O LORD, I lift up my soul; in you I trust, O my God. PSALM 25:1–2

One of the most obvious differences between Saul and David is seen in their respective attitudes toward God. Saul wanted to be king on his own terms and had little patience for waiting on God and God's timing. David, despite his sins, seemed to understand that life was at its best when he was trusting in God and that trusting in God sometimes meant waiting.

As we go about our daily routines, don't we often push to do things—and to get things—sooner rather than later? Don't we often lose sight of the value that can come with waiting?

Certainly there are times to act and act decisively (see Ecclesiastes 3:1). But it is God Who directs the action. If we act without God's direction, then we act in vain (Psalm 127:1).

To trust in God sometimes means we have to wait. And Psalm 25 shows us that in waiting, we are assured promises of . . .

- *Honor:* We won't be put to shame (v. 3).

- *Direction:* If we ask, God will teach us His ways (v. 5).

- *Protection:* God will free us from our enemies (v. 15).

- *Moral fortitude:* "Integrity and uprightness" will protect us (v. 21).

This doesn't mean life will be easy and trouble-free, but by trusting in God and waiting on Him, we find ourselves equipped to handle whatever troubles come our way.

Mission Statement

One thing I ask of the LORD, this is what I seek: that I may dwell in the house of the LORD all the days of my life, to gaze upon the beauty of the LORD and to seek him in his temple. PSALM 27:4

A mission statement is like an organization's North Star. It is the fifty-year goal a group always reaches for but never quite attains. A good mission statement inspires organizational leaders in their strategic and tactical decision-making. It keeps them on track when situations are difficult or ambiguous. It is the corporate marching orders.

Not many companies have a good mission statement. Most sound similar and are filled with meaningless language about quality, value, creativity, and diversity. Few inspire and even fewer are actually known by leadership, let alone the employees of the company. All too often, creating a mission statement is little more than an empty exercise at an executive retreat.

But this does not mean the idea of a mission statement is bad. It just means that its execution is often sloppy or misunderstood.

In Psalm 27 we see a profound personal mission statement. David articulates that his chief aim is to dwell in God's house forever. This passionate plea is more than just a request for life after death; it is an approach to life itself. David's goal was to reside in the presence of the Lord all the days of his life. He wanted to spend every waking moment gazing into the beauty and holiness of the Lord. He wanted his every effort and endeavor in life to bring him closer to God, understanding Him more, discovering Him more.

Is this our life's mission? How can we integrate a passionate pursuit of the Lord with our sixty-hour workweeks? Is it possible? The answer must be yes. And figuring out how is a very good mission statement.

To Whom Credit Is Due

Ascribe to the LORD, O mighty ones, ascribe to the LORD glory and strength. Ascribe to the LORD the glory due his name; worship the LORD in the splendor of his holiness. PSALM 29:1–2

What do we give God credit for?

Typically it is for supernatural activities in our lives that we cannot explain or those things that look like coincidences. We meet someone at just the right place and time. We receive a word of encouragement, a check in the mail, or a call from a friend just when we need it. We dodge a disaster, survive a close scrape, or live through a serious illness. All of these would make our list of things for which we give God credit.

But is this all He does?

Consider the sun and the moon and the stars. The seasons, the oceans, the birds in the air. Dew in the morning and sea foam lapping at our feet. The smell of cut grass and the feel of a kitten's fur. The Grand Canyon, a rose, rain, sleet, and snow. The autumn leaves and the taste of an apple. All of these simple pleasures in life are so amazing, and He designed them for us.

But is that all He has done?

What about love and laughter, faithfulness, holiness, peace, patience, and joy? Consider the way He faithfully provides for us. His protection and deliverance. His salvation and holiness and glory and strength and honor. God does it all because He is, and He is all that He does. There is no falseness within Him. His character and His actions are one and the same.

In our worship and praise, let's remember not only the huge things that He has done, but also the small things He has done and the awesome way that He is.

Thankful Key

You turned my wailing into dancing; you removed my sackcloth and clothed me with joy, that my heart may sing to you and not be silent. O Lord my God, I will give you thanks forever. PSALM 30:11–12

If there is a key to a joyful life, it has to be thankfulness. A heart of ingratitude will derail our spiritual growth and journey quicker than anything else in our life. Ingratitude fails to acknowledge the reality of God's provision in our lives. It spits in the face of our Savior. It says that His sacrifice means nothing in light of the situation we are currently facing.

If we are ungrateful, it is because we have lost sight of Who He is and what He has done. Nothing in our lives, regardless of how tragic, will ever compare to what Jesus went through on our behalf. Our situations cannot be even half as bad—they are not even on the same plane. And yet, at every turn Jesus walked in submission to the Father. He marched willingly to His own death, asking for the forgiveness of the ungrateful masses who stood around Him mocking while He hung in agony.

A heart of ingratitude is the ultimate arrogance. It is a created being elevating itself to the level of the Creator. It is a pot on a shelf refusing to give thanks to the potter who lovingly formed it from a lump of cold, useless clay into an object of beauty and use. It is the pride that brought down Lucifer, the angel of light, who in his heart determined that he was equal to God. It is a dangerous sheet of thin ice, and nothing but cold, icy water lies beneath.

There is nothing like giving thanks to battle gloom and despair. Thankfulness will drive out self-pity. It will restore strength and perspective. It is a spiritual shot in the arm protecting us from the disease of the world. It is a spiritual vitamin giving us strength for the day. It is recommended that you take it daily and often for best results. And now is a great time to start.

Putting Your Enemies in the Pit (Part One)

May all who gloat over my distress be put to shame and confusion; may all who exalt themselves over me be clothed with shame and disgrace. PSALM 35:26

There are those who view capitalism as a particularly harsh economic system, one that offers little sympathy for those who are unable to keep up with the competition. In fact, work often is described in military terms. Companies battle each other for market share and often take a win-at-all-cost approach to meeting their strategic objectives. Even within organizations, battles can turn ugly.

The cold, harsh reality is that most of us have enemies—outside of our organizations, inside of our organizations, or both. Jesus, of course, teaches us to love our enemies and to turn the other cheek, but this isn't always easy. Consider, for instance, one of Jesus' human forefathers—King David. When David prayed about his enemies, as he did in Psalm 35, it wasn't exactly in glowing terms.

"May those who seek my life be disgraced and put to shame; may those who plot my ruin be turned back in dismay. May they be like chaff before the wind, with the angel of the LORD driving them away; may their path be dark and slippery, with the angel of the LORD pursuing them. Since they hid their net for me without cause and without cause dug a pit for me, may ruin overtake them by surprise—may the net they hid entangle them, may they fall into the pit, to their ruin" (Psalm 35:4–8).

There certainly was no love lost between David and his enemies, was there? We might be tempted to judge him for his attitude, but before we get too uppity, we need to remember one thing. David didn't spread rumors about his enemies, badmouth them, or try to hurt them himself. He didn't hesitate to share his true feelings in his prayers, but he left all vengeance right where it belonged—with God.

Where do you go to express your feelings about your enemies—to other people or to God?

Putting Your Enemies in the Pit (Part Two)

May all who gloat over my distress be put to shame and confusion; may all who exalt themselves over me be clothed with shame and disgrace. PSALM 35:26

D avid was a warrior. He knew all about battles. He knew how to handle his enemies in times of war. And as a human, and thus a sinner, he sometimes acted rashly and in ungodly ways. But as we learned yesterday, he got one thing right. He didn't try to settle the score with his enemies—he left that up to God.

He didn't, however, shirk at reminding God of his circumstances over and over again because he knew that, ultimately, God was the only one Who could rectify the situation. And in the midst of his prayers for deliverance, he never failed to praise God for His goodness.

"O Lord, how long will you look on?" he prayed. "Rescue my life from their ravages, my precious life from these lions. I will give you thanks in the great assembly; among throngs of people I will praise you. . . . May all who gloat over my distress be put to shame and confusion; may all who exalt themselves over me be clothed with shame and disgrace. May those who delight in my vindication shout for joy and gladness; may they always say, 'The LORD be exalted, who delights in the well-being of his servant.' My tongue will speak of your righteousness and of your praises all day long" (Psalm 35:17–18, 26–28).

Now let's turn the focus to your work world. How often do you mutter mild (or strong) curses against your boss or a client or a coworker or a competitor? What do those thoughts say about you and your walk with the Lord? Are you bitter and angry or just frustrated? What do you do with those feelings? Do you take it upon yourself to settle the scores you have with others? Or do you follow David's example and bring them all to God?

His Love

An oracle is within my heart concerning the sinfulness of the wicked: There is no fear of God before his eyes. . . . Your love, O LORD, reaches to the heavens, your faithfulness to the skies. PSALM 36:1, 5

Love is often defined as always making the best decision regarding a person. There are many other definitions that we could consider, but let's ponder on this one for a moment. If God is love, then He is always making the best possible decision for you. His desire for you is always the best. His intentions for you are the best. His plans for you are always the best. His direction for you is the best. His calling, provision, protection, defense, and shelter for you are the best. Everything that the Lord has in store for you is the best. Nothing could be better. He is love. It is impossible for Him to make an unloving decision or to think an unloving thought.

But we can have an unloving response to Him.

In His design, God allows us to choose our response to Him. Inasmuch as He is powerful and sovereign with the entirety of existence operating under His command, He still has given us a choice in our lives. Our spiritual journey is an "if/then" equation. And all too often, we are either too proud or too ignorant to choose Him.

Our pride blinds us to our need. And we desperately need Him. Without Him, we are in a bus headed for a cliff. It may not happen tomorrow or next week, but the edge of that precipice is coming, and without Him we are surely headed for disaster.

Our ignorance keeps us from understanding God's character. It blinds us from the realization that even though He is awesome and fearful, He is also the perfect loving Father Who has adopted us and loves us as His own children. Everything that He has is ours. He has written us into His will, and we will receive a full inheritance.

Don't let pride or ignorance keep you from walking fully in the abundant life that He has planned for you. It is perfect—not trouble-free, but truly perfect.

Leap of Faith

Delight yourself in the LORD and he will give you the desires of your heart. Commit your way to the LORD; trust in him and he will do this: He will make your righteousness shine like the dawn, the justice of your cause like the noonday sun. PSALM 37:4–6

A life following Jesus is full of paradoxes: We lose to win, give up to get, and sow to reap. It takes a supernatural act of faith energized by the Holy Spirit to accept that a full surrender of our lives—body, mind, will, emotions, and spirit—will result in a deep abiding joy, peace, and sense of purpose in this life *and* an eternity with the Lord. That is too big a leap for man to make alone.

But this is not the only leap that we will make in our walk with Jesus. Beyond our salvation is our vocation—the thing that He made us to do in life. Here again, is another paradox. In order for us to fully discover that thing that will be most fulfilling in our lives, we have to do nothing more or less than delight ourselves in Him. When our satisfaction and fulfillment come from Him, when we are listening to and following His voice, when we are surrendered fully to His will, then He will bring to pass the deep longings in our hearts. He will unleash the pure motives that He hard-wired inside of us from the day we were born. We will find ourselves thinking, *I was made to do this.*

How do you delight yourself in the Lord? Many ways. One example is to allow every desire and longing of your heart to be wrapped up in Jesus, not in your career, your hobbies, or even your family. When He becomes the end and not the means, you are finally in a position for Him to use you. This is not easy, but He is loving and just and faithful to complete the work that He began in you.

Are you ready to delight yourself in the Lord? The good news is that regardless of your current season of life, it is never too late to begin. He is a God Who can redeem the time no matter how much you have left.

Patient Ambition

Be still before the LORD and wait patiently for him; do not fret when men succeed in their ways, when they carry out their wicked schemes. PSALM 37:7

If you are a follower of Christ and you are ambitious, then you have to walk a tightrope that takes an intentional approach to master.

Many people think that spiritual life and personal ambition are mutually exclusive—but they are not. Jesus sought to do everything that the Father wanted Him to do, but He did not operate in a unilateral fashion. Instead, He always submitted to the Father's will for Him, a will that led Him to His own death.

The business climate today is very competitive. There are battles to be fought on every front, both inside our organizations and out. Success in business is not certain; neither is it evil. What is certain for the follower of Christ is the will of our Father. And this means that we cannot always use the strategies and tactics of the world to get ahead. There will be times when others will beat us, move ahead of us, make more money than us, and seem to succeed even at our expense.

Nowhere does the Bible say that following Christ will not cost you something while you are here on earth. In those seasons, the correct response is to wait on the Lord. He is not unaware. He sees. He is familiar with everything that is going on in your life. He is not caught by surprise. He is still in control. Now is the time for you to rejoice and give thanks and praise Him. For great is your reward, not only in this age, but also in the age to come.

Simply be still. And wait on the Lord.

God-Help

Why are you downcast, O my soul? Why so disturbed within me? Put your hope in God, for I will yet praise him, my Savior and my God. PSALM 43:5

Self-help is not total hogwash. Just partial. Popular psychology has become a national obsession since the 1960s and has gathered steam into the twenty-first century. We spend hundreds of thousands of dollars annually on books, tapes, and seminars to help our way out of obesity, depression, and family dysfunction. Like scores of generations before us, we are troubled and desperate people. What is unique to us, however, is our self-reliant attitude toward tackling the tough issues and pains in our lives.

Not all self-examination is a bad thing. God has given us the ability to step outside of ourselves and examine our attitudes and actions in the third person. In balance with the rest of life, this is a good and healthy practice. If it is done in conjunction with the Holy Spirit, it can be a revolutionary force in our lives. In Psalm 43, the psalmist performs some introspective surgery and refines his self-talk. Realizing that he is slipping into a state of despair and possibly even depression, he bolsters himself and points his weary disposition back to the source of its hope and strength—the Lord.

This type of prayer is a healthy and underutilized expression of our faith. God has given us these emotions, and we need to take them under the control of our renewed minds and God's Word. Often, this requires some rigorous personal work and self-talk. Think of it as God-help versus self-help.

Where is your attitude today? What are your thoughts about where you are in life? Your work? Your family situation? Your colleagues? Your boss? Are you up or down? Take a quick inventory and work on your attitude in areas that need it. Begin to rewire your internal conversations with yourself and with the Lord, Who is your Savior and your God.

Reconnecting with God

Why are you downcast, O my soul? Why so disturbed within me? Put your hope in God, for I will yet praise him, my Savior and my God. PSALM 43:5

Do you ever get so frustrated with your own humanness that you put yourself on trial? *What's your problem? Why are you acting this way?*

It usually happens like this: After a period in which things are going pretty well, we hit some roadblocks. A career that was sailing along smoothly suddenly is filled with headaches. A family life marked by nothing but joy begins to experience heartache. A spiritual life that was vibrant and active has become dull and passive.

Depression sets in. And because we've experienced the fullness of God in the past, we begin to ache to get it back. We can relate to Psalm 42:1: "As the deer pants for streams of water, so my soul pants for you, O God." Some believe those words were written by someone who was living in the northern kingdom of Israel and thus prevented from worshiping in the Temple in Jerusalem. He felt cut off from his God and depressed, especially as he thought back on all the wonderful moments: "[H]ow I used to go with the multitude, leading the procession to the house of God, with shouts of joy and thanksgiving among the festive throng" (v. 4).

Three times in this song, the writer pauses and asks a question of his soul: "Why are you downcast, O my soul? Why so disturbed within me?" (Psalm 42:5, 11; 43:5). You can almost picture him staring at his reflection and shouting: *What's your problem? Why are you acting this way?* Yet despite his frustration, he knows the answers to his inner sufferings. *Put your hope in God,* he tells his soul, *for I will yet praise Him, my Savior and my God* (Psalm 43:5).

Are you feeling separated from the God you love? Is something keeping Him from being part of your work? Of your family? Of your faith?

Put your hope in God. Praise Him. He is your Savior and your God.

Don't Be Too Impressed (Part One)

Do not be overawed when a man grows rich . . . for he will take nothing with him when he dies, his splendor will not descend with him. PSALM 49:16–17

Once when I (Tom) was on a trip with my parents and siblings, we stopped for supper at the home of some family friends. As we pulled up to their very large house (it was a mansion, really), my father said to my mother, "That's quite a shack!"

They didn't realize that my brother, who was about five years old, was eavesdropping. And much to my parents' chagrin, the first thing out of his mouth when he met the man of the house at the door was, "That's quite a shack!"

We laugh, but this little story aptly illustrates how natural it is for us to give great deference, either in our words or our actions, to people who are wealthy. Think about what you say when you meet a rich person: "Wow, your house is amazing!" "You must be really good at what you do." "You clearly know how to manage your money." "Man, you've really accomplished a lot here." We praise them—simply because they have a lot of money.

Measuring a person's value based upon his or her bank account is not an invention of modern society; people have been doing it for thousands of years. Even Job, the first book of the Bible to be written, begins with a description of the main character's wealth. But it does seem that society's emphasis on money is stronger now than it's ever been. The more money you have, the more valuable you are to society. The larger your stock portfolio, the more important you are. When was the last time you saw a listing in *Forbes* magazine of the five hundred poorest Americans? It would never happen; the rich are always the ones who are elevated in our culture.

Even those of us who know where our worth really comes from tend to get awed by wealth because we've grown up with such a mind-set. But in Psalm 49:16–17, David brings us back to reality. He doesn't say wealth is bad or evil; he just tells us not to be overawed when someone gets rich because when he dies, he'll end up just like the rest of us—with nothing.

Keep that in mind next time you visit the home of a wealthy friend who seems to have everything!

Don't Be Too Impressed (Part Two)

Do not be overawed when a man grows rich . . . for he will take nothing with him when he dies, his splendor will not descend with him. PSALM 49:16–17

We're always going to be around people with more money than we have. Unless we bear the title of "richest person in the world," there will always be someone with a bigger house, a nicer car, and a larger stock portfolio.

This passage makes the point that other people's wealth should not be a big deal to us. We are not supposed to use the money gauge to determine how we act toward others. Sheer bank account volume tells us very little about people. We might be able to determine how *much* money they have, but we may have no idea how they got it, how they handle it, or whether they're about to lose it all. Rather, we should evaluate them based on their characters, their levels of self-control, their hearts for God, their generosity, and the ways they handle their relationships.

Psalm 49:20 tells us "a man who has riches without understanding is like the beasts that perish." This gives a big clue why people with money shouldn't overawe us—if they refuse to acknowledge the ultimate source of their blessings, then they're no better than an animal. In addition, no matter how financially secure they might be, they could lose it all tomorrow. That thought should help you keep things in perspective, too.

David doesn't tell us to snub people with money, but he does ask us to examine our motives. Next time you're tempted to give deference to a rich person, ask yourself, *How would I be treating this person if he didn't have any money? Am I hoping to build a relationship with him simply because he is wealthy and powerful and influential?*

Going before the Judge

For I know my transgressions, and my sin is always before me. PSALM 51:3

Who holds you accountable at work and in life? And, of equal importance, how do you respond when you are held accountable?

One of David's primary accountability partners was the prophet Nathan. When David sank to an all-time low in arranging to have a man killed after committing adultery with that man's wife, it was Nathan who confronted him (2 Samuel 12:1–14). David had given in to temptation, and Nathan wouldn't stand for it.

It was in response to this confrontation that David wrote Psalm 51. Unlike his predecessor on the throne, Saul, David had a heart for God that always caused him to seek a right relationship with his Maker. While Saul would deny his sins, avoid responsibility, and conspire to control situations for his personal gain, David found a way to put on the brakes.

David was a sinner, he had always been a sinner, and he would always be a sinner. Just like you. Just like me. But when confronted with the reality of his sins, he didn't close his eyes. He returned to God and sought forgiveness and restoration.

Do you have someone in your life who isn't afraid to walk into your office and tell you that your behavior isn't appropriate? If not, you're most likely living a dangerous lie—that you can guard your own heart without the help of others.

The first order of business is to find someone who will hold you accountable. Next, understand and expect that you will be confronted by your own sins. As David expressed in Psalm 51:5, sinning is inevitable as long as we are on this earth. "Surely I was sinful at birth, sinful from the time my mother conceived me." Finally, return to God. He's waiting for you.

Fill Me with Your Presence

Create in me a pure heart, O God, and renew a steadfast spirit within me. Do not cast me from your presence or take your Holy Spirit from me. Restore to me the joy of your salvation, and grant me a willing spirit, to sustain me. PSALM 51:10–12

Even when we are doing everything we can to follow Christ and obey His commands, we are going to mess up. We are going to rebel. We are going to sin.

If we truly are in a right relationship with Jesus, such behavior will create a sense of heaviness in our hearts. We will feel guilty because we know we have violated God's laws. We will be sad because we know our actions have brought Him grief.

Because of what Jesus did on the cross, our relationship with God is secure even when we sin. But when our fellowship with Him is broken because of sin, our hearts are devoid of joy and gladness. And even after we confess our sins and do whatever we can to make it right, that heaviness sometimes remains. That's when we need come to Him in prayer, imploring Him to erase the black cloud of guilt that covers our hearts. We need to ask Him to make our hearts pure, to bring the joy back to our souls.

That's what David was asking for in this psalm. He wasn't asking God to restore him because he was weary and tired. He was begging God to restore the relationship between them that had been broken by his sin. He wanted to take joy in his salvation again, and he wanted God to make his spirit steadfast so that he wouldn't fall again.

We deceive ourselves if we think we're never going to fall into the kind of behavior that creates that kind of heaviness in our hearts. We might not succumb to adultery and murder like David did, but we'll succumb to sin. When that happens, we need to throw ourselves at the feet of Jesus and ask Him to cleanse our hearts and bring back our joy. We can pray such prayers when we're kneeling beside our beds, while we're sitting at our desks at work, or while we're in the middle of a conference call. It doesn't matter *where* we do it. But if we want to be effective for Christ, we *do* need to do it.

What Do You Dread?

There they were, overwhelmed with dread, where there was nothing to dread.
PSALM 53:5

There are days when our work overwhelms us. The boss, with that unmistakable look in her eyes, pulls up a chair and delivers some piece of unwelcome news—the project must be redone and the deadlines are two weeks earlier than they were before. Or the client calls with an urgent request. Or the computer system crashes, taking a month's worth of financial planning with it. The list of work-related stresses is nearly endless, but what these stresses hold in common is a sense of dread—an inner anxiety—about what's to come.

How often do you feel such anxiety and live with such dread? Once a month? Once a week? Once a day? More often?

King Jehoshaphat probably felt it the day he learned that a massive army was gathering to attack Judah. He knew that he and his countrymen were no match for these forces. The Scripture says he was "alarmed" (2 Chronicles 20:3). But Jehoshaphat was a godly leader, and his response provides a wonderful action plan for dealing with unwelcome news. First, he resolved to inquire of the Lord and proclaimed a fast for all of Judah (v. 3). He convened an assembly (vv. 4–5). Then, on behalf of the assembly, he turned the matter over to God (vv. 6–12). Next, he obeyed God's directive, even though it made little sense in human terms (vv. 15–26). Finally, he gave God the credit for saving the day (vv. 27–28).

People who don't believe in God don't take this approach. Eventually, instead of trusting and obeying God, they are overwhelmed by their own sinful nature and give in to the worry and the dread of stressful circumstances. But if we believers choose not to trust and obey God during difficult circumstances, are we that different from the agnostics and the atheists? Aren't we just as likely to end up dreading the troubles that come in life?

How do you respond when trouble comes? Do you have the type of faith needed to say to God, as King Jehoshaphat said, "We do not know what to do, but our eyes are upon you" (v. 12)?

Soothing Words Meant to Destroy

My companion attacks his friends; he violates his covenant. His speech is smooth as butter, yet war is in his heart. PSALM 55:20–21

Controlled speech is good. If you're in the middle of a heated meeting and you disagree with someone else, you are to be commended if you speak slowly and thoughtfully, refusing to fly off the handle and say things you might regret later.

Although it might seem so initially, that is not the kind of speech David is talking about in this verse. When he speaks of someone whose speech is "smooth as butter," he's describing a person whose speech says one thing but whose intentions are totally different. To put it in legal terms, it's premeditated speech with the intent to do harm. This person speaks with a gentle smile and a soothing voice, but his words are meant to destroy. He's learned that he can't accomplish his dirty work if his tone of voice is angry and he has steam coming out of his ears. He has the ability to cloak his words in such a way that his listeners walk away smiling despite the fact that he has just plunged a dagger into their hearts.

People like this are self-controlled in an evil sort of way. They're steady and careful, not impulsive. They leave you with the impression that they're reasonable, but if you really listen to what they say, you realize that you totally disagree with them. This type of behavior often manifests itself in the workplace. Buttery speech often serves people well as they maneuver and manipulate their way up the corporate ladder.

We may not be able to read someone else's intentions to determine if he's drawing a sword or practicing genuine self-control, but we do know our own intentions and motivations. At the end of the day, we're not responsible for someone else's words and actions, but we are responsible for our own.

Have you been using buttery words to disguise a sword in your heart?

Watching Your Tongue

My slanderers pursue me all day long; many are attacking me in their pride.
PSALM 56:2

What causes us to say nasty things about other people? What starts us down the road to slander?

Slander occurs when we verbally communicate to others lies that harm someone's reputation. Slander is a brother of libel, which is slander in the written form. We hear those terms mostly in legal contexts, where one person charges another with slander or libel. Slander is extremely hard to prove, especially when it involves public figures. In cases of libel and slander, ill intent generally must be shown. In other words, you have to prove that someone meant to cause you harm.

But if we hold to the dictionary definition and not the legal definition, slander happens far more frequently than we might admit. It shows up in common gossip and intense battles of office politics. It might start with a whisper. It might start as a joke. At its worst, it grows into vicious power plays that end up damaging reputations and ruining careers.

Do you see it happening around you? Do you see it happening to you? Do you see it happening in you?

Again, what causes us to say nasty things about other people? What starts us down the road to slander?

Look in your heart. Check your pride. Is your pride in God or in yourself? And if it's in yourself, what fruit is it producing from your tongue?

Being Paranoid

All day long they twist my words; they are always plotting to harm me. PSALM
56:5

There's an old saying that goes something like this: You aren't paranoid if they really are out to get you.

There were times when David, as the heir apparent to the throne of Israel and as the king, sounded paranoid. And maybe there were times when he was unduly concerned about those who were attacking him. Then again, all indications are that David never lacked for enemies. They spread nasty rumors about him. They tried to kill him. They tried to bring him down.

His primary pursuer, however, was King Saul, a man who became so attached to his positional power that he couldn't distinguish his friends from his enemies. Everyone was out to get him, even those who were not. He had no more loyal servant than David, and yet he became obsessed with bringing David down.

What type of paranoia do you pack in your briefcase? Do you spend your time preparing for battle or fending off attacks from imaginary enemies? Is the person who reports to you scheming to take your place? Is your supervisor stealing your best ideas and plotting to ruin your career?

And, perhaps, most important, if you truly have reasons to be paranoid, what are you doing about it? Are you constantly plotting your defense? Are you building secret alliances to strengthen your power base? Or are you doing what David did: trusting in God?

Psalm 56 describes David being attacked by those who were out to get him, and yet he never declares what he will do to these enemies. Instead, he turns his fears over to his Lord. "In God, whose word I praise, in the LORD, whose word I praise—in God I trust; I will not be afraid. What can man do to me?" (Psalm 56:10–11).

Indeed, what can man do to any of us when we put our faith in the Lord?

Under Authority

I am under vows to you, O God; I will present my thank offerings to you. For you have delivered me from death and my feet from stumbling, that I may walk before God in the light of life. PSALM 56:12–13

When a soldier is "under orders," he is obligated to follow those orders. It doesn't matter if another person tells him to do something else; he answers to the one who gave him the orders, and his job is to carry them out completely.

This same idea is presented in this passage. To be "under vows" is similar to being under orders. Biblically, a vow is a pledge or promise that is elevated above any circumstances that would give someone an excuse not to fulfill it. When we are under vows to God, it means that ultimately, we are taking orders from Him and no one else. We owe our loyalty and attention to Him, as well as our thank offerings when we are successful. That doesn't mean we can't thank our bosses or express gratitude to our coworkers if something goes well at work, but it does mean that in the end, all the praise for what happens must go to God.

Regardless of our personality types, physical attributes, or family backgrounds, we all suffer from a reckless spirit of autonomy and independence. Inside every one of us is this notion that we don't need anyone over us telling us what to do or keeping track of us. Like David, however, we must willingly place ourselves under orders of God if we want His direction and protection in our lives.

Private vows lead to public surrender. Has the pledge that you made to God when you met Christ resulted in a public demonstration that you are actively seeking to follow Him in all areas of your life?

The Cry of Our Hearts

I cry out to God Most High. PSALM 57:2

It's a common question: How can a follower of Jesus survive in a work environment that is filled with nonbelievers? There are all sorts of settings that are hostile to people who acknowledge their faith in Jesus. The hostility can come from owners, managers, coworkers, or even subordinates. It can come from a few bitter individuals, from a large group, or from formal policies. It can be found in privately owned companies, publicly held companies, nonprofit companies, and all branches of government.

What does this type of situation look like?

David describes it often, but he expresses it particularly well in Psalm 57:4: "I am in the midst of lions; I lie among ravenous beasts—men whose teeth are spears and arrows, whose tongues are sharp swords."

Notice the enemy's weapon. It's not a club or a gun; it's words.

Words, too, are our weapon. But to whom do you direct your words during times of trouble? To the government? ("Fix this with a program!") To your parents? ("Why did you raise me with so much baggage?") To your boss? ("I can't work with that woman!") To your friends or your spouse? ("Everyone at work is out to get me!")

Seeking wise counsel is one thing, but whining is another. And whether you are seeking counsel from friends or just venting your frustration, ask yourself: *Have I first cried out to God Most High?*

What's the Plan?

I cry out to God Most High, to God, who fulfills [his purpose] for me. PSALM 57:2

So your life is filled with trouble. So you have problems. So you have enemies at work who pursue you with tongues as sharp as swords. So you can't finish everything on deadline. So your boss is unreasonable. So your coworkers are incompetent. So . . . so . . . so.

So you cry out to God Most High.

What is it about crying out to God in times of trouble that makes us feel better about life? Or, if crying out to God isn't providing much comfort, what's the problem? Is He not there? Does He not care?

Part of the comfort can be found in the second part of Psalm 57:2, which tells a little about Who God is and why we cry out to Him in the first place.

Is it because He will solve our problems to our satisfaction? He might, but, then again, He might not. There is no guarantee in Scripture that God will give us what we want, only that He will give us what we need. That's the character trait of God that David seems to find comfort in as he cries out—that He is the God Who promises to fulfill His purpose for David.

Isn't that the same God you worship? Doesn't He make you the same promise?

Help!

Hear my cry, O God; listen to my prayer. From the ends of the earth I call to you, I call as my heart grows faint; lead me to the rock that is higher than I. For you have been my refuge, a strong tower against the foe. I long to dwell in your tent forever and take refuge in the shelter of your wings. PSALM 61:1–4

There are times in our work lives when we just really need help. We might be really discouraged. We might be totally stressed out. We might be trying to meet impossible deadlines. We might be in the middle of conflict with supervisors. We might be facing opposition from coworkers. It doesn't matter what the problem is, Psalm 61:1–4 reminds us that we have access to God's 911 system anywhere, anytime.

As he wrote these verses, David's heart was growing faint. He was going down. If the paramedics didn't get there in the next few minutes, he would be history. It was at that point that he called for help, knowing that God—his Refuge and Strong Tower—would hear and answer.

Some days at work beat us up so badly and confuse us so terribly that we feel as if we're about to drown. We're desperate for someone to rescue us, to shelter us, to set us on high ground. When we have an automobile accident, we automatically call 911—it's practically second nature to us. But somehow we forget that God also has a 911 system—prayer—that is available 24/7. And the best part of it is that we don't have to have a cell phone or be near a pay phone to reach Him. He'll hear us from anywhere, even from the ends of the earth.

Are you feeling overwhelmed and stressed? Cry out to your Refuge and Strong Tower. He will hear and answer.

A View from the Heart

With their mouths they bless, but in their hearts they curse. PSALM 62:4

Some people are horrible liars, usually because they simply lack the practice. With a little effort, they no doubt could develop the skill.

All it takes for starters is a few honest compliments, and those are easy enough. *Nice dress. Good work on the Boatman account. Are you losing weight?*

Pretty soon, everybody loves Mr. Nice Guy because he always has a kind word. And what's wrong with being Mr. Nice Guy? Nothing, if you have a pure heart. Too often, however, we find ourselves slipping into the mode of giving compliments and providing encouraging words because we think we will get something out of it.

We don't act like Mr. Nice Guy because we like people. We just want a raise. We just want more power. We just want to get ahead. If the people around us could only read our minds, they would know how we really feel: We actually think her dress is ugly. We're mad because he was two weeks late closing the Boatman account. And there's no way he's lost weight; he's only wearing bigger clothes.

Is this how we are called to treat each other? Do we really think God won't notice that the words of our lips don't match the motivations in our hearts?

This doesn't mean you have to verbalize every thought that comes to your mind. If you think your coworker's dress is ugly, just don't say anything about it at all. Ditto for any other situation in which you might be tempted to tell a lie to flatter someone who might be able to do something for you later. Limit your praise for occasions that truly deserve it. That way, your lips will match your motivations.

Sitting on the Balance

Lowborn men are but a breath, the highborn are but a lie; if weighed on a balance, they are nothing; together they are only a breath. PSALM 62:9

Some people are born to money. Others are born to poverty. Some think they are born to poverty; then they see a glimpse of a Third World country and find that they are rich. Some live in the filth of forgotten dirt streets but think themselves better off than the ones around the corner curled up in the ditch.

Some start life with nothing and end it with great wealth. Others begin with a huge inheritance and squander it, dying penniless and alone. Some work hard and honestly to get their material wealth. Others obtain it through devious means: lying, stealing, and cheating.

But regardless of how their wealth is obtained and how much is left when they die, all of them have one thing in common: They are nothing; together they are only a breath.

Therefore, "do not set your heart on" such possessions, whether you have them and love them or lack them and covet them (Psalm 62:10). Instead, shout to the Lord the song of the psalmist: "My salvation and my honor depend on God" (v. 7). This is the only way you will be able to maintain a godly perspective on wealth, no matter the size of your bank account or stock portfolio.

The Tender Warrior

One thing God has spoken, two things have I heard: that you, O God, are strong, and that you, O Lord, are loving. PSALM 62:11–12

Stuart Weber penned the book *Tender Warrior* to describe the manner in which a godly man should live. What an apt description and foundational philosophy for how to treat others—with strength and with love.

In a single breath, God conveyed this twin thought to David, and David poured it into a psalm: "One thing God has spoken, two things have I heard: that you, O God, are strong, and that you, O Lord, are loving" (Psalm 62:11–12).

What a picture of God's character. God is mighty, but He's also gentle. He's powerful, but He's also kind. He is the epitome of a tender warrior. What a model for how we should carry ourselves around our families, our friends, our coworkers, and our customers.

Ask yourself the hard questions about your own character. What is it about you that is strong? Make a list. Do others see these things as strengths? And are these strengths of God? If so, they will be balanced by love. What is it about you that is love? Make a list. Do others see these things as love?

Could your coworkers look at you and say that in your words and actions they see a consistent theme in your character—both the love and strength of God? In other words, are you a tender warrior?

And Thank You for the Toothache

Because your love is better than life, my lips will glorify you. PSALM 63:3

It's easy to glorify God when things are going well. A healthy baby is born: Praise God! A new client agrees to a significant deal: Praise God! The Arkansas Razorbacks beat the Tennessee Volunteers in football: Praise God! (Unless, of course, you're a Tennessee fan.)

Yet, God wants—and deserves—our *unconditional* praise. And not only does He not promise us an easy life if we believe, He promises that things will be difficult (John 16:33). Even after he became king of Israel, David knew pain and suffering. He had to deal with his own sins. And his family was more dysfunctional than anything modern television could dream up. At one point his own son plotted against him and forced him to flee his palace.

So why did David spend so much of his time praising God—even when his team was losing its earthly battles and nothing seemed more certain than his impending death? How did he find so much comfort in those trying times?

The answer is simple: David knew God. "I have seen you in the sanctuary and beheld your power and your glory," he wrote in Psalm 63:2. David knew of a promise from God that left him filled with a passion for praise, a promise of an everlasting love that is better than life itself.

Are you able to praise God in the midst of difficulties? Perhaps you need to get reacquainted with a heavenly Father Who loves you, knows what you need, and promises never to leave you or forsake you.

A Little Whine with That Cheese?

Hear me, O God, as I voice my complaint. PSALM 64:1

What's the most important skill in effective communication? Speaking articulately? Having meaningful content? Making sound arguments? Or, perhaps, is it listening?

It is all of these, and more. But what ties it all together is timing—that wonderful sense of knowing not only what to say, but when to say it and when to say nothing at all.

God is a good listener. Thus, when He communicates to us, it's all the more powerful. But there's one phrase you never hear God saying to you: "I'm tired of listening!"

Our God has a good ear and a comforting shoulder, strong arms and a tender heart. He loves us, and He listens to our complaints—even when we have no good reason to complain.

But ask yourself: Why do you complain? How do you present your complaints? What do you expect from your complaints?

The psalmist voiced his complaints by praising God. He complained about his condition by acknowledging God's character—His power, His sovereignty, His glory. He asked for relief, but from bended knee. "Hear me, O God" wasn't a command; it was a plea. It was a humble request from a humble servant. It was an act of faith.

Are your complaints arrogant and self-serving, or are they voiced with the foundation of praise? Do you trust that God is listening? And do you trust that in His perfect timing, He will make things right?

Listening to God's Music

Blessed are those you choose and bring near to live in your courts! PSALM 65:4

How does God bless us in our daily routine?

In this love song to the Lord, David outlines several provisions that should give peace to our souls as we wrestle with life. First and of greatest importance, there is redemption: "When we were overwhelmed by sins, you forgave our transgressions" (Psalm 65:3). That blessing was fulfilled through the death and resurrection of Jesus.

Some other blessings to consider throughout the day:

- The blessing of answered prayer (v. 2)

- The blessing of good things in the house of the Lord (v. 4)

- The blessing of awesome deeds of righteousness (v. 5)

- The blessing of an earth made to sustain us (vv. 9–13)

If we each made our own list, it might include the love of a spouse and family. It might include health. It might include a job we enjoy. It might include the opportunity to see God work in us and through others. The list would go on and on and on. This is why we praise God in all that we do—because we long for the opportunity to stand before the Father and say, "Thank You!" Or, as David put it, "Praise awaits you, O God, in Zion; to you our vows will be fulfilled" (v. 1).

What are the blessings in your life for which you thank God today?

Make My Life a Song

Where morning dawns and evening fades you call forth songs of joy. PSALM 65:8

Some psalms overwhelm us with the passionate love for God that is offered up by the psalmist. This is one of them.

Psalm 65 is a love song to the Lord that showers its readers with a sense of inspiration. David had many skills and talents, but his passion was for God. He loved to write and sing about God's character in ways that showed God as much more than an invisible omnipotent being who rules from some distant quadrant of the universe. God was very real to David, and so David loved Him, feared Him, and worshiped Him with a tremendous degree of energy.

When we read this psalm, we don't just know about David's passion for God; we feel it. And surely those who encountered David felt it as well.

So, where is the source of our passion? And what things are the objects of our passion?

We can love our work, our play, and our families. And we can feel immense passion for those things. There's nothing wrong with that. But how do those passions relate to our passionate love for Jesus? One of the themes of the Book of Hebrews is this: Jesus is better—better than the prophets, better than the angels, better than anything. So when we show the world our passion for our hobbies, for our families, and for our work, we have the opportunity to show by extension our passion for God.

Your life can become a love song to the Lord, overwhelming and inspiring all who encounter it. Go and sing that song.

Can I Help Today?

Praise be to the Lord, to God our Savior, who daily bears our burdens. PSALM 68:19

The God we serve literally asks us on a daily basis, "Can I help?" He's not pushy. He doesn't demand to help; He's just always available. Notice that David did not say, "Praise be to the LORD . . . who *bears* our burdens." He said, "Praise be to the LORD . . . who *daily bears* our burdens."

Life is so daily. That is especially true in the work context. When we drive to the office in the morning, we're not really sure what's going to happen to us that day, but we have enough experience in life to know that it might not all be good. There may be computer troubles to deal with, perplexing problems to solve, deals that fall through, or people who don't do their jobs correctly.

Whatever the situation, Jesus wants to help us bear our burdens. He offers to be a pack mule for the stuff in life that we'd rather not carry and we're not sure we can handle all by ourselves. "Come to me, all you who are weary and burdened, and I will give you rest," he says in Matthew 11:28. "Cast all your anxiety on him because he cares for you," writes the apostle Peter (1 Peter 5:7).

In the Sermon on the Mount, Jesus instructs His followers not to worry about tomorrow because each day has enough troubles of its own (Matthew 6:34). If we follow His advice and live for Him one day at a time, Psalm 68:19 says we have a daily Volunteer Who is ready and willing to help us. If we choose not to worry about tomorrow and instead focus on today, Jesus says, "I'm here."

Bring the Good Times Back

Your righteousness reaches to the skies, O God, you who have done great things. Who, O God, is like you? Though you have made me see troubles, many and bitter, you will restore my life again; from the depths of the earth you will again bring me up. PSALM 71:19–20

One of the most refreshing things about Scripture is that it doesn't gloss over the fact that life has its ups and downs. It acknowledges—often in vivid language—that there will be times of poverty and times of riches, times of stress and times of rest, times of pain and times of joy.

Such cycles also exist in the business world. There are times when the economy is strong and times when it's bad. There are times when cash flow is great and other times when it's iffy. There are times when profits are up and times when profits are down.

Such is the course of life, regardless of our spiritual condition: "He causes his sun to rise on the evil and the good; and sends rain on the righteous and the unrighteous," Jesus said in Matthew 5:45. But while it's true that God makes the good times as well as the bad times (Ecclesiastes 7:14), that in no way means that if we're in a downturn, we can't ask Him to restore the good times again. In Psalm 71:19–20, David was not at all embarrassed to ask God to rescue him from the depths of the earth, to grant him a reprieve from the troubles that had been "many and bitter." He's seen the good life, and he wants to go back.

There will be seasons and times of life that are darker and heavier and drier than other times. If you're in one of those times, don't become overly discouraged. Stay the course, guard your heart, and keep connected to the people around you. And don't be afraid to ask God to let the good times roll again.

Why Bother? (Part One)

Surely God is good to Israel, to those who are pure in heart. But as for me, my foot had almost slipped; I had nearly lost my foothold. For I envied the arrogant when I saw the prosperity of the wicked. They have no struggles; their bodies are healthy and strong. They are free from the burdens common to man. . . . Surely in vain have I kept my heart pure. PSALM 73:1–5, 13

Have you ever looked around and wondered, *What's the use in being righteous?* Every way you turn, wicked people are getting ahead. As Asaph writes in this passage, "They have no struggles, their bodies are healthy and strong, they are free from the burdens common to man, they are not plagued by human ills" (Psalm 73:4–5). They're "always carefree, they increase in wealth" (v. 12).

In the meantime, you're working hard to follow God and obey His commands. You're focused, you're disciplined, and you honestly desire to please Jesus. Yet unlike the wicked, who always seem to be winning, you never seem to gain very much. You often feel that you're spinning your wheels, dealing with the same problems and burdens over and over again, while the people who have no regard for God seem to be living life on Easy Street.

This inequity is strikingly obvious in the business world. Many times the most successful people also are the most arrogant and corrupt. Their businesses churn out profits as they ruthlessly destroy their competitors. They turn on the charm when they're called upon to appear on television news shows, yet they treat their employees like dirt. And while they're jetting around the world, sailing yachts, eating caviar, and showing off their Rolex watches, you continue to struggle just to get by.

It gets frustrating. It gets tiring. It gets old. It makes you throw up your hands and wonder, *Why bother?*

There is an answer, of course. But it involves taking your eyes off other people and fixing them solidly on the God Who is good to "those who are pure in heart" (v. 1).

Why Bother? (Part Two)

Whom have I in heaven but you? And earth has nothing I desire besides you. My flesh and my heart may fail, but God is the strength of my heart and my portion forever. PSALM 73:25–26

When Asaph asked, "Why bother?" he found his answer when he entered the sanctuary of God. There he finally understood the final destiny of the wicked.

"Surely you place them on slippery ground; you cast them down to ruin," he cried. "How suddenly are they destroyed, completely swept away by terrors! As a dream when one awakes, so when you arise, O Lord, you will despise them as fantasies" (Psalm 73:18–20).

This realization may have provided him some comfort, but it wasn't until Asaph reflected further on his *own* relationship with the Almighty that he was able to accept the apparent inequities he was witnessing. "I am always with you; you hold me by my right hand," he said. "You guide me with your counsel, and afterward you will take me into glory. Whom have I in heaven but you? And earth has nothing I desire besides you" (vv. 23–25).

Asaph realized that all the triumphs and pleasures the world had to offer paled in comparison to the joy of being in the presence of God. Compared to the wicked, his bank account wasn't as big, he had larger medical bills, and he didn't wield as much influence. And yet, he realized that none of that mattered because in God, he had everything he needed.

Are you having trouble keeping your eyes fixed on Christ when everyone around you seems to be taking no thought of Him? Don't forget their ultimate destiny: "Those who are far from you will perish; you destroy all who are unfaithful to you" (v. 27). And when you're tempted to ask, "Why bother?" be ready with Asaph's answer: "[A]s for me, it is good to be near God" (v. 28).

A Mature Faith

"Will the Lord reject forever? Will he never show his favor again? Has his unfailing love vanished forever? Has his promise failed for all time? Has God forgotten to be merciful? Has he in anger withheld his compassion?" PSALM 77:7–9

No one enjoys difficulty, conflict, and hard times. We like for things to go well. We like for the waters to be smooth and the road to be straight. It gives us a sense of God's blessing and favor upon us. We know then that He is opening doors for us and making situations and circumstances come together. We can see His hand at work, which confirms our decisions and lets us know that we have heard His voice and answered His calling correctly.

But what happens when things change?

At some point, winter will come. Night will fall. Things will not go as planned. Where is God then? Has He pulled back His blessings? Did we miss His directions? Are we outside of His will for our lives?

Sometimes this is the case. After all, we are only human. Our ability to discern and follow God's direction is flawed at best. It is a skill we have to learn—a relationship we must continually nurture and cultivate. Otherwise we will go astray. But what about those times when we know we heard His voice and then suddenly all hell breaks loose? What happened?

More than likely, nothing. Following Christ is a mysterious and wonderful thing. It is filled with risk-taking, faith-stretching adventure, and it is also filled with times that seem lonely, isolated, and confusing.

But a mature faith knows that this too shall pass. A mature faith does not require a sign to be convinced of God's direction, and does not abandon the call at the first sign of conflict. A mature faith expects troubles along the path, and holds on through the night—calling out for the One Who can lead him to the light.

Our faith will mature during the trials of life, not during the high times. High times are the breaks in the action. They are the resting points along the path, not the destination. If you are in or entering one of these seasons, do not give up, lose hope, or let go. This too shall pass, and the increase of your faith is worth the wait.

Don't Forget

Then I thought, "To this I will appeal: the years of the right hand of the Most High." I will remember the deeds of the LORD; yes, I will remember your miracles of long ago. I will meditate on all your works and consider all your mighty deeds. PSALM 77:10–12

In the business world, we always look forward. We try to predict the future. We plan for the future. The future is our hope. It's everything we have. We spend all our time, effort, and money on things in the future. Strategic planning is all about anticipation—how we're going to get from here to there.

None of that is wrong unless we start assuming that we can actually *know* the future. But in the middle of all our forecasting and predicting, the psalmist jerks us out of the future and sends us back to the past. Scripture instructs us to remember the past. We're not supposed to rehash our sins or rest on the laurels of what we did right; we're supposed to remember all the good things that God has done for us.

Time and time again throughout Scripture, the nation of Israel recounted how God took them out of slavery in Egypt into the Promised Land. They remembered the miracles He did along the way, and they meditated on the mighty deeds He accomplished. Such recollections kept God's power and holiness fresh in their minds and kept them in the correct frame of mind for worshiping Him.

This kind of reflection is still beneficial for us today. Remembering what God did for us in the past helps us have faith to face an uncertain future. The things we remember may not be as dramatic as the miracles God did for the children of Israel, but they are no less significant when it comes to building our faith.

Take a few minutes to reflect on your past. What has God done for you? Whether it was the time He saved you from making a bad decision or the time He restored a broken relationship, remembering such events gives you a sense of confidence that the same God Who did things for you in the past can and will intervene for you in the future.

A Teaching Agenda

O my people, hear my teaching; listen to the words of my mouth. I will open my mouth in parables, I will utter hidden things, things from of old—what we have heard and known, what our fathers have told us. We will not hide them from their children; we will tell the next generation the praiseworthy deeds of the LORD, his power, and the wonders he has done. PSALM 78:1–4

Sometimes we think that the Christian life should be characterized by our personal relationships with God: what we think of Him, how we meditate on Him, how He answers our prayers, what He says to us, etc.

That certainly is a big part of it—we should make the most of moments of prayer and meditation that are just between us and God, whether we're on airplanes jetting between cities, listening to a boring presentation at a board meeting, or just sitting at our desks at the office. But in this passage, Asaph identifies another agenda for our lives with Christ. We should take all the wisdom and insight we have gained through our walks with Jesus and intentionally pass it on to others. Whether it's through a mentoring relationship at work or with our own children at home, we are to express what God has done in the past, both in Scripture and in our own lives. In order to do this, we have to know what those praiseworthy deeds are. We have to know what He did in the Scriptures, and we have to pay attention to what He's done for us.

Then we have to figure out appropriate ways to pass them on to the next generation. We can bring them up in a teaching context, or we can inject them into casual conversation with friends and coworkers who are confused, angry, hurt, or uncertain about life. Over lunch or an afternoon Coke, we can encourage them by relating cases when God came through for *us* in uncertain times. Perhaps hearing how God answered our prayers will give them the extra faith boost they need to press forward into a cloudy future.

Make a list of specific times in your life when God showed up and made a crooked road straight or a bumpy path level. And don't forget to mention these praiseworthy deeds of the Lord the next time you have the opportunity to advise or encourage someone.

The Call of God

He chose David his servant and took him from the sheep pens; from tending the sheep he brought him to be the shepherd of his people Jacob, of Israel his inheritance. And David shepherded them with integrity of heart; with skillful hands he led them. PSALM 78:70-72

In these three verses, we get a snapshot of our work lives as we see a glimpse of David's calling and gain valuable insights into the way that God works in the lives of men. This psalm shows us a basic pattern that is reflected over and over again in the Scriptures: God's calling, equipping, and sending.

The word *vocation* is taken from the Latin word *vocare,* which means "to call." From the earliest times, man sensed that he was designed for work in general and his profession specifically. There was a sense of calling. But this is not the primary call in our lives.

In life, there are two callings: salvation and vocation. The call of salvation is the most important call you can answer. It is a call to relationship and restoration with the One Who created you—a call from darkness into light, from death to life.

You have done nothing to deserve this call. It is His desire to call you—all you have to do is turn and answer. Once you have answered, nothing you can do will separate you from Him. And nothing you can do will endear you to Him more—you are His.

But you are not done answering His call. The second call is vocation. Vocation is essentially an assignment from God. It is what we do once we surrender our lives and futures to Him. We have relinquished control of the wheel, given up the captain's chair. We have been purchased. Our lives are not our own. So now what? Listen and follow.

In the Bible, God called men and women in different ways. Some He called directly by name, some were born into their calling, some had their hearts stirred, and still others had an attractive option arrive on the scene. There is no one right answer, but we do have to answer. We are followers of Christ, not just believers in Christ. Our faith incites us to action; otherwise, as we are told in James 2:17, our faith is dead.

The call of God is risky business indeed. It requires finely tuned hearing and the courage to answer. Are you up to the challenge?

The Equipping of God

He chose David his servant and took him from the sheep pens; from tending the sheep he brought him to be the shepherd of his people Jacob, of Israel his inheritance. And David shepherded them with integrity of heart; with skillful hands he led them. PSALM 78:70–72

David must have spent many days and nights on his father's property tending his sheep. He rescued them from lions and bears. He fed them and gave them water. He found them when they wandered astray.

We do not know what David was thinking all this time, but we can imagine that he dreamed of faraway places, battles, and heroes. Little did he know that caring for smelly, simple-minded sheep was preparing him for his future career. He probably never imagined that the songs he composed and sang before the Lord under starry skies would someday be read by millions of people.

Are you in a position that doesn't make sense? There are times in life that seem puzzling to us, phases when we seem to be idling or spinning our wheels. In our haste for progress and promotion, we often fail to learn the lessons that we are being taught.

David learned how to be a king in the pasture. He became a warrior by fighting bears. He became a man after God's own heart out under the stars. His life is proof positive that God does not call the equipped; He equips the called.

David was created to be a shepherd. But it still took preparation to bring out these skills and form his character. Finally, when his training was complete, David was promoted from shepherd of sheep to shepherd of the nation of Israel, God's chosen people.

God does not make us one way and ask us to be another. Instead, He tends to use us in our areas of strength. He does, however, stretch our faith at times by putting us in situations in which we need Him or we will fail.

It is risky to follow God. He will not allow you to sit still. You will constantly be pushed out of your comfort zone and into something new.

Do you feel that you are spinning your wheels? Be open to the lessons that you are learning. Are you being stretched beyond what you think you can handle? Hold on tight—you will get to see God come through.

The Sending of God

He chose David his servant and took him from the sheep pens; from tending the sheep he brought him to be the shepherd of his people Jacob, of Israel his inheritance. And David shepherded them with integrity of heart; with skillful hands he led them. PSALM 78:70–72

After you have answered God's call and attended His training program, you are ready to be sent into the fray. God does not call you just to fill you with wisdom. He has somewhere for you to go, and you have to get on the road and go there. Your spiritual journey will be just that—a journey. And it's hard to sit still on a journey.

No matter the destination God calls you to, your responsibility is to go. And once you arrive, there are a few principles that will make your work successful.

First, *do what you are*. When David became king, he did not pretend to be something he was not. It would have been easy for him to feel that way. He was the youngest of his brothers. His only real experience for the job was as a lowly shepherd and occasional warrior. It would have been easy for him to try to operate outside of his skills or personality, but he stayed true to what he was and God used him mightily.

Second, *pursue integrity of heart*. David had a good heart; in fact, God called him a man after His own heart. We see David's heart and passion for the Lord in the psalms that he wrote, and we see his integrity in the way he led his people. David was a passionate and caring king who dearly loved his God and his people.

Third, *develop skillful hands*. David was a good king because he was a good shepherd. He was a hard worker. He cared about what he did, and he did it with all his might. David understood that God was his boss, and he knew that he would stand before Him and Him alone to give an account for his life. We often settle for being "good enough." But as followers of Christ, we work for the same unseen Boss that David worked for. And we, too, must have a commitment to excellence and a passion to learn and grow the skills that God formed within us.

We are all somewhere in the cycle of being called, equipped, and sent. We need to learn this cycle and figure out where we are in it. It will make us more fruitful and productive workers in the eternal kingdom.

Some Things Are Worth Repeating

Restore us, O God; make your face shine upon us, that we may be saved. PSALM 80:3

These days, it seems we are on perpetual information overload. We're barraged with facts, figures, formulas, and opinions from television news and talk shows, magazine and newspaper articles, e-mail, friends and coworkers, and the Internet.

Even though there's more information floating around out there than we could ever possibly know or use, we're constantly looking for the latest, most up-to-the-minute data that will help us grow our businesses, beat our competitors, improve our marriages, become better parents, stay in shape, and so on.

In the middle of this onslaught of new information, however, some things are worth repeating. Some thoughts need to serve as anchors for our days, our weeks, our months, and our lives. No matter how much new stuff there is to know, we need to keep returning to these bedrock thoughts. Through the din of forgettable information, we must not forget these timeless truths.

A phrase like this shows up in Psalm 80. As Asaph recounted God's glorious deeds in different situations, he kept returning to one key thought: "Restore us, O God; make your face to shine upon us, that we might be saved" (v. 3; cf. vv. 7, 19). The fact that he repeated this prayer three times in nineteen verses is a good indication that he thought it was pretty important. Perhaps he needed to remember it himself, or maybe he felt he had to drive it home to his audience. Either way, he felt it was worth repeating.

What phrases or verses from Scripture do you need to start repeating in your life? Perhaps you need to make 2 Timothy 2:15 your motto: "Do your best to present yourself to God as one approved, a workman who does not need to be ashamed and who correctly handles the word of truth." Or maybe Philippians 2:3—"Do nothing out of selfish ambition or vain conceit, but in humility consider others better than yourselves"—bears repeating in your life. Whatever the text, make it a habit of remembering it. After all, some things are worth repeating.

He Sees Us

Return to us, O God Almighty! Look down from heaven and see! PSALM 80:14

In 1927, a theoretical physicist named Werner Heisenberg dropped a bomb that shook the scientific community to the core. The aftershocks still rattle us today. In layman's terms, Heisenberg's Theory of Uncertainty, as it is called, reads something like this: We cannot truly know what goes on at the subatomic level, because the very act of viewing these microscopic particles changes their path as they orbit an atom. Said differently, just looking at something changes it.

Ah, the power of vision!

Vision affects our momentum and direction—it forges a new path. Vision is a catalyst, a power that jolts us off our sleepy routine and headlong into a new adventure in life. Vision lures. It is the nucleus of our ministry around which we (and our organizations) orbit.

God's vision is the most powerful force in the universe. His eyes are always upon us. A revelation of this will radically explode our present state and catapult us onto a path beyond what is currently imaginable. Actually, it transports us *to* the imaginable: to dreams lying dormant in our hearts. And it scatters them broadly in rich earth to germinate and take root.

In biblical times, prophets were called *seers*. Their words were known as *oracles* or *visions*. These divine revelations transformed entire nations. The prophets were God's change agents for the human race. They knew the power of vision to act as a procession for the hand of God. Call it the Certainty Principle: Where His eyes rest and His lips speak, His hand acts.

Where are the "seers" today? The dawning age desperately needs men and women who have forged this deep, powerful gift and tempered it with discernment and humility—individuals who can say with Isaiah, "I saw the Lord" (Isaiah 6:1).

Ears to Hear

If my people would but listen to me, if Israel would follow my ways, how quickly would I subdue their enemies and turn my hand against their foes!
PSALM 81:13–14

We don't have to learn how to hear. Our ears are always open and always turned on. We hear automatically. Of course, it takes time to *understand* what we are hearing. But through repetition and instruction, we can discern the difference between words, music, and noise. Specialists say that a mother's voice is one of the first things a newborn will recognize. If you are a parent, then you know the joy of seeing your little one respond to your voice.

As we become older, however, we develop the ability to hear without listening. This is evident in children, but adults are just as guilty. Every day at work we hear ideas we disagree with and receive assignments that we don't like. We hear them, but we do not take them to heart; in short, we don't listen.

We have that same problem in our spiritual lives. Our spiritual ears can hear God's Word and yet act as though we never heard. We hear, but we do not understand. We read His Word, but we fail to tuck it away in our hearts where it will lodge and take root. In the parable of the sower (Luke 8:5–15), Jesus tells us that many different forces are conspiring to rob us of our ability to hear and listen—the devil, the cares of this world, the hardness of our hearts, and so on.

But it is not just enough to listen and consider the Lord's words. We also must act upon them. We must follow Him and His ways. We must do what His Word says. Otherwise, we are like the man who looked in a mirror and, when he left, immediately forgot what he looked like (James 1:23–24).

If we are listening and following, then God will act on our behalf. He will intervene in situations and circumstances that are blocking His will and purpose in our lives. He will right relationships and subvert the plans of people who are coming against us. He will be our Defender and protect our lives and our reputations. In short, He will be our God, and we will be His people. It is His promise. We have His Word on it.

Deciding Where to Live

Better is one day in your courts than a thousand elsewhere; I would rather be a doorkeeper in the house of my God than dwell in the tents of the wicked. For the LORD God is a sun and shield; the LORD bestows favor and honor; no good thing does he withhold from those whose walk is blameless. O LORD Almighty, blessed is the man who trusts in you. PSALM 84:10–12

Scripture clearly teaches that we have to choose whether we're going to serve God or Satan, whether we're going to obey God's law or go our own direction, whether we're going to submit to Christ's authority or remain in the captain's seat ourselves.

The choice presented in Psalm 84:10–12 is similar: We have to choose where we're going to live—in the house of our God or in the tents of the wicked. To say that it is better to spend a day in God's courts than a thousand elsewhere does not mean that working in a church should be our ultimate career goal. The issue here is not where we literally spend our days. The issue is whether we'd rather live in God's presence or hang around with evil people.

In God's presence we find peace, a clean conscience, clear direction, a refuge, forgiveness, warmth, acceptance, help, advice, joy, and numerous other positive benefits. In the tents of the wicked, we might find short-term pleasure and gain, but we also find confusion, guilt, insecurity, unforgiveness, and strife.

The correct choice seems obvious. Why would we ever want to forgo all the blessings that are found in God's presence in exchange for all the pain that exists in the tents of the wicked? Again, the answer is simple. We leave God's presence because we're still attracted to the things the world has to offer—the lust of the flesh, the lust of the eyes, and the pride of life (1 John 2:16 KJV). We find security with God, but we also love being autonomous. We love living with God, but we're pulled to live elsewhere. No matter how long we've known Jesus, we can all relate to the words the apostle Paul wrote in Romans 7:19: "For what I do is not the good I want to do; no, the evil I do not want to do—this I keep on doing."

Where are you living? Have you strayed from the courts of God? If so, now is a good time to come home.

Sun and Shield

For the LORD God is a sun and shield. PSALM 84:11

What does it mean that the Lord is our sun and shield?

The sun is the center of our solar system. All of the planets revolve around it and derive their heat from it. For earth in particular, the sun is absolutely necessary to sustain life. It determines our seasons and climates, our days and nights, and to some degree even our moods and attitudes. Throughout the ages, people have even worshiped the sun in some form or other. It is essential to life as we know it.

Is the Lord the center of our universe? We often hear people talk about priorities. They mention that they want God to be the top priority in their lives. This is totally the wrong perspective and paradigm. He is not on the top of a list—He is at the center of every item on the list, whether it is work, family, church, friends, hobbies, or anything else. The Lord is our sun. Without Him we would not exist. He is not a priority in life; He is life itself.

In this day and age, we do not have much experience with shields. But in Old Testament times, if you were a soldier or warrior, you knew what a shield was and you knew how to use one. If you didn't, you were as good as dead in battle. A shield was a miniature wall of armor behind which you hid to protect yourself from the arrows and swords of your enemy. Arrows could be launched from quite a distance, so keeping your shield up and protecting yourself was important. When you became engaged in hand-to-hand combat, a shield could help protect you from direct attacks with a sword or club. It was an essential defense weapon.

Is the Lord our protector and defense? We should look to Him when the attack is at hand or when it is launched from afar. He is our Protector. Nothing can take us from His hand of protection. We are safe within His care. This does not mean that we will not face hardship, but through it all we are under His watchful eye. He desires our maturity in Him, not our independence from Him. At all times and in all ways, He will be there to protect, defend, and shield us from the enemy of our souls.

An Undivided Heart

Teach me your way, O LORD, and I will walk in your truth; give me an undivided heart, that I may fear your name. PSALM 86:11

One of the things that God wants most from His children is wholehearted love and devotion. Throughout Scripture (Jeremiah 32:39; James 4:8), it's clear that He places a premium on an undivided heart.

So what exactly is an undivided heart? Several years ago, a popular gospel tract entitled "My Heart, Christ's Home" compared a person's life to the rooms of a house. It's an analogy that works well here. When we have divided hearts, we give God one or two rooms of our lives, but we keep the other ones closed off to Him. From a business standpoint, having a divided heart would be like pledging full loyalty to your current employer while you were negotiating a relationship with your company's closest competitor.

When we have undivided hearts, however, we give Him the keys to all the rooms. It doesn't mean we're sinless; it just means that we're not trying to hide anything from Him. We're laying our whole household of thoughts and feelings on the table: all our fears, thoughts, concerns, agendas, and ambitions. And as He reveals areas of our lives that need work, we willingly uncover them and do what we can to put them in order.

Only a man or woman who is working hard to live a holistic, integrated life can ever hope to pledge a wholehearted, single-focused devotion to Jesus. Why is that? As long as we split up our lives, closing off work in one room, church in another room, our finances in another room, and our family in still another, our focus will always be divided. We can't concentrate on one thing first and another thing later. We must bring all our worlds together and realize that it's just as possible for God to be in the middle of our mundane, Tuesday afternoon work world as it is for Him to be involved in our family lives or church activities.

Examine the rooms of your life. Do you need to pray and ask God to give you an undivided heart?

It Might Hurt, but the Love Never Leaves

If his sons forsake my law and do not follow my statutes, if they violate my decrees and fail to keep my commands, I will punish their sin with the rod, their iniquity with flogging; but I will not take my love from him, nor will I ever betray my faithfulness. PSALM 89:30–33

If you've ever taken care of children—either yours or someone else's—you know that kids will do things for which they need to be punished. It's just part of life, part of the pattern that began when Adam and Eve sinned in the Garden of Eden.

As God's children, it's also inevitable that we also will do things for which we need to be punished. As we see from this passage, God's discipline isn't especially comfortable—there's nothing particularly *nice* about a flogging. But God is in the business of providing individualized instruction and discipline that is designed to help us return to Him as quickly as possible. In other words, even when it hurts, God's discipline really is for our own good.

In a way, it's like getting a performance review at work. If the boss truly has our best interests at heart, he or she will give negative feedback as well as positive; otherwise, we would never improve. A poor manager never bothers to correct his employees, while a manager who gives feedback that it honest yet gentle is an excellent boss indeed.

The good news, spiritually speaking, is found in Psalm 89:33: No matter how hard the discipline, God will never—under any circumstance, conceivable or otherwise—take His love from us or be unfaithful to us. As Romans 8:38 says, "I am convinced that neither death nor life, neither angels nor demons, neither the present nor the future, nor any powers, nor height nor depth, nor anything else in all creation, will be able to separate us from the love of God that is in Christ Jesus our Lord."

As a result, even when the discipline is particularly painful, we truly are able to smile through our tears.

The Ultimate Motivator

Teach us to number our days aright, that we may gain a heart of wisdom. PSALM 90:12

The idea of numbering our days can seem like a fatalistic preoccupation with the end of our lives, especially when we're young. Who thinks about death when it seems so far away? And besides, with average life spans in the midseventies, we are talking about having ten-thousand-plus days left when we're forty-five. That is almost as many days as Jesus walked on this earth. And yet, we are exhorted to number them correctly.

Three admonishments and benefits spill out of this verse.

First, numbering our days helps us to think comprehensively and strategically. It does not come naturally for most people to think holistically about their lives, but as followers of Christ, we must. It is not an option for us to be a one-dimensional success story with a fantastic career and a family in ruins or to have an incredible family life with a string of job failures. All of life must get our attention and our intention. We have to take notice of all areas and think about the big picture even while we are bogged down in the minutiae of everyday living. Otherwise we will get to the end of the road and discover that it led us in the wrong direction. Do not let life pass you by. Take time to think.

Second, numbering our days motivates us to work diligently and passionately. Realizing that life has an end inspires us when nothing else will. As followers of Christ, we do not labor under a burden of guilt, trying to work out our salvation. Instead, we see our life and work as an expression of love and worship toward a God Who has loved us unconditionally. In light of that reality, our short turn here on this earth becomes so important. We must be found at work on His agenda when that final day arrives for us, always seeking to gain more in His kingdom than in our own.

Finally, numbering our days will allow us to live wisely and compassionately. Relationships are all that we will take out of this life. We need to spend our emotional and physical energy on loving and serving others. This is easier said than done, but it yields a return far above all others.

Are you counting your days? More importantly, what are you doing to make your days count?

Defining Success (Part One)

May the favor of the Lord our God rest upon us; establish the work of our hands for us—yes, establish the work of our hands. PSALM 90:17

Grace is the unmerited favor of God that rests upon us when we respond to His call and believe in Him. Its benefits and blessings are beyond compare and comprehension. Grace is an unsearchable mystery that deserves our meditation and devotion. It also is a reality that alters the very nature of our work.

In our go-go economy full of excitement and energy, we have created an unrealistic and unhealthy preoccupation with success. We read about "success stories" in the news; we travel many miles and pay thousands of dollars to learn how to become "successful"; we buy books promising the ingredients of "success." But for the follower of Christ, what does success look like? In God's economy of giving and receiving versus buying and selling, how do we define success?

We'll look at one way today and two more tomorrow.

Success is about grace. When God's favor rests upon you, success is at your doorstep. You have transitioned from one kingdom into another. Your future is secured in Him. You are His child. His inheritance is yours. Your life is radically and permanently altered. You did nothing to warrant this, nothing to earn it. You can do nothing to lose it. Your salvation is given, received, signed, sealed, and delivered.

But you also will have difficulty. You will be opposed. You will struggle and labor and toil. Your life will be marked by hardships and pain. You are no longer callous to the hurts and needs of others. You will share them in a new way—you will feel other people's hurt with them and understand their sorrow. You will encourage, exhort, heal, soothe, and comfort others. You are blessed, and in return, you bless. You give grace the way it was received.

Are you giving God's grace to others through your words and actions at work? If so, that is success.

Defining Success (Part Two)

May the favor of the Lord our God rest upon us; establish the work of our hands for us—yes, establish the work of our hands. PSALM 90:17

This may come as a shock to some, but rest is a key ingredient in success. Most people think that success requires hard work and a little luck. Yesterday we learned that it is grace, not luck, that is involved, but what about hard work? Yes, you will have to work, and work hard, in this life. Nothing is free, and everything around us tends toward atrophy. But you will not be successful in God's economy unless you also rest—and work hard at it.

Life is hectic, and many people think that time spent resting is either an expensive luxury or a wasted opportunity. But rest is a necessary part of the cycle of work—six days on, one day off—that God established by example in Genesis. We must take time to renew and refresh ourselves, our relationship with Jesus, and our relationships with family and friends. The key is rest.

Success also is about legacy. Too often, we find ourselves working toward the next big thing in our lives. For some of us, it can be the weekend or the next paycheck; for others, it is the next promotion or closing a deal. But success is always just ahead, a little ways down the road, just out of reach, tomorrow, next week, next year. But we can spend our entire lives looking ahead at what is yet to be and miss an opportunity to build something today that is worth passing on.

God is more interested in today than tomorrow. He wants to establish the work you are doing now, not the work that is to come.

Do you want to be successful? It's not easy, but if you want to be successful, you must learn to live in the moment, giving your passionate best today and letting tomorrow take care of itself.

Powerful and Intimate

"Because he loves me," says the LORD, "I will rescue him; I will protect him, for he acknowledges my name." PSALM 91:14

If God were merely omnipresent, omniscient, and omnipotent, He still would be awe-inspiring. He is bigger than the universe; it resides in the palm of His hand. He is more powerful than the strongest storm, the erupting volcano, or the trembling earthquake. He is everywhere all at once, and He is right beside us now. He knows our past, present, and future; and He sees all our hopes and fears and desires.

But He is even more magnificent than this. Every time we discover something new about the universe, whether in the realm of science, medicine, or psychology, the gap between Him and us grows.

On the other hand, if God were merely intimate, He still would be comforting. He has the hairs of our heads numbered. His love alone is beyond compare. What Jesus accomplished on earth apart from His death and resurrection is remarkable. He walked among the lowly and the sinner. He fought for the oppressed and those without a voice. His life alone is worthy of emulation.

The amazing and wonderful thing is that God is both all-powerful and personally interested in us. When we couple these two realities together, it is beyond our ability to understand. All we can do is develop metaphors that don't even begin to scratch the surface of what it all means. His love for us, His intimate knowledge of us, and His care and concern for us, together with His majesty and power and strength and might—it's incomprehensible.

Our response to God is a balancing act. We cannot be too familiar and forget that He is wholly other than us, but we cannot be too afraid to approach His throne of grace. We will never get this quite right, but the good news is that our Father so desires relationship with us that He will forgive our shortcomings—even our shortcomings in relating to Him.

Hidden Camera and Concealed Microphone

Does he who implanted the ear not hear? Does he who formed the eye not see?
PSALM 94:9

Many portions of our lives don't come under scrutiny from other people because they're hidden. Some, such as questionable activities we might participate in while away on business, are hidden because we conceal them on purpose. Others, such as our thought lives, are hidden simply because they're internal.

It's sometimes easy to think that nobody—not even God—really knows about these secret things. But He *does* know. As this verse indicates, it's ludicrous to think that the One who made our ears can't hear everything we hear, and the One Who made our eyes doesn't see everything we see.

The issue here is one of accountability. We must be careful what we listen to and what we see, because there will come a day when we will have to explain to Him why we listened and why we looked. Every word and deed will be brought out into the open and judged.

This does not mean that God rejects us if we see or hear something bad. It does mean that we invite God's discipline when we intentionally, consciously, and regularly choose to engage in hearing and seeing things that are dark and sinful.

The bottom line is this: We need to do everything we do—whether we're at home, at work, or at play; whether we're in a group or by ourselves—as if God is our audience, because He is. We shouldn't just remember this when we're out on the road and have access to pornographic movies in our hotel rooms. It also applies when we're balancing our checkbooks, when we're working on solo assignments at work, when we're driving to business meetings, and when we're waiting for phone calls.

What are the hidden camera and concealed microphone of God picking up in your life that you'd rather He not see and hear?

Honest to God

When I said, "My foot is slipping," your love, O LORD, supported me. When anxiety was great within me, your consolation brought joy to my soul. PSALM 94:18–19

Bad decisions or circumstances have a way of compounding into personal or professional disaster. Once we have started down the wrong path, it is hard to get off. Cover-ups, deceit, and continual hardening of our hearts war against repentance and restoration.

The world is no help in these matters. It communicates a "don't-ask-don't-tell" message regarding sin and indiscretions, in which getting caught is the only cause for remorse. And the idea of catching yourself is out of the question.

On the other hand, there are times when ill circumstances have a way of finding us even if we are living the way we're supposed to. There is no guarantee of easy times or the good life for the follower of Christ. The rain falls on the just and the unjust. In a moment, we can find ourselves without work, without a home, or without a spouse or loved one. These events forever alter the course of life and require great faith and perseverance.

When life goes awry, either through our own poor decisions or the random circumstances of life, it is important that we cultivate a healthy and honest life of prayer. We need to learn to be completely transparent with the Lord. He always knows what is going on in our lives, but He often chooses to wait until we bring an issue before Him until He responds on our behalf. It is a testament to His desire for relationship with us above all else. He is a jealous God, and He wants to be the first and preferred stop for all our issues.

How are we doing at gut-level honesty with God? Start today, whether your foot is slipping or not.

A New Song

Come, let us bow down in worship, let us kneel before the LORD our Maker.
PSALM 95:6

You are God's idea.

It is a simple idea, but profound when you fully grasp all that it means. You are His idea. He thought of you, created you, formed you, and designed you perfectly. He took the time to consider the color of your hair, the shape of your nose, and the sound of your voice. You are His idea.

When He looked at this generation, He decided what was really needed was you. Then He set about the task of designing you. He gave you the gifts that you have, exactly what you will need to fulfill His purpose for your life. You lack nothing that His grace cannot give you. He is incapable of mistakes—He has given or will give you everything you need to accomplish what lies before you.

The road ahead will be difficult. It will be fraught with hardship and heartache, personal and professional setbacks, and hurdles galore. But God knows about all those obstacles, and He has given you what you need to overcome them. In Him, you live and move and have your being. He will see you through. Through Him you can finish—and finish well.

He owns the trademark on you as well. This means that you are 100 percent His, whether you realize it or acknowledge it. In our economy, a person's ideas and trademarks are worth more than hard assets. They are capital that pays huge dividends to its owners. In God's economy, His ideas recognize Him as Creator and give Him the credit and worship and honor that He deserves.

You are God's idea—and a good one, too. Think about it.

In the Line of Fire

Fire goes before him and consumes his foes on every side. His lightning lights up the world; the earth sees and trembles. The mountains melt like wax before the LORD, before the Lord of all the earth. PSALM 97:3–5

A previous home of our partner, Sean Womack, had a gas-lighting fireplace. He recalls that he and his wife had a key to insert into a tiny hole onto a hidden fitting. Once it was inserted and they turned the key, the gas would begin to pump out of the pipe running just beneath the logs. Carefully, they would stick a match inside and—*poof!*—the gas would light and eventually catch the logs on fire.

This was a great system, mostly because it was easy. Or at least it was easy until the family lost the key. One day it was there, the next day it was gone. Then they couldn't turn on the gas. Gone were the days of easy-light fires. They had to try to light them with a match and paper. They finally bought a new key, and things went back to normal.

Then one day, Sean's wife cleaned the ashes out of the fireplace and found the original key. Their son had thrown it into the hot coals one day. It was melted beyond repair. Shriveled and deformed, the key was completely different and no longer useful for turning on the gas.

Fire does that. It changes things. It consumes them and alters them completely. Once something has been through the fire, it will never be the same. Including us. John the Baptist said that while he baptized with water, Jesus came to baptize with fire (Luke 3:16). He changes us, makes us new. We are permanently altered. We're no longer useful for sin; we have a new purpose. His purpose. His call. His assignment.

Has your life been transformed by Jesus' renewing fire?

Party Time

Shout for joy to the LORD, all the earth. . . . Enter his gates with thanksgiving and his courts with praise; give thanks to him and praise his name. For the LORD is good and his love endures forever; his faithfulness continues through all generations. PSALM 100:1, 4–5

Psalm 100—all five verses of it—is an unabashed testimony that a relationship with God deserves a party. It's short, it's intense, and it's an awful lot of fun.

As believers we have lots of responsibilities and commitments. We're concerned with following God's law and knowing His Word. We have to remember that He can see and hear everything we do. We're focused on keeping an undivided heart. We understand that discipline is part of the equation in the Christian life.

We take none of this lightly. But there comes a time when our relationships with Jesus overwhelm us with so much gladness that all we can do is "shout for joy to the LORD" (Psalm 100:1). It's not work time, it's not accountability time, it's not discipline time—it's party time! It's time to acknowledge that God is good and His love endures forever (v. 5). It's time to revel in Who God is and what He does for us—including all those things that we take for granted or don't even realize He's doing on a daily basis.

We might think such parties can only be had at church or maybe late at night as we gaze up at the stars. But you can schedule one at work anytime! You might have to leave the bells and whistles at home—you wouldn't want to distract the people around you too much—but there's no law against having your own private party in your heart.

Your face will be full of joy, your words will be bright and cheerful, and your actions will be loving and kind. Your coworkers might think you've gone crazy, or they might be so intrigued that they ask you what's going on. And then you have an open invitation to tell them—and to invite them to join the party.

Joyful, Joyful!

Shout for joy to the LORD, all the earth. Worship the LORD with gladness; come before him with joyful songs. PSALM 100:1–2

Someone once said, "You cannot share the good news if you are the bad news." Religious people can be the most sour and pious people on the earth. We can allow pride and self-righteousness to so consume us that we are not only unpleasant to be with, but we can actually hinder the spread and growth of the gospel.

Ask any waiter or waitress about waiting tables for Sunday lunch and you will get the same standard reply: "The folks who come in after church are rude and bad tippers." This is beyond shameful; it is sinful. Too often our attitude is a stumbling block for those whose faith is weak—or nonexistent.

Jesus performed His first miracle by keeping the wine flowing at a wedding feast. Pious people are seldom accused of being gluttons and drunkards who eat with sinners, but Jesus was. It is hard to imagine Him not living joyfully while He was on earth.

So what about us? Most of us live and work in very similar circumstances. We pay bills, keep the grass cut, play with the kids, go to church, and eat out with our friends. But are we embracing life exuberantly? Are we living with a song of praise in our hearts? Does an infectious joy spill out of us? If not, it might be a good time to ask why. We are not intended to live a Pollyanna life of foolish and insincere optimism. Instead, we are to walk in the joyful reality that this is not our home and that our future is secure in Him.

Let's start that walk today.

Everything I Need

Praise the LORD, O my soul; all my inmost being, praise his holy name. Praise the LORD, O my soul, and forget not all his benefits—who forgives all your sins and heals all your diseases, who redeems your life from the pit and crowns you with love and compassion, who satisfies your desires with good things so that your youth is renewed like the eagle's. PSALM 103:1–5

While many psalms repeat the same thing over and over again, this one is more of a laundry list of the wonderful things that God does for us.

He forgives our sins, He heals all our diseases, He redeems our lives from the pit, He crowns us with love and compassion, and He satisfies our desires for good things. In other words, everything we need to make our lives complete and fulfilled, God ultimately provides. There is nothing we can obtain on our own or from anyone else that will provide more meaning than what He willingly gives us.

Our jobs might give us satisfaction, but they are from God. Our families may give us meaning and companionship, but they are from God. Our ministries might provide fulfillment, but they also are from God.

When God bestows all the blessings enumerated in Psalm 103:1–5 on us, our youth will be renewed like the eagle's. Have you ever seen an eagle struggling and flapping in the air? Of course not. It flies effortlessly, using the currents of the wind to transport it. The same is true for us. Once we experience all the extravagant benefits that a life with Christ offers, we are infused with His strength, and we can soar with the eagles.

Take some time to remember all the benefits that accompany your life with Christ. He truly is everything you need, and knowing that should make your heart break out in a song of praise to Him.

Who Owns You?

Let the redeemed of the LORD say this—those he redeemed from the hand of the foe. PSALM 107:2

You have a new owner. You have been sold, purchased by the Master. The title has been transferred, and all rights have been assigned. God owns you now, completely. He has the title, the deed, the rights, the trademark, the name, and the assets. In short, He has everything.

Your previous owner took no interest in your well-being. In fact, his goal was your demise. He was intent on your destruction. He was your foe, but then you were bought away from him.

You were "hungry and thirsty" (v. 5) and "sat in darkness and the deepest gloom" (v. 10). You "rebelled against the words of God" (v. 11), and so you worked in "bitter labor" (v. 12). But when you "cried out to the LORD in [your] trouble" (vv. 6, 13, 19, 28), He saved you, delivered you, and brought you out. He redeemed you.

When work is bitter and circumstances are against you, when everything is dark and despair begins to creep in, cry out to the Lord. Don't give up or wish things were better; cry out to the Lord. Reach out to Him, call His name, and cling to His word. He will redeem you.

There are times when desperate and aggressive prayers are warranted: when you experience or witness injustice or cruelty at the hands of others, when you've lost a loved one, when you're facing unemployment or bankruptcy, or when you're in utter defeat and all your hopes and dreams have been dashed.

Do you desperately cling to Him? If not, then maybe you do not see the reality of your condition clearly enough. Perhaps you do not understand the depths from which you were saved—or you have forgotten the price that was paid for you.

Desperate times can stem from many sources: our own foolishness and rebellion, our enemies, life circumstances, or the Lord's testing. Regardless of the source, the solution is the same: Cry out to Him. He will redeem you.

Whose Battle Is It?

Give us aid against the enemy, for the help of man is worthless. PSALM 108:12

Where do you turn for help in times of trouble? What is your first reaction when adversity strikes? There are occasions when another person can comfort, encourage, and advise, but when it comes to fighting the enemy, "man is worthless" (Psalm 108:12). Salvation belongs to our God alone. He can destroy any enemy with a word.

God does not need to muster up courage or convince Himself that He is up to the challenge. He is not engaged in a kind of cosmic battle, struggling to defeat evil. The outcome is clear, certain, and decided.

We are the ones in the midst of a daily spiritual battle. We find ourselves fighting for our very lives. But where is our victory? *Who* is our victory? And why are we still fighting this war alone? We have not enlisted Him, and until we lay down our weapons and take up His, we will suffer defeat. As we continue our solitary struggle, He patiently stands by, loving us enough to allow our defeat. But when we call on God, His sheer size and awesomeness strikes fear in His enemies. The universe rests in the palm of His hand. He makes earth His footstool.

His anger and wrath once brought Egypt to its knees and allowed a nation of slaves to walk out as free men and women. And when Pharaoh and his army pursued Israel, expecting to enslave them again, God swallowed them whole in the Red Sea.

Why do we not call on Him? It's often because we want to win the war; we want the glory. We crave recognition and want the attention focused on us. When God shows up, however, the battle is immediately over—and we didn't lift a finger. That's hard on our egos. Our pride can't take that, so we fight on—while the One Who "trample[s] down our enemies" (v. 13) waits to hear us say, "Give us aid."

Who is fighting the battles in your life—you or God?

The Strength of Weakness

Let [my enemies] know that it is your hand, that you, O LORD, have done it.
PSALM 109:27

David certainly had an unusual number of enemies. His psalms are filled with pleas to God to destroy his enemies and rescue him from his foes. And you don't hear him talk about his victories apart from a description of how God helped him.

It's interesting that a man who was accustomed to war and battle, who had victory upon victory to his credit, who as a boy slew the giant Goliath, now sees himself as one "shaken off like a locust" (Psalm 109:23). Is this the posture of a great man of God? Does admitting weakness and frailty befit a warrior and a king? Absolutely. In fact, he is doomed without it. He would be utterly destroyed if he stepped out of the cloak of humility. Yes, this is a paradox. Yes, it is counterintuitive. And yes, it's easy to discuss and difficult to practice.

We live in an age that rewards progress and achievement rather than humility and weakness. This is not the stuff of résumés; no one hands out trophies for frailty. But let's face it—we *are* frail. We are clothed in weakness. Our days are a vapor. Our best is still inadequate. Realizing this should never lead us to despair but to salvation. A clear understanding of our shortcomings only serves to magnify the awesome redemptive work of God.

How do you view your weaknesses? Do you look at them as liabilities, or do you view them as vehicles that God can use to demonstrate His power through you? Have you fully grasped the knowledge that when you are weak, He is strong and that His strength is made perfect in our weakness? (2 Corinthians 12:9). Put away your ego and trust in Him. Only then will you find true strength.

The Work of God (Part One)

Great are the works of the LORD; they are pondered by all who delight in them.
PSALM 111:2

We work because God works. Work is a part of His image that is written upon our hearts. But how does God work? What does He do?

As Author and Creator of life, God sets the standard with His work. He does not simply do His work well; His work is the very essence of perfection. His actions define His character, and His character defines His actions. Whatever the Lord does flows from Who He is. His work is memorable, satisfying, powerful, faithful, redeeming, holy, and awesome. He is and always will be infinitely beyond us in all that He does. His least far surpasses the sum total of our best.

The revelation of this should prompt two reactions within the heart of a thinking man: despair, and then fear. If God is so majestic and awesome, so completely set apart from us in His perfection, how can we ever do anything to please Him, to earn His affection, or to get His attention?

Quite simply, we cannot do anything. And yes, this should strike a chord of fear within us. This should get our attention and cause us to look closer at His Word, to understand and know Who He is, to discover what He expects of us and our work here on earth. This fear is, as the psalmist says, "the beginning of wisdom" (Psalm 111:10).

Have you ever thought of God as a worker? More specifically, have you ever thought that He could be a role model for you in your professional life and career? We strive to be like Christ in every other way—why shouldn't we strive to achieve excellence in our work just as He did? We will never achieve perfection—we are incapable of meeting His standard of excellence. But we can do our best.

The Work of God (Part Two)

He provided redemption for his people; he ordained his covenant forever—holy and awesome is his name. PSALM 111:9

It is the nature of God's work—its completeness, beauty, and power—that brings about the purpose of His work: redemption. The chasm between Creator and creation requires a bridge. And so we see that God is in the business of restoring relationships, building bridges, and preparing His kingdom. We would do well to join Him.

Restoration is hard work. It's demolition work. There are walls to knock down, debris to sweep up, trash to haul. And there are no shortcuts. The workplace is often full of these projects—and they usually take the form of broken relationships. Building and restoring relationships is an essential activity in any business. We need to clear up misunderstandings. We need to really listen to others. We need to invest time in people. In short, we need to restore relationships.

Building bridges is about understanding. The bridge that God built required that He come down and live among us. He had to experience life on earth for the work to be complete. He had to walk in our shoes, feel our pain, and live our lives. How are we at understanding? Building bridges? Walking in someone else's shoes? This is all difficult but necessary work.

Ultimately, Jesus' work was the work of His Father's kingdom, which He came to establish. It was the focus of His teaching, His death, His resurrection, and His life.

Is our work kingdom work? Are we kingdom-minded? These questions apply more to a frame of mind than to a set of actions. What is our focus? Where is our focus? We all have a choice: our kingdom or His. We need to choose wisely.

Finding Delight

Blessed is the man who fears the LORD, who finds great delight in his commands. . . . Wealth and riches are in his house, and his righteousness endures forever. PSALM 112:1, 3

As believers, we must never allow our focus to be on the accumulation of wealth. Our focus must be on the Lord and His commands. As a result, righteousness becomes a natural by-product of centering our lives on God.

But there is a search involved, and we need to search until we find. Great treasures are hidden within His commands, and those who search them out will discover them.

Are we searching? Of course we are searching. Everyone, it seems, is searching for something. But what are we searching for? And where are we looking: in the right places or in places where there's no chance we'll find what we're seeking?

Work can become a search site. Unfortunately, if we look for an eternal answer in the temporal work we do, we will come up short. The answer—the long, satisfying drink—is found in the commands of God.

Not in suggestions. Not in principles. Only in His commands.

Think of following His commands as following military orders. A superior officer expects a soldier to obey his commands willingly. As followers of the Lord, we need to take several steps beyond willing obedience. We must obey His commands with delight—in fact, with *great* delight, with joy. And we must not confuse joy with happiness. Happiness depends on circumstances; joy soars above circumstances.

Joy at work. Does that sound like an oxymoron, an improbability if not an impossibility? Have you seen anyone around the workplace exhibiting joy lately? If so, you know that joy stands out. It gets noticed.

Look to have a joyful impact on your colleagues. Joy is contagious. And it is to be found in God's commands. Start searching.

Is Your Work Praise?

From the rising of the sun to the place where it sets, the name of the LORD is to be praised. PSALM 113:3

Is your work praise? The question is not, "Are you praising God at work?" The real question is about the nature of your work. Is it praise? This question is essential—and it's not intended just for pastors, missionaries, and worship leaders. Accountants, farmers, and bus drivers need to consider this question carefully as well. Too many times, people who are not in "full-time ministry" are relegated to a second-class calling, and we lower our expectations of the spiritual output of their work. Why? Because of our misunderstanding of both work and worship.

In today's thinking, there is spiritual work, and there is necessary, earthly, secular work. The clergy perform spiritual work all the time; the laity does their spiritual work on Sunday mornings and when they pray, read the Scriptures, or perform acts of service. Secular work is the work the laity does for income. But in this psalm, David exhorts us to praise the Lord all day long, from the rising to the setting of the sun, both now and forevermore. Anybody with a job will tell you that this is impossible if you plan to get any work done. Or is it?

What does it mean to praise the Lord? This is where our misunderstanding of worship comes into play. To many people today, worship means singing in church on Sunday mornings. Adventurous types may try to worship during their quiet times; perhaps you were even planning to engage in that kind of worship after you finished reading this. But worship stems from the focus of our singing—*why* we sing, and *Whom* our minds are fixed upon while we sing. It doesn't involve what we sing, but to Whom we sing.

This can take place at work. You can worship while you're making a presentation. Closing a deal. Hiring and firing. Building a house. Fixing a faucet. This is how we praise the Lord all day long.

Drinking from a Rock

[W]ho turned the rock into a pool, the hard rock into springs of water. PSALM
114:8

A rock is about as different from a pool of water as you can possibly get. Have
you ever been in a place that's as different as it can possibly be from the place
where you need to be? That's where David was when he was hiding from Saul in
the caves that dotted the landscape. When Moses was wandering in the desert, and
Joseph was trapped at the bottom of a well, they, too, were like David—men who
were "buried" and "resurrected" by God's hand at work in their circumstances. On
different levels, each of these men experienced physically what we experience spiritually—death and rebirth.

Joseph lay in a well, waiting to be sold into slavery by his own brothers. He
knew what the future held for him. But his doting father and his own lack of discretion enraged his jealous siblings, and he found himself on a journey to the bottom—slavery and then prison. Joseph experienced the rock.

Moses delivered Israel out of Egypt only to wander around the desert until a generation of his peers had died. And that was his *second* experience of death and rebirth.
The first was the time he spent in Midian, learning how to shepherd a dull and obsti-
nate flock. Far from the palace in Egypt where he grew up, he experienced the rock.

David was anointed as king. He received the promise of royalty from Samuel.
He knew what his future occupation would be. He knew the power, position, and
perks he would have. But first he had to die. Not literally, but symbolically. Slinking
around in caves, fearing for his life, he experienced the breaking effects of the rock.

Are you experiencing the rock, that place that is so far from where you know
you were meant to be? Do you find yourself being broken on its sharp edges? That
is part of God's plan, because only through this breaking will springs of living water
flow forth from your life.

What's in a Name?

Not to us, O LORD, not to us but to your name be the glory. PSALM 115:1

Names matter. They matter to us, and they matter to God. Adam, Eve, John the Baptist, Jesus. God at times changed a person's name to emphasize a hidden quality. Abram became Abraham, Jacob became Israel, and Simon became Peter. God the Father spoke directly to Moses and Samuel, calling them by name. And He demands that His name not be used in vain.

Even today, family names are often handed down, regardless of how old-fashioned these names may sound. Expectant parents pore over baby-name books touting sixty-thousand-plus entries. We put our names on business cards, on plaques, and on office doors. Companies spend millions of dollars each year developing brand names and identities—and an even greater amount infusing meaning into those names, building equity so that the mere mention of the name conjures up a whole host of associations. Companies go to great lengths and amass huge staffs for the sole purpose of building and protecting equity in a name.

Are we this serious and committed about "building equity" in the name of the One Who is exalted above all the earth? His name is to be praised and exalted, worshiped and reverenced. To His name goes honor for all the things He has done. Are we making those deposits, building up that account so that the mere mention of His name conjures up a host of associations and memories? In essence, we are all on staff to build (worship, praise, honor) and protect (fear, revere, defend) the name of the Lord.

How do you treat the glorious name of God? Do you handle it with reverence and awe, or do you throw it around carelessly, without a second thought about how your use of it might affect a coworker's impression of your heavenly Father?

The Living God

But their idols are silver and gold, made by the hands of men. PSALM 115:4

Are we following a blind god? Are we talking to a deaf god? Are we following a god without feet, thinking that we are going somewhere? Are we lulled by the illusion of progress? We must guard against letting the work of our hands become the object of our worship. The work of our hands is an offering to the true God—not a god in and of itself.

The God of Abraham, Isaac, and Jacob is a living God. He has a mouth and a voice. When He spoke, the world came into being. At the very sound of His voice, the earth was created. When He speaks, the mountains tremble and the oceans roar. He whispers in a still, small voice, and our hearts are satisfied, filled with His deep secrets.

God has eyes. He sees us. He searches for us as He did for Adam and Eve in the Garden of Eden. He sees beyond what human eyes can see. He is not impressed with outward appearances. He is not intimidated by strength or size. His piercing gaze sees straight to the heart. He sees our innermost thoughts and senses our subtle attitudes.

God has ears. When we cry out to Him, He hears and answers. He heard the cries of Israel in bondage. He listens to our prayers. He hears us.

God has hands. With them He fashioned us in the womb. He holds the universe in the palm of His hand. He shelters us under His wing. With one wave of His hand, all His enemies are vanquished. His hands held Him in place on the cross, pierced with nails, fashioned by the work of our hands.

We follow a living God Who is present and active. Where do you see Him at work? You would do well to join Him there.

Cultivating a Public Life

I will fulfill my vows to the LORD in the presence of all his people . . . in your midst, O Jerusalem. PSALM 116:18–19

Some aspects of our spiritual lives are private, but the greater portion is to be lived out in the presence of other people. A public life does two things: It protects us, and it allows others to witness God's activity in our lives.

We live life in many layers of personal existence: public, private, blind, and subconscious. Others know our public lives. Often we have blind spots that others see and point out to us. This requires close, courageous friendships. Our private lives are known to us—and possibly no one else. Here are the secrets, often laden with guilt and shame, that hold us hostage. Again, we need trusted friends whom we allow to poke around in the dark closets and turn on the lights. Finally, the subconscious is a mysterious place that bubbles up in our dreams and through longings and urges that are difficult to categorize.

A healthy life, however, is lived primarily in the public arena. This keeps us free from blind spots and secret sins that can entangle us. When we publicly live out our faith—filled as it is with hopes, fears, successes, and failures—others will witness our actions. If they witness a man or woman truly following Christ, they witness something more powerful than words can convey.

Our lives at work are filled with opportunities to walk a different path—graciously and lovingly. Many jobs are filled with deadlines, tensions, and conflicts. How do we navigate these? We have bosses, peers, and subordinates. How do we treat them? What about vendors, partners, and suppliers? If we are witnessing with words alone and no one witnesses Christ in our lives, we are nothing more than an annoying racket. Allowing Christ to live through us is the best way to be salt and light at work.

Is your life at work a flavor enhancer, or is it simply leaving a bad taste in the mouths of your coworkers?

The Big Picture

Praise the LORD, all you nations; extol him, all you peoples. PSALM 117:1

Out of the shortest psalm in the Psalter—the shortest chapter in the Bible—comes a foreshadowing of hope for the Gentiles and for all nations. Paul recognizes this in his letter to the Romans and quotes this tiny chapter as evidence of salvation come to us all (Romans 15:11).

The scandal of the inclusion of Gentiles in Christ's salvation is lost on us today because of elapsed time and cultural ignorance. But it ushered the entire world into a new era. Its force divided human history in two. It shifted the balance of power. It changed all of life. This small idea sparked a revolution, a revelation.

Big ideas sometimes hide in small packages. There are enormous blessings in unsuspecting places. And we miss them because we look for the wrong things in the wrong places. We look at people and size them up based on appearance and presentation—"He looks like a leader." We size up opportunities based on what we will get out of them—"I should take that assignment; it will give me the 'stripe' I need." All the while, we miss great people and incredible opportunities. We miss them because we are looking and not listening.

A picture may be worth a thousand words, but appearances can be deceptive. Things are not always what they seem. Just go to church any Sunday morning—everyone looks great, but nobody knows what's really bubbling just beneath the surface.

Our words betray what is really going on inside. Unless a person is a pathological liar, it is hard not to hear the hurts, needs, dreams, and desires in his or her voice. But we only hear if we are listening to others and to the Holy Spirit. If we fail to listen to Him, we will miss the big opportunities hiding in tiny places.

The Lord, Our Refuge

It is better to take refuge in the LORD than to trust in man. PSALM 118:8

Has a colleague ever let you down? Disappointed you? Hurt you? Betrayed you? Stabbed you in the back? Slandered you? We've all experienced at least one of these, and it's possible we've seen them all. The workplace is a competitive, pressure-cooker environment filled with wounded individuals who misunderstand work and its place in their lives. In short, it's a recipe for conflict—a battleground.

So where is our retreat from this battlefield?

For some, it is family—the comfort of personal, familiar surroundings. Children, full of life, energy, and love, provide solace. The loving, sympathetic ears of a spouse bring comfort. Family means safety and security.

For some it is recreation—getting lost in a favorite sport or hobby. The challenge and the competition provide a welcome distraction.

For others, it is a darker retreat—addiction, compulsion, secret habits. Alcohol, drugs, or the alluring trap of sexual temptation provide escape.

All of these fall short in meeting our need to retreat from the battle. We need refuge to rest and regroup. We are like a people without a home in a strange land—refugees in need of safe harbors.

There is no better refuge than the Lord. He will not take advantage of our weakness—He strengthens you in it. He will not betray our trust—He bolsters it. He will not leave us or forsake us—He is faithful. He is our refuge.

Who or what is your refuge? It's not wrong to enjoy family or recreation, but do you find yourself seeking your ultimate comfort in those venues? Have you started down the slippery path of a darker sort of refuge? Think about it. Then turn your eyes and heart toward the Lord.

Terms of Agreement

[A]ccording to the law. . . . who keep his statutes. . . . walk in his ways. . . . laid down precepts. . . . obeying your decrees. . . . consider all your commands . . . . according to your word. PSALM 119:1–9

A friend told the story of an Indian man who was visiting the United States for the first time. When he was asked what struck him most about being in the States, he knew immediately. "People here obey the law," he said simply.

The rule of law undergirds Western civilization. It protects us as it liberates us. This is certainly true in business, where the rule of law and the freedom of capitalism go hand in hand. Contractual relationships, corporate structures, and terms of agreement protect shareholders and clarify expectations. Yet as great as this system is, most of us fall short of worshiping it. Unless you are a lawyer, the very idea of studying a contract is a tedious proposition. And the idea of longing for the Constitution is silly.

But not for the psalmist.

The first nine verses of Psalm 119 give us eight distinct words for what is commonly referred to as God's law. Most of these words are laden with what we might call "legalese." They are conventional contracts that God made with Israel and ultimately fulfilled in Jesus Christ.

In fact, in Jesus, God fulfilled the terms of His agreement completely. He did everything He said He would do. On top of all this, He completely forgave, and He even paid our end of the deal. Now Christ has drawn up a new agreement. No longer are we living under a heavy load of rituals, ceremonies, and impossible expectations. Our only requirement is faith and confession. And, just as He was before, He is meeting perfectly His end of the deal, all the while helping, forgiving, and carrying our end as well.

When was the last time you expressed thanks to God for fulfilling the requirements of His law through His Son, Jesus Christ? Do it today!

The Art of War

I am a man of peace; but when I speak, they are for war. PSALM 120:7

Most, if not all, wars are fought over conflicting and deeply held ideologies and philosophies about life, religion, economics, and so on. The inability to reach an understanding or come to terms can escalate any situation from a disagreement to a full-blown conflict, whether it is geopolitics or office politics.

We live in the age of information, and most of it is incomplete or inaccurate. If we are going to survive and thrive in the marketplace, we must cultivate two key skills: communication and discernment.

The ability to communicate is so valuable (and rare) that one employer recently confessed to hiring more college grads who had majored in English than in business simply because they could communicate clearly. Words matter. Each one is laden with meaning and context. We must choose them wisely—with discernment.

Discernment is equally important in speaking and listening. We must know to whom we are talking and gauge what, when, and how much to tell a person. There is a fine line to walk between withholding information and telling too much, especially in communications about other people. If we live among those who hate peace, we must be especially discerning. You cannot retract words. And starting a war at work damages your credibility for the kingdom.

Be wise in your responses as well. The psalmist constantly runs to the Lord for defense and action against the slander of others. If you intend to defend yourself and right every wrong communication about yourself, be prepared for a full-time job. People will say harmful and untrue things to you and about you at work. But a right and discerning heart is able to forgive the offense and let God take care of the defense.

130 THOMAS G. ADDINGTON AND STEPHEN R. GRAVES

Bogged Down

I lift up my eyes to the hills—where does my help come from? PSALM 121:1

Work is about getting things done. Yes, it is about ideas and innovation. But, as Peter Drucker said, eventually those ideas are reduced to a pile of work for someone. Usually, this work is not glamorous, but tedious—more implementation than inspiration. We have to focus on the details—the small things—and get them right.

Execution is king. But if that is all we do—if our noses are always to the grindstone, if we just keep plodding along and never raise our eyes or take time to gain perspective—we will run into a dead end and never know what hit us. Worse yet, we might run right off a cliff without seeing the warning signs.

The new economy made many promises that it did not keep. One of them is the idea that we will be freed from the tedium of details and implementation and allowed to work solely in the world of ideas and innovation. Anybody with a to-do list will tell you that it simply isn't so. What the new economy missed is Genesis 3:17–19—the curse aspect of work that will always be with us.

Yes, we are called. Yes, we can have purpose, satisfaction, and fulfillment. But we also have to deal with sweat, toil, and thorns. So what are we supposed to do when we are so bogged down and overwhelmed that we think we will not be able to endure another thing? Here, the psalmist offers encouragement.

Help is coming. Lift up your eyes to the hills. The Lord sees us. He sees you. His vantage point gives Him a clear picture of your situation. He will lift you out of the pit and out of the miry clay (Psalm 40:2). He is faithful in the big battles and the smallest detail. Nothing eludes His watchful eye. Not our work. Not us.

The Power of Positive Company

I rejoiced with those who said to me, "Let us go to the house of the LORD." PSALM 122:1

Take a moment and reflect on your closest colleagues, those people with whom you work most closely and those who know you best. It is probably a half-dozen men or women. Now think about them as people. What do you know about them? Their families? Their philosophies of life? Their views of the world?

In the movie *It's a Wonderful Life,* we see how the life of one person—George Bailey—changed the lives of literally everyone around him. This fictional story is born out of a profound truth—we affect others and they affect us. The people who surround us will mold and shape us. They will sway our decisions and influence the direction we take at critical junctures.

This is a two-edged sword. If your colleagues are of like mind and faith, they will lead you into righteousness, but if they hold opposing views on the central tenets of faith, the results may not be so positive.

The problem is that most of us live and work in the world (and rightly so). When we walk through dusty streets, it's only natural that our feet get dirty and need to be washed frequently. You may feel that way about your work environment. There are places and cultures that leave us feeling soiled. So what are we to do? Should we retreat into the hills to live among people like us? Or should we just give in and start living like those around us?

The answer, of course, is neither. We must live in both worlds at once, surrounding ourselves not only with wise and trusted counselors, but also with needy seekers in search of a better way.

The world does not need our condemnation or our sponsorship of its activities. Instead, it needs to witness a thoughtful follower of Christ living and working in the world. It needs to see a person who is engaging culture—not a person who is shrinking back from it or criticizing it without thought, but someone who is looking carefully at every interaction as an insight into the hearts and minds of searching people, people who need someone to live that better way in front of them each day.

Slave Wages

As the eyes of slaves look to the hand of their master, as the eyes of a maid look to the hand of her mistress, so our eyes look to the LORD our God. PSALM 123:2

Slavery is a dark spot in the history of our country. While we still live in its shadow, we are largely free from living in master/slave relationships. We do, however, still have employers, customers, and clients. Although we're not their slaves, we are beholden to regard their interests above our own.

What is your relationship with your employer? Would you characterize it as hostile? Tolerant? Cordial? Does it really matter? The answer is a resounding yes! It matters—a lot. But the real trick is keeping in balance the right kind of relationship with our "master."

As followers of Christ, we have a mandate to serve others that is not lifted when we check in at the office. We are not exempt from following Christ from nine to five. In fact, this is where the rubber meets the road in our journeys of faith. Our attitudes and our approaches to those in authority speak volumes to those around us about the veracity of our walks with Christ. In small and subtle ways, our language and posture betray our hearts toward those who would lead us. How are we doing in that regard?

On the flip side, we cannot look to our work, our companies, or our bosses for the security and assurance that only God can provide. Job security is a big issue in our downsized and restructured corporate environments, and it is easy to pay lip service to the Lord while we are anxiously polishing our résumés and networking "just in case." Taking "our" careers into our own hands (and ultimately out of His) is an act of pride. Certainly following Christ and concerns about career are not mutually exclusive activities, but they are dangerously close. The surest career path is not a great résumé, but a great relationship—with Jesus.

It is His hand that sustains us, saves us, feeds us, houses us, and clothes us. His way is best. It is more fulfilling, not less. And while the metaphor is that of slavery, the reality of the relationship is that of a son, a brother, and an heir. Definitely not slave wages.

Building Your Team

If the LORD had not been on our side . . .   PSALM 124:1

Team building is a key skill for business today. Employers are looking far and wide to acquire people who understand how to harness a unique and talented group of people and lead them to accomplish great things, people who know how to motivate, recruit, and lead. And when they find them, they pay big salaries to get them and keep them.

If you manage or run a business, you understand the value of great people on your team. They are worth their weight in gold. Once you find them, you will do whatever is necessary to keep them. They are the keys to your success.

But what about your team for the rest of your life? This is your life team, the people around you who keep you on firm footing and headed in the right direction: your spouse, family, closest friends, advisers, and colleagues. They are invaluable to you. They help you in success and failure, celebrating and correcting, laughter and tears. You could not make it without them.

But if those are the only members of your team, then you have fallen short.

"If the LORD had not been on our side . . . ," the psalmist declares. The rest is obvious. If the Lord had not been on our side, then He would be on the other side. Against us. Opposing us the way He opposes the proud. The very idea should make us shudder and drive us to our knees. And yet even the idea of having God on our side falls short. Again, way short.

In reality, it is not God Who has signed on to our team for the salary of our faith in Him and the bonus of our occasional worship and devotion. Quite the contrary; we are on His side. Not only that, He recruited us when we were too blind and dumb to understand what a good deal we were getting. He vouched for us when we had nothing to offer. He gave us gifts we didn't work for. And He overpaid us lavishly—with His very life.

Yes, the team that is being built is His. The talents we possess are from Him. And the victories we enjoy as our own are in reality His. Let's hold loosely to what seems to be ours and worship Him fully for what we know to be His.

Stirred, Not Shaken

Those who trust in the LORD are like Mount Zion, which cannot be shaken but endures forever. PSALM 125:1

Who doesn't want to be calm, cool, and collected? To walk through the trials and tribulations of life without anxiety? To ease the fears of others when the sky is falling? To remain at peace and rest when the world runs out of control? We all want that. But how do we find it?

The psalmist says quite simply, "Trust."

"Trust me," you can hear a salesman saying as he makes a false and empty promise to lure you into a sucker deal. The phrase is so overused and misused that it has lost most, if not all, of its meaning. A new phrase is needed to convey the concept of "trusting in the Lord."

"Letting go" comes close—releasing our hold on possessions, people, and situations and letting God take care of them. But it does not go far enough. "Giving God the reins" is another good metaphor. This is the idea that God is in control of the carriage and we are just along for the ride. But this misses out on our part in the equation. *Control* is a big word. Giving God control over our lives is a beautiful sentiment, but it breaks down when we try to make it practical.

Perhaps the best word is *abandon.* The mental picture that accompanies it is one of jumping off a cliff without a net or parachute. You run full speed to the edge of a cliff and right over the edge. You experience a moment of flailing and exhilaration, and then the terrifying reality of falling hits you. Your stomach gets lodged in your throat as you begin to accelerate, and finally, you feel the sensation of flying as you are seemingly suspended in space and time—never falling, never landing. There, at that exact moment, is a picture of what it means to trust.

If you are not living at the place where you absolutely need God to sustain you or you will meet the harsh reality of the ground below, then you are somewhere short of trust. And when you find yourself there, with nothing to lose because you willingly gave it up already, you cannot be shaken. Just like the mountain you jumped from.

Change Is Coming

Restore our fortunes, O LORD. . . . Those who sow in tears will reap with songs of joy. PSALM 126:4–5

Life is a series of crests and troughs. It has ebbs and flows, ups and downs. Seasons change. And as followers of Christ, we have to be adept at change. Our walk with Him is initiated by the most significant change in our lives. In fact, we exchange our lives completely for the new one that He gives us.

If we walk with Him long, we will see this at work over and over again. Life will not always work out as we planned. A project will turn south. A business will fail. Our health will decline. Life seemingly deteriorates right before our eyes.

But we follow a God Who is in the business of restoration. He's like a builder who looks at an old run-down house and sees the potential, not the need to condemn. God sees beyond our circumstances to the day of His deliverance. He sees our restoration and brings it to pass.

Many of us will face, have faced, or are facing dark days—days of tears that seemingly will never end. But they do and they will. Our Deliverer is faithful. Just as the seasons hearken change in the world around us, the Holy Spirit hearkens change in the hearts of men. Just beyond the cold, dormant winter lie the new life of spring and the long warm days of summer when God will, as He promises, restore our fortunes.

Are you in down time in your life right now? How are you responding? Are you blaming God and complaining about your difficulties? Or are you trusting that He knows exactly why you're going through the valley, even if you don't? It's easy to focus on circumstances and lose sight of the big picture. Don't do it. Remember, if you sow in tears, you'll reap with songs of joy.

God in the Middle

Unless the LORD builds the house, its builders labor in vain. PSALM 127:1

God is integral to our success in life; He's not ancillary. He is either in the middle of a circumstance, or He's not there at all. It is His activity, or it is not. And contrary to popular belief, the choice is not up to us.

Too many times we bring our plans before God and ask for His blessing as if it is a stamp from a review committee. He is not a vendor or a supplier. He is not an asset or a resource. He is God. He is outside of our plans, our system. He is altogether different from us. The work that He does is supernatural because He is supernatural. It is not a matter of His conjuring this up. It is a reality.

He is the builder; we aren't. He does not hand us the plans and ask us to build. He builds. He understands the intricacies of the smallest atom. He holds the vast expanses of the universe in the palm of His hand. He knows how it all works because He built it.

Thankfully, He has given us a part to play because He loves us and wants us to be in right relationship with Him. We can carry lumber, swing a hammer, or lay some block. But building is in the realm of God. He makes things happen.

He is not a redundant system. God is not our backup plan in case we can't deliver. It merely looks as though we are building, but we know better—or we should. If what we are building does not originate with Him, it is an empty exercise.

Are you grounded in this reality? Do your activities originate with Him? Get out your to-do list and run it through that filter. Ask Him for discernment and eyes to see where He is at work. Find out what He is building and join the crew. Those are great projects to work on.

The Real Blessing

Sons are a heritage from the LORD, children a reward from him. PSALM 127:3

Our culture is built largely on the premise of dissatisfaction. Media and marketing companies spend billions of dollars annually to persuade you to try their products in order to find consumer Nirvana—the ultimate bliss of the perfect purchase. The cult of the shopper has become a national epidemic. Today the question, "How much is enough?" is followed by the answer, "A little more."

The problem with consumption is that it completely misses the real blessings that God has for us in life. It blinds us to them. It keeps us completely away from them in a numb state, unable to feel or to sense how lost we have become.

And so our lives are spent working in jobs that pay well but don't quite fit our passions so we can afford the things that we think will fulfill the deepest needs in our lives. But once we get those things, we find that our end condition is worse. The ache deepens, and we try to soothe it with other things that we are certain will provide relaxation for the whole family despite the mounting debt we incur. And so it continues.

Is this endless cycle merely a way of life in affluent Western culture in the twenty-first century? To a degree, yes, it has become a way of life. But is this all that life has to offer? If by "life" you mean this world, then yes, all it has to offer are creature comforts and an endless line of experiences designed to numb you from the reality that life is hard, lonely, and unfulfilling.

The psalmist recounts over and over the blessings of the Lord: salvation, victory in battle, land, cattle, and children. The real blessings are found in the things that we take for granted. God has designed a system of blessings that grows and multiplies over time. Land yields crops, which give seed for more crops that can be used as feed for cattle, which multiply as well. Children are born, grow up, and have families of their own. All around us, the self-perpetuating blessing of God is multiplying.

So should we all move out to the country and start a farm? Probably not. But today, begin to open your eyes to the real blessings of God all around you—the sunlight and the rain, seasons, friendships, children, spouse, and yes, even the satisfaction of a job well done.

A Life of Impact

Blessed are all who fear the LORD, who walk in his ways. You will eat the fruit of your labor. PSALM 128:1–2

Everyone wants to know how to share his or her faith at work. What do they say? How do they say it? When is it appropriate?

The questions go on, but they're always centered on the words that they will use. They never focus on the life that they will use. But here, the psalmist beautifully describes the impact of one man walking in right relationship with God. The ripples are felt by those around him and stretch out in geography and time. This man's life is in sharp contrast to that of Adam, who ate the fruit of the tree, walked in his own ways, and then fled from the Lord. This man's life is centered on God—not only his relationship, but also his response, his being, and his doing:

A life like this has an impact on five spheres of influence:

Yourself. The immediate impact of a life following God is personal. Enjoyment and satisfaction from your work is a gift from God. It is not the by-product of hard work, but of right relationship and response.

Your spouse. Next the ripples spread out to the person closest to you in life—the "flesh of your flesh" and "bone of your bones." The idea is that when you walk correctly, your spouse reaps the rewards.

Your children. Your children also benefit, not only from living within a house that is enjoying the blessing of God, but from receiving the blessing of a godly inheritance in the form of their own family.

Your community. Your influence flows from you to your family and then out into your community and eventually into the nation. The impact of one life walking in right relationship and response literally can affect the prosperity of a nation.

Your lineage. Finally, the impact of this life is felt across time, blessing not only those in your generation, but also the generations beyond.

So the next time someone asks you how he can start sharing his faith at work, tell him that if he's living life in right relationship and response to God, he's already begun.

Down but Not Out (Part One)

[T]hey have greatly oppressed me from my youth, but they have not gained the victory over me. PSALM 129:2

In Old Testament times, God's people were held captive as slaves, extracted from their homeland, and forced to live in exile. They wandered in the desert. They were lied about and attacked on all fronts.

Later, the early Christians were persecuted in unspeakable ways—scattered to the farthest reaches of the earth, beaten, imprisoned, slandered, and executed. Down through the ages, countless known and unknown martyrs have given their lives for the cause of Christ. Even today the persecuted church thrives in the midst of discrimination and calculated extermination.

But God's grace truly is sufficient and results in a people who cling to Him out of desperation and necessity with a common tenacity that will not let go. Regardless of, or maybe in spite of, any seemingly decent characteristics that any of us ever display, we are safe because He protects us, and we are here because He saved us.

If we were honest with ourselves, we would have to acknowledge that the bumps and bruises we suffer on the job are mere surface scratches when compared to the suffering that the children of Israel, the early believers, and the later martyrs had to endure. But sometimes our trials can seem difficult indeed. Our coworkers, friends, and loved ones question our motives, mock our faith, and scheme to defeat us. Circumstances discourage us, disappoint us, and beat us down. Events spiral out of control and we're faced with a barrage of pain and anxiety.

As we go through such struggles, we have only one viable response: We must cling to Christ with desperation and tenacity. We must remember that we might be down, but we're not out. Our enemies may have just won the battle, but they're not going to win the war. That's guaranteed.

Down but Not Out (Part Two)

[T]hey have greatly oppressed me from my youth, but they have not gained the victory over me. PSALM 129:2

External enemies are not the only source of oppression in our lives. Our own flesh wars against us, fighting against what we know to be good, right, and holy. Despite our best efforts, we do what we don't want to do (Romans 7:15).

The world and its desires run contrary to our faith and besiege our eyes, our ears, and our minds with their persuasive and seductive call. It is nearly impossible to resist. As if that weren't bad enough, our enemy, the devil, prowls around like a roaring lion seeking whom he may devour (1 Peter 5:8). There is a real but unseen enemy who wants more than anything to see us fail miserably. That any of us finish at all, let alone finish well, is truly a miracle and a testimony to the faithfulness of God.

As followers of Jesus, we are white as snow and wearing the white robes of righteousness bestowed upon us, not by our own works, but by faith alone in Christ alone. And yet we still have to live and work in a fallen world. If we are going to be effective in our ministries, we have to go to war. We have to put on the armor of the Lord (Ephesians 6:10–17) and face our enemies, whether they are internal or external, seen or unseen. We cannot simply stand on the sidelines and shout encouraging words onto the field. It won't work. We have to be willing to get down and dirty. This is a war, after all, not a social gathering.

Are you aware of the enemies that come at you from every side? Are you passively letting them attack you, or have you enlisted the help of the only One Who can win the war for you?

Beyond Self-Help

Out of the depths I cry to you, O LORD. PSALM 130:1

Self-help has never been bigger in our culture. Every year, we spend countless millions of dollars on self-improvement conferences, books, tapes, and videos. Psychology has become our national religion. And there does not seem to be any end in sight.

Self-help products—when they tap into truth—can be helpful, but they are not the solution to every problem. In fact, we sometimes fall to depths that we cannot "self-help" our way out of. There are times in life when things look so bleak that we cannot raise up our heads, when circumstances are so dark that we cannot see the road ahead. These are not the times for self-help. In these moments, only God-help will do.

When we find ourselves in the depths where only God can reach us, what do we do? How do we get His attention? The psalmist instructs us to do three things; the rest is up to God:

First, *we wait for Him.* This is not a popular thing to do. We'd much rather follow three easy steps for a quick solution. Unfortunately, life is difficult, and solving problems is messy and takes time. The good news is that God is never late. The bad news is that He is rarely early. But He is faithful. If you wait, then He will come.

Second, *we get in His Word.* We can't just read it; we have to delve into it. How are you as a student of the Bible? If you do not cultivate your love of Scripture when skies are blue, you will not turn there when the skies grow dark. Those days *will* come; so let's ready ourselves by reading, studying, soaking, meditating, chewing, and digesting His Word until it literally becomes food that sustains us.

Third, *we hope in Him.* We have to have hope, especially when life is grim. Loss of hope is not tragic; it's dangerous. Misdirected hope is foolish. All other gods are mute, deaf, dumb, and immobile beings fashioned by the hands of men. There is one—and only one—true God, and it is in Him that we should hope and trust.

If your days are dark and despair is creeping in, rest assured that He is coming. His rescue is imminent and sure. His covenant is lasting. His faithfulness is certain.

Our Place (Part One)

My heart is not proud, O LORD, my eyes are not haughty; I do not concern myself with great matters or things too wonderful for me. PSALM 131:1

It is tough to find our place in this world when it comes to calling. Understanding our purpose in life and then discovering where we are to live out that purpose takes many years of searching, discovery, and prayer. It is not an overnight project. We cannot cram for it at the end of the semester.

But finding our calling is not enough.

In addition to finding our place of work in this world, there is another place that we must find—a place with a proper view of ourselves and of others. Veering to the left or to the right is perilous. If we get too close to one side, we run into the danger of thinking too little of others. If we veer the other direction, we run the risk of thinking too much of ourselves.

Putting people down—either verbally or mentally—is the heart of arrogance. God opposes the proud, but He gives grace to the humble (James 4:6). Have you thought about what it means to be opposed by God? Whatever you try to do, He comes against and thwarts. There is nothing beyond His eye, His ear, or His hand. He can be in all things at all times—opposing you. That's not a pleasant thing to consider, is it?

God made each of us in His image. He knit us in our mothers' wombs. He numbers our days and the hairs on our heads. He sent His Son into this world to live among the least of us and die on a cross for all of us. No one is insignificant. Thinking too little of someone else is to think too little of God Himself. Remember that next time you're tempted to belittle a coworker or put down a colleague.

Our Place (Part Two)

My heart is not proud, O LORD, my eyes are not haughty; I do not concern myself with great matters or things too wonderful for me. PSALM 131:1

Thinking too little of others, as we learned yesterday, can be a dangerous practice. But thinking too much of ourselves is equally as hazardous.

As always, Jesus Christ should be our example in how to think of ourselves. According to Philippians 2:6–8, Jesus did not consider equality with God something to be attained. Instead, He made himself a servant and died on a cross—for a bunch of people who were totally undeserving.

Jesus was born humbly, He lived simply, and He died cruelly. His was not a life of privilege, of taking what He deserved or what He had earned. His was a life of serving, of giving what was rightfully His. For all that Jesus was, He did not think of Himself very often.

As if this tightrope were not hard enough to walk, there is another dimension added to it. We must walk this out not only in action, but also in attitude. God is not looking at what we do, but at the source of our actions—our hearts. What is going on in there? How are you thinking about others? What are you thinking about yourself? You can hide those innermost thoughts from everyone else, but you can't hide them from God. He can see it all, down to the very last prideful thought and motive.

How would your life change if this thought were at the top of your mind? Would you begin to think differently about others? About yourself? Why don't you give it a try? If you humble yourself as Christ did, perhaps God will lift you to heights you've never known.

Across the Divide

How good and pleasant it is when brothers live together in unity! PSALM 133:1

In Scripture, the concept of brotherhood extends beyond blood relatives who have the same parents. As believers, we are all adopted sons and daughters of God. So in a spiritual sense, we are all "brothers" and "sisters" in Christ.

We don't just spend time with these brothers and sisters in the faith at church. We also rub shoulders with them where we work, live, and play. And there's a good chance the brothers and sisters we come in contact with outside our homes and churches are from a denomination or spiritual tradition that is different from our own. Scripture teaches that other people will know we are Christians by our love—and although we sometimes wish it weren't so, this includes our love for other believers.

This presents an interesting question: Are we living in unity with our spiritual relatives?

This type of unity only comes from God, and it results in blessings that descend from God.

Take a minute and think of your coworkers whom you know to be Christians. Are you living in unity with them, or do you spend your lunch hours arguing over whose understanding of eschatology is correct, whose church has the correct kind of music, or whose view of speaking in tongues is right? If the latter is the case, have you ever thought about how your disagreements might sound to your nonbelieving coworkers? Chances are, such discussions are not making anybody else want the faith that you share.

Let's major on the majors of the faith—the lordship of Christ, our faith in His salvation, and our love for and devotion to Him—and not let the details divide us. This will make our lives more fragrant and attractive to those who are surely watching us at work.

24/7 Worship

Praise the LORD, all you servants of the LORD who minister by night in the house of the LORD. PSALM 134:1

Day and night, the Levites of old worshiped God and offered up praise and thanksgiving to Him in the Temple (1 Chronicles 23:30). Today, we are the royal priesthood (1 Peter 2:9), and our bodies are the temple of the Holy Spirit (1 Corinthians 3:16). So is worship going up day and night in our lives?

This is easy on Sunday morning, during personal devotional times, or when we're on spiritual retreats. But what about other times—especially at work? Are the altars burning and the incense rising to the Lord Monday through Friday from nine to five?

How would you worship the Lord in the following situations:

- at a lunch meeting with a client of the opposite sex?
- during a discussion with a colleague who likes to gossip about folks in the office?
- during a dinner out with your largest customer who wants to go to a strip bar?
- alone at night in a hotel room with adult entertainment just a remote click away?
- in a meeting alone with your boss when you were just given credit for an idea you know was your colleague's and not yours?
- when you are tired, angry, or lonely?

Worshiping God 24/7 is certainly the ideal, but we must also guard against becoming religious. Our worship of Him cannot become a ritual. It cannot become a burden. It cannot become legalistic. We have to intentionally cultivate a worshipful attitude in our hearts.

Learning to worship God 24/7 will be hard work. There will be frequent failures. But you will be blessed.

Acts of God

I know that the LORD is great, that our Lord is greater than all gods. The LORD does whatever pleases him. PSALM 135:5–6

When a hailstorm riddles your car with dents and dings, the insurance adjustor might file the claim as an "act of God."

As people, our understanding of God is so limited. And our responses to situations in life tend to betray our theology. Many people who do not follow Christ assign natural disasters, terrible circumstances, and tragedy to the "acts of God" category, while many believers assign natural beauty, wonderful circumstances, and blessings to the same category.

So who is right? That's a good question. Your response probably has more to do with your own current circumstances and personal experiences than with a scriptural understanding of God's character.

It is kind of a trick question—the answer is *both*. God did create a world with incredible beauty, majesty, and grandeur, but it also has fires, earthquakes, and storms. What kind of scientist would you be if you only studied the good and not the bad?

For all of the successes and triumphs, there are also losses and failures. But in each and every one of these God has the ultimate "sign-off." There is nothing that is outside of His purview, His jurisdiction, and His control. He is high and above all things, but He also is intimately involved in the details. He knows. He cares.

What kind of circumstances do you find yourself in? Depending on which area of life you are talking about, there is probably tragedy and success going on simultaneously. It is not unusual to have a family situation going well (the birth of a baby, perhaps) while a work situation is going south (the loss of a job).

The reality is that God is aware of both, in control of both, and has signed off on both of them. This is a difficult and mysterious aspect to His character, but it is one that we must acknowledge and live in even if we do not fully comprehend it.

Our Confession

Give thanks to the LORD for he is good. His love endures forever. PSALM 136:1

"Give thanks" is more appropriately translated "confess" or "acknowledge." The concept of confession brings to mind the movies and TV shows that have cops trying to coerce a confession out of a suspect in a stark, smoke-filled room lit by a bare light bulb hanging from the ceiling.

Here, however, the psalmist has us alone in the room and is about to lay out all of the evidence in front of us about God and His acts.

God is above all other gods and lords on earth or in heaven. He alone does great wonders, wonders that cannot be duplicated. He created the earth and oceans. He hung the sun, moon, and stars in the sky. He delivered the Israelites from Egypt by striking down the firstborn in Egypt. He parted the Red Sea, brought the children of Israel through the desert, and defeated many kings to give them a land flowing with milk and honey. As if this were not enough, He remembers us when we are down; He rescues us, and He feeds us.

Given the preponderance of evidence of God's faithfulness and provision, what else could our response be?

But we are living and working in the twenty-first century. We're surrounded by all the "wonders" that man has created. We're confronted every day by a barrage of endless information and unprecedented opportunities. But we are dangerously close to becoming blind and deaf to Him, His word, His works, and His love that never ends.

You don't have to make your confession in a stark, smoke-filled room lit by a single bulb hanging from a ceiling. But before the day ends, find a quiet place where you can reflect on Who God is and what He has done for you. Acknowledge aloud that He alone is God of all gods and King of all kings. Confess that you are nothing without Him.

The Good Old Days

By the rivers of Babylon we sat and wept when we remembered Zion. PSALM 137:1

Have you ever done anything that you regret? Have you ever been in less-than-desirable circumstances and pined for days gone by? It is hard for us to relate to the idea of being captured by a foreign country and living in exile. But the concepts of regret and longing are familiar to everyone.

In this psalm we find the psalmist remembering Zion—God's city, Jerusalem—with great longing and emotional outpouring. But it is too late. Once again, the wayward affections of Israel have resulted in national catastrophe and defeat. Now God's chosen people find themselves in a strange and foreign land, forced to eat foreign food and smell the incense offered to foreign gods. They're wed to the mistress they found so desirable, but they're also fully realizing the devastation this has wrought upon their families, their children, and their inheritance.

It is unlikely that you will ever make choices that will so radically affect those around you, let alone an entire nation. But every day, in small and significant ways, you are faced with the opportunity to choose to be faithful. How are you doing? What are the affections of your heart? What is your ambition tied to? What do you desire? What are you working toward? The answers to these questions will have serious outcomes in your life. They need to be considered.

Work offers unlimited chances to come face to face with our own shortcomings and character faults. It pulls at our affections, our desires, and our ambitions. But work also offers us a chance to prove our faith, to test our convictions. There may be no better place to walk out our relationship with God or to experience Him.

Let's live these days with our hearts, minds, and strength directed toward Him. Let's live faithfully to the One Who calls us His bride, the One Who has covenanted with us to redeem us, the One Who has made us beautiful. Let's live and work faithfully to Him and avoid the pain and regret of exile.

Walking in Trouble

Though I walk in the midst of trouble, you preserve my life; you stretch out your hand against the anger of my foes, with your right hand you save me.
PSALM 138:7

We will walk in the midst of trouble. This is a reality we all know in our heads, but we have to experience it firsthand to really understand it fully.

At best, life is difficult. Other times, it is desperate and even tragic. Markets change. Businesses fail. Relationships come apart. People lose jobs, their health, and their loved ones. Life moves naturally from order to chaos.

Some of this difficulty and trouble is merely circumstantial—it is just happening that way. There seems to be no rhyme or reason to it. We can wonder if God is still in control or if He really knows what is happening in our world. No matter how hard we try or how much we pray, the situation remains unchanged. In these times, He will preserve our lives. If we stumble and fall, we must get up and keep walking.

Some trouble is relational, caused by others who wish us ill. We live in a competitive environment, yet we follow a God Who serves. Often these two will come into conflict, and guess who seems to lose? We cannot expect everyone to like us. They won't. We cannot expect to like everyone. We won't. But when people are actively pursuing our demise, He is there for us. In these times He will stave off our enemies and save us by His hand. He is our Defender, our Shield, and our High Tower. He will rescue us from our foes, ultimately and here on earth.

But even so, like all believers, you will walk in the midst of trouble. The question is, How are you walking?

Ethics of the Heart

O LORD, you have searched me and you know me. You know when I sit and when I rise; you perceive my thoughts from afar. You discern my going out and my lying down; you are familiar with all my ways. Before a word is on my tongue you know it completely, O LORD. You hem me in—behind and before; you have laid your hand upon me. PSALM 139:1–5

An ethical life comes down to myriad tiny decisions that we make every day. These decisions form patterns that develop the habits that shape our characters. While we may not see the effect of today's indiscretion right now, looking back over years of shortcuts and compromises reveals ugly patterns and scars in our characters.

It would be impossible to anticipate each one of these decisions. Life is moving too rapidly. Change is constant, and even the nature of change is changing. The black and white seems to have muddied into a river of gray. So how do we improve our ability to make right decisions in the heat of the moment or the daily grind?

Heart work.

Jesus was very clear when He said that it is not what a man puts into his mouth that makes him unclean, but what comes out of his mouth. We may be able to fake it in the short run, but over time our true nature oozes out of us. It will show up in what we say, what we do, and the decisions we make. These decisions spill out of our hearts. Generally speaking, if the heart is good, then the decisions are good; and if the heart is bad, then the decisions are bad.

How do we examine our hearts? We don't. We ask other people to help us do it, people who know us well and who aren't afraid to point out blind spots. More important, we invite the Holy Spirit to do it, frequently and thoroughly. This is a brave request. Don't make it lightly. It *will* be answered.

Success Warning

[D]o not let [the wicked's] plans succeed, or they will become proud. PSALM
140:8

We live in a day and age of success. Chances are, you are working right now in a competitive environment, trying to get ahead, to make your goals, to close a deal, or to earn another stripe or promotion.

Every company—from the large multinational corporation to the start-up in the garage down the street—faces intense pressure to succeed. Regardless of the setting, everyone is working toward success—to be bigger, faster, better. It is an alluring goal, to be sure.

Does this mean that we should not be success-oriented? Quite the contrary. Jesus succeeded perfectly at everything He came to earth to accomplish. We need to know what our calling is and work toward achieving it. But although we need to design our lives for success, we also need to guard against the downsides of success: self-sufficiency and self-indulgence.

The Lord warned the children of Israel that when they had taken the Promised Land, built their homes, had their families, and eaten from the fat of the land, they would forget the Lord their God if they weren't careful. And that's exactly what happened.

This process was not limited to the Israelites. It's a hazard for us, as well. When times are good, we tend to drift away from God and get distracted. We can become off-balance, pursuing our own fulfillment over the call of God in our lives. We might start thinking we don't need God anymore. We can do it on our own. We'll be fine by ourselves.

Is your pursuit of success causing you to lose your focus on Jesus? Has your achievement of success made you a little bit too comfortable with the status quo in your spiritual life? Perhaps it is time to revisit the Old Testament and see what happened to the Israelites when they forgot about God. Any way you look at it, it's not a pretty picture.

Calling Out

O Lord, I call to you; come quickly to me. Hear my voice when I call to you.
Psalm 141:1

When is the last time you called on the Lord? What was the situation? Did He respond? How? When?

The fact that the Lord knows about us individually is remarkable. That He can hear our voices and respond to our needs is supernatural.

But then again, maybe it isn't. Most of us lead our lives in such a way that we rarely need to call out to the Lord for anything. Our need for Him is relegated to the disaster areas of life—death, disease, or despair.

But what about the proactive side of calling out to Him? Are we pushing ahead toward a vision that He has birthed in us? Are we living by faith? Are we on the edge of whatever He is calling us to? Are we desperate for His intervention in our lives? What about the simple need and desire for relationship and intimacy with Him? Are we calling out for that?

Usually the idea of calling is reserved for our vocational lives. This is the inward calling. It involves discovering what He has planted within us and then nurturing it so that it grows and flourishes.

But if we are to fully realize the inward call, there must be an outward call. This outward call is the life of prayer and devotion. It is a life that realizes that its daily bread must come from Him if we are to survive. We must abide in the vine through prayer, God's Word, meditation, devotion, and service.

The outward call also is an attitude and an approach to life. It is a life that sees its sad state and clings desperately to the hope of our salvation—Jesus. We are nothing without Him, but we are completed with Him. We are now saints and conquerors, seated in the heavenly realms with Christ.

Are you in a time of need? Call out to the Lord. He will hear, answer, and come.

Lodging a Complaint

I pour out my complaint before him; before him I tell my trouble. PSALM 142:2

One of the beauties of the psalms is David's honesty before God. His gut-wrenching pleas for justice, mercy, deliverance, success, and blessing strike a chord within all of us. But rather than nodding in assent with David, we should be praying—and complaining—right next to him.

Yes, you read that right. We should be complaining—to God.

Most of the time, we lodge our complaints with friends and family members. We burden our loved ones with the tedious details and petty discrepancies of our lives. More often than not, these details cause us to cast others in a bad light or to disclose too much information about a situation. This is unwise in a networked society. For the follower of Christ, it is wrong.

If we think that we must sanitize our prayers before we speak them, then we have a serious misunderstanding of what it means to pray. Any close inspection of prayer in the Scriptures will surface numerous examples of people wrestling honestly before God. Prayer is the proper venue for complaints. God knows our thoughts, attitudes, and intentions before we speak them. But laying them bare before Him in prayer is healthy catharsis, not irreverence.

Our work environments move rapidly. Communication happens on the fly. Our relationships and networks are key to getting anything done. Project deadlines are tight. Tempers flare. Conflicts are inevitable, if not required, for the work to get done. But how, where, and with whom we process these feelings is up to us.

Too many times, we carry the stress of a misunderstanding or tense relationship for days before we even think to pray about it. When we finally go to Jesus, He lifts our burden, but only when we are completely and passionately honest.

If we want to walk closely and enjoy a deep relationship with Jesus, then we must master the ability to communicate to Him what is on our hearts. Otherwise, we are left with nothing more than shallow interactions and pious platitudes.

God Is My CEO

Show me the way I should go, for to you I lift up my soul. PSALM 143:8

Organizations need strong leadership. They need people at the helm who can determine where to go and how to get there. Then these people have to rally the troops around a common purpose and execute against a plan to make the vision a reality. This takes strong leadership.

People are not different. Everyone needs to be led—collectively and individually. In our own lives, we need a compass and an anchor. We have to know which direction to head. Without a compass, we are just running in circles. We also need an anchor so we are not tossed about on the open seas during the storms of life.

Many of us are self-directed or self-led. We are self-starters who, with little information and direction, can forge a course through the wilderness. Some of us have made great careers out of doing this and even of convincing others to follow us. We go where we want to go and do what we need to do. We're self-made men and women who run our own shows.

But there is another way. If we have answered the call of God on our lives, then we have relinquished the control as well. We have submitted to a new form of leadership. We still need to be led, but now we need to be God-led. He is our CEO, our commander in chief. Even more than that, He is our Master, having bought us with the price of His own life. He is fully in control.

So are you living under His leadership? This is tough work that takes soul surrender—total relinquishment of mind, will, and emotions. You have to align your mind with His and learn to think His thoughts. You have to align your will with His and learn how to submit yourself to Him. And finally, you have to rein in the emotions that so often deceive you or lead you astray when they are not in alignment with His will and ways.

The good news in all of this is God's character. He is more loving, faithful, and caring than any leader you could ever have at work. You can trust His decisions and follow them fully. No earthly CEO can live up to those expectations.

God Is My CEO: The Surrendered Mind

I remember the days of long ago; I meditate on all your works and consider what your hands have done. PSALM 143:5

If God really is CEO of our lives, with the directional authority and the right to disrupt our routines, then He is also in charge of our thinking. We must have surrendered minds. It is not enough just to do the right thing; we must be the right things. This requires more than a passing action or quick regard for something. To be fully surrendered in mind means we are committed to the complete and total renewal of our minds. You cannot halfway renew something—it's either renewed or it's not.

So how can you renew your mind?

First, *we must learn to think His thoughts.* Thankfully, He has given us a book full of them. Do you love His Word? Not the ink on the paper—that is just a book. Do you love the Spirit, the Person Who embodied those words? You must develop a passion for Scripture. It will change who you are and how you think.

Second, *we must remember what He has done.* Do you keep a journal? It is the best way to keep track of God's hand in your life. We are all busy, but this is one investment of time that will pay dividends to you and your children and their children. Your words do not have to be formal or eloquent. Just capture briefly what He is doing—prayers answered, changes He has brought about in you and others, situations He has altered.

Third, *we must consider Him.* We need to give time and mental space to Him. The brain is basically a muscle, and we are either teaching it good habits or bad habits. Of course, God can supernaturally restore any damage or years of bad thinking. But there will always be habit and thought patterns that need to be rerouted. Fixing your thoughts upon Him is the best way to do this. Consider Who He is and what He has done. You will be amazed by Him and the effect He has upon you.

If you have answered His call, then you have a new CEO. It is time to get to know the leadership a little better.

God Is My CEO: The Surrendered Will

Teach me to do your will, for you are my God. PSALM 143:10

If God is our CEO, then we have surrendered our will to His. Do we plan? Absolutely. We plan tenaciously, but we remain open to His supernatural redirection. How many times do we have things figured out but end up missing His real provision?

God has the directional leadership of our lives. His hands are on the steering wheel, not ours. He knows the way. In fact, He is the Way (John 14:6). There is no better place we can be. If we know Him and His character, then trusting Him is second nature. He cannot lead us down a wrong path because He is perfect. He will not take His eye off the road because He is faithful. We can trust Him fully and completely. It's a learning process, but He will teach us.

First, *He will teach us in His Word.* Scripture contains dozens of stories of men and women who followed the Lord against all odds and saw Him come through time and time again.

Second, *He will teach us through others.* We need to surround ourselves with people who will challenge us in our faith. Do you have someone who pushes you spiritually, a faithful friend who calls out blind spots and holds you to your commitments?

Third, *He will teach us through our circumstances.* It is very easy to follow Him on good days. But what happens when the bad week turns into a bad month and then a bad year? How we respond to prolonged difficulty says a lot about our character, our theology, and our walk with Jesus.

If we are going to surrender our will to Him, then we have to know His will. This takes a discerning ear, one that can hear His voice in the many different ways that He speaks to us. Being able to correctly handle the Word of God, the words of friends, and the situations of life is essential.

If we are going to surrender our wills to Him, then we have to carry out His will. This takes courageous faith. It's not a sit-on-the-sidelines kind of faith, but a roll-up-your-shirt-sleeves-and-get-to-work kind of faith. Faith requires action. As the saying goes, "Work as if it all depended on you. Pray as if it all depended on Him."

God is My CEO: Surrendered Emotions

Answer me quickly, O LORD; my spirit fails. PSALM 143:7

Leadership is, by very definition, a disruptive activity. A great leader knows that the status quo is not the road to victory. You have to constantly push the envelope, press the boundaries, and stay on the edge. Otherwise you will atrophy into complacency. You will wither and die. A good leader knows that the key to progress is change.

Change can bring better, worse, or different circumstances for us. But things will not stay the same. It sets you on a new course, putting you into unfamiliar territory that is at once exhilarating and terrifying. And, if you do not learn how to manage your emotions, change will make you respond in ways you never thought possible.

In times of change, focus is key—keeping our focus not on the situation, but on the One Who can change our situation, the One Who has already ultimately changed our situation from desperation and despair into hope and faith, the One Who exchanged our wretched past for an overwhelming future. Fix your gaze, your heart, and your attention on Him. Keep Him as the center of your world.

During change, we need an anchor in His character and His Word. We need to know Who He is and how He responds to us. We want to know if He has been in this situation before and if He came through (He has and He did).

Ultimately, we have to respond to Him, not to how we feel. We have to follow Him when we don't want to. We have to trust Him when everything inside us wants to run away. We have to believe that He will come through when all around us is doubt. He is faithful, loving, and sure—and in control.

Your Training Department

Praise be to the LORD my Rock, who trains my hands for war, my fingers for battle. PSALM 144:1

Most organizations spend money to train their people. Whether it is computer training for office assistants or an MBA program for senior executives, companies realize the need for great training. Spending on training continues to escalate, and many predict that the Internet will cause it to grow well into the future.

David was in training as well. He was training for his future line of work—being king. His was as thorough a program as you could want. It was custom-designed for him, his needs, and his future role. His Teacher was the best in the business, and He is still teaching today. In fact, He's available if you are willing. He's ready to teach you to have "hands for war" and "fingers for battle" (Psalm 144:1).

Winning wars was crucial for kings. It was how they maintained and eventually expanded their kingdoms. In David's day, if you could not win a war, you were doomed as a king. The wars we fight today are the big objectives that we keep in front of us to keep our lives progressing forward. In God's training program, you will learn the strategy that you need to be victorious in the wars in your life.

Wars are comprised of battles in much the same way that hands are comprised of fingers. In God's training program, you will not only learn strategy, but you'll also be taught the tactical execution to win the battles—those tiny skirmishes that can undermine your footing and get you off balance. You will leave this program on the sure footing of the Rock.

Your foundation will be built on the Rock, the Lord. He knows the smallest details of your life, and He cares enough to help you with them. He is also very interested in the wars you are fighting, and He knows the strategies for winning them. He is a solid foundation to build your life upon, and He will rigorously and faithfully train you. All you have to do is ask.

The Character of God

The LORD is gracious and compassionate, slow to anger and rich in love. PSALM
145:8

Is there a God, and if so, what is He like? This question is in the heart of seekers around the world, regardless of their ages, backgrounds, or nationalities. It is a central question in life, one that is of ultimate importance because of its effect on who we are and what we do.

If God does not exist, then we are random accidents, living on a meaningless globe, hurtling through a vast empty universe toward nothingness. We should pursue our own interests and pleasures. Our work is without meaning unless it satisfies us. Whatever we desire we should obtain by any means necessary. We are beyond the law because the very idea of law is ridiculous. Ethical considerations are thrown out the window. The only rule is to take care of yourself and get all you can.

Another option is that God does exist, but He is a ruthless and angry tyrant Who is hard to please. In this case, we had better work especially hard to garner His approval. Everything we do must be perfect or we are taking steps backward in His kingdom. Life is short and there is much to accomplish if we are going to be found worthy.

Thankfully, there is a third option, one that comes from God Himself. When Moses was on Mount Sinai, he asked to see God. The Lord denied his request because Moses would have died, but He did allow His glory to pass in front of Moses. While the Lord passed by Moses, He uttered these words: "The LORD, the LORD, the compassionate and gracious God, slow to anger, abounding in love and faithfulness" (Exodus 34:6). God described the essential nature of Himself: gracious, compassionate, patient, and loving.

Fortunately, the third picture is the only true and accurate one. As a result, our work is a response to God's grace given to us in the form of His Son, Jesus. It means that He is not giving up on us despite our shortcomings and failures. It means that He is concerned about the things that concern us. And finally, it means that His response to you today and every day comes from a heart that is love itself. Not a bad picture at all.

Mere Mortals

Do not put your trust in princes, in mortal men, who cannot save. When their spirit departs, they return to the ground; on that very day their plans come to nothing. PSALM 146:3–4

As a culture, we are enamored with leaders. We read their books, listen to them speak, join their companies, and follow them just about anywhere. They are our heroes, the men and women we emulate and hope to be like someday. But they are just mortals. They're here today and gone tomorrow. And when they are gone, they have no ability to lead, guide, or direct us anymore. They are just a memory.

Yet life goes on. We find someone else to follow.

As workers in this leader-driven economy, we have to keep our leaders in the right perspective and give them the appropriate place in our lives. God moves people in and out of positions of authority as He sees fit. They are just men and women with a job to do that happens to carry the weight of power and responsibility with it. We should honor and respect them, but we should not fear them. Ultimately, we are accountable to the Lord for our lives and our actions.

A friend told the story of getting to have a brief visit with the president of the United States one day. As he sat outside the Oval Office, he became very nervous about what he would say. He would have five minutes with the leader of the free world. What could he say that would be memorable or significant to the president?

At once, he sensed the still, small voice of the Lord, saying, *You are nervous about meeting a man, and yet you rarely give Me this kind of attention or consideration.* Convicted by this realization, he purposed in his heart not to worry about the presidential encounter. That was a good thing, because just then the president's secretary stepped into the hall to inform him that the president had to take a call and would not be able to see him.

Let's commit to honor, respect, and pray for our leaders. But let's also commit to fear, love, and worship the Lord. Keeping these two in balance will keep you on the right path.

Praise at Work

Let Israel rejoice in their Maker; let the people of Zion be glad in their King.
PSALM 149:2

Sometimes we just need to celebrate! We need to throw a party with balloons, confetti, streamers, singing, and dancing. It is a great way to enjoy success or to honor someone's accomplishments. We need to be generous with our praise and lavish with our affection for the people God has brought into our lives.

We also need to celebrate the Lord. We need to praise Him with singing and worship and prayer and work. Yes, with work. Our work should be a celebration to God, reflecting Him at every turn. Our love and devotion to Him must be seen in the work of our hands. If it is not, then we do not understand our work or worship very well.

Our work is a direct result of the Lord's work within us. As He knit us together in our mothers' wombs, He put together our basic wiring and gifts. He decided what our aptitudes would be and what would motivate us. He carefully crafted us so that we would have the raw materials we needed to fulfill our purpose here on earth.

No detail was too small for Him to fashion perfectly. As we grew older, He brought about circumstances that developed our characters and directed us down a path for our lives. All along the way, we continue to gather new skills and experiences that prepare us for what He has next. Our work lives are adventures when placed totally in His gracious and loving hands.

Our worship is the focus of our hearts upon the Lord. It is expressed physically through singing, music, acts of service, and work—if our work is a response to Him. Answering His calling to a certain profession, to a different city, or a new career path is an act of worship. So is serving a client, delivering a presentation, helping a coworker, or building a spreadsheet or an apartment complex. If we are doing what He made us to do and responding to His call, then we are worshiping.

Today, ask yourself if the work you do is in response to how He created you and called you. If it is, then begin to do your work in a way that would please Him. If it is not, then start to assess your skills, passions, and calling. You may be in for a big change.

3

Proverbs

Practical Instruction for the Daily Grind of Work

Introduction to Proverbs

While the Book of Psalms deals with the vertical relationship between God and man, the Book of Proverbs addresses life on the horizontal. Written primarily by King Solomon—arguably the wisest man who ever lived—it addresses everything from handling money, business strategy, and dealing with sexual temptation to making good decisions, controlling our speech, and living with our neighbors.

"Without a doubt, Solomon's sayings offer the most practical, down-to-earth instruction in all the Bible," writes Charles Swindoll. "The entire book of thirty-one chapters is filled with capsules of truth . . . short, pithy maxims that help us face and, in fact, apply God's wisdom in real-life situations. These sayings convey specific truth in such a pointed, easily understood manner; we have little difficulty grasping the message."[6]

It is biblically incorrect to view the Book of Proverbs as a list of commands that apply to everyone or a collection of promises that always come to pass. It is neither. Rather, it is a wonderful compilation of truisms and nuggets of wisdom—guidance that is generally true but that carries no guarantees. Take, for example, the oft-quoted saying about raising children: "Train a child in the way he should go, and when he is old he will not turn from it" (Proverbs 22:6). This bit of wisdom is generally true, but to hold fast to it as if it were guaranteed to produce godly children is flawed theology and will only lead to disappointment and disillusionment.

Written in poetic form, "the most commonly employed style of expression in Proverbs is the 'couplet'—two ideas placed next to each other."[7] In *contrastive* couplets, the two ideas are usually linked by the word *but:* "The eyes of the LORD keep watch over knowledge, but he frustrates the words of the unfaithful" (Proverbs 22:12). In *completive* couplets, the second idea completes the first: "A lying tongue hates those it hurts, and a flattering tongue works ruin" (Proverbs 26:28). And in *comparative* couplets, one idea acts as a comparison for the other: "As water reflects a man's face, so a man's heart reflects the man" (Proverbs 27:19). According to Swindoll, this final category of couplets, identified as such by phrases such as "better . . . than," "as . . . so," and "like . . . so," are among the most graphic sayings in the book.

Many of the proverbs appear to contradict each other, but that is because they each have a point to make about a particular area of life. A couple of common non-biblical sayings illustrate this well. One says, "If you snooze, you lose," while the other says, "Haste makes waste." The former addresses initiative, which is generally thought of as a good thing, while the latter deals with the area of caution, which is also often necessary. Both apply to different scenarios; if we were to view them as absolute promises, we would never be able to reconcile the two. The same is true for the sayings in the Book of Proverbs. They are simply observations about life through the eyes of Solomon and the other wisdom writers.

The fact that there are thirty-one chapters in the Book of Proverbs makes it easy to use as a daily devotional guide each month. To keep it from becoming too familiar, switch translations every few months. You just might be surprised at the impact such a practice will have on your life. "I can't promise you that a chapter a day will keep the devil away," Swindoll quips, "but I can surely tell you it'll help keep him at arm's length!"[8]

The Book of Proverbs holds tremendous application for the follower of Christ in the twenty-first-century marketplace. Within its pages we find advice about listening, gossip, ethics, forgiveness, planning, mentoring, wealth, praise, dealing with adversaries, borrowing money, philanthropy, and success, just to name a few. Whatever we happen to be facing at work on any given day, we can probably find a proverb that will help us deal with it correctly. As Robert L. Alden writes, the sayings in the book have a wonderful way of adapting themselves to any situation. "How often we feel tension between overwork and industry, laziness and relaxation, discipline and encouragement, spending and saving, and even generosity versus waste. Yet these are the very tensions of life itself. The way of wisdom teaches us how to achieve perspective and balance in that tension."[9]

Never Lost

The fear of the LORD is the beginning of knowledge, but fools despise wisdom and discipline. PROVERBS 1:7

When was the last time you were lost? Maybe it was when you flew into an unfamiliar city and didn't know where to go. Fortunately, your Hertz rental car was equipped with the Never-Lost navigation system. "Proceed to the highlighted route" is Hertz's gentle way of telling you that you're using a multimillion-dollar satellite system and you're still lost. Not a good feeling.

Even so, being lost in a car is not a really big deal. We check the map (or listen to the voice on the navigation system), make a U-turn, and we're on our way. The stakes aren't that high. But when we are lost in our lives and the futures of our families and organizations, the stakes skyrocket.

When we're navigating through life's twists and turns, we often focus solely on the destination. But according to Proverbs, it's equally important to remember the starting point. In this passage, the starting point is the much-avoided emotion of fear. In our culture, we are taught to conquer fear, or at least to act as if we don't have it. Yet on the road to knowledge (and real life), the starting point is fear.

Fear isn't always a negative thing. It depends on the object and the circumstances. God is a worthy object of fear, not because He's out to get us, but because He is the source for all things holy and pure. His power is unfathomable. He is larger than all we know. When the writers of Scripture speak of "fearing God," they are referring to reverential awe. But take a look at the initial reaction of the disciples when Jesus calmed the storm (Luke 8:25). Mixed with their reverential awe was outright fear about what had just taken place.

As with the disciples' fear, our fear turns quickly to worship. God wants to interact with us. And every time He does, we are changed. We grow toward knowledge. We travel the intersection of His instruction. The "highlighted route" starts with the Source for real knowledge and life. Life can be a long, hard road. Don't try to start somewhere else.

A Legacy of Grace and Honor

Listen, my son, to your father's instruction and do not forsake your mother's teaching. They will be a garland to grace your head and a chain to adorn your neck. PROVERBS 1:8

What did your father or mother teach you when you were growing up that helps you in your current role? Think about your answer carefully. Make a quick list.

Perhaps that's a difficult assignment for you. Maybe your mom and dad weren't around much, or maybe they weren't very good role models. Or maybe your list could turn into a book. Either way, God wants to step in. Whatever your foundation, He wants to build on it. He might step in by introducing you to His Son, Jesus. He might step in by showing you principles for life through His Word. He might step in through the lives of other people: parents, mentors, coaches, friends, or spouse. He wants to step in to teach and instruct you.

Now, let's flip the question. What legacy of learning, love, and grace do you want to leave the children in your life? Think about it. Make a quick list. Don't ignore the question. Decide now that you are going to influence them while they are young and then consider how you might serve as a coach to them when they move into the marketplace.

To attain that eventual goal, you have to have a relationship with these children. You have to earn their trust. You have to know them beyond their surface interests. Do you? What are their passions and skills? What areas of their character need your loving nurturing?

To fill the role of workplace mentor to the children in your life, you also need their respect. What would you not want them to emulate about your current business practices? Decide to change. Tell them about the mistakes you've made, what you've learned the hard way, and how you are correcting your mistakes. You have something to offer them. What they learn from you will be their crown of grace and honor.

What kind of legacy are you leaving for the children in your life?

First Things First

Honor the LORD with your wealth, with the firstfruits of all your crops; then your barns will be filled to overflowing, and your vats will brim over with new wine.
PROVERBS 3:9–10

There is no feeling like seeing the results of hard work for the first time—that sense of satisfaction when our toil and determination at last yield a tangible result. A farmer or gardener experiences this sensation when the first tender vegetables sprout from the earth. An entrepreneur experiences it the first time she turns a profit and sees black ink on the balance sheet. An author feels it when he pulls a printed copy of his book out of the box from the publishing company.

These are first fruits—the promise of more to come. They symbolize potential turned into reality, and they indicate that we may become wealthy, or at least have enough for our needs. It's only natural, then, that we treasure our first fruits. We step back and admire them from every angle with a deep sense of fulfillment, thinking, *I did that.* But that's when God taps us on the shoulder and reminds us, "No, *I* did that." He gave us the ability and blessed us with the right circumstances.

In the Mosaic Law, the Israelites were required to bring a portion of their first fruits to the priests as a sacrifice to the Lord. This offering represented the finest produce of the land. The result, God promised, would be blessing and prosperity for the nation of Israel and God's continued presence among His chosen people.

God asks the same of His children today: We are to give Him the first and best of what we have. Unfortunately, our tendency is to clench our fists around our first fruits and give what's left over. But a grudging gift doesn't honor God (remember Cain?), so He doesn't pry our hands open. He doesn't need our offering, but in His perfection He knows that giving what's most precious to us changes our hearts. When we learn to let go of what we most desire—when we look for ways to honor the Lord with the best of our resources—our lives will brim over with blessings.

What do you value the most? Your money? The first hour of your day? Time with your family? When you're tempted to give God the leftovers, consider whether that honors Him and what abundance you're missing by holding on to it so tightly.

Just Say Yes

Do not withhold good from those who deserve it, when it is in your power to act. Do not say to your neighbor, "Come back later; I'll give it tomorrow"— when you now have it with you. PROVERBS 3:27–28

Most of us aren't as cold-hearted as Charles Dickens's Ebenezer Scrooge, who, when asked for a charitable gift, told the collectors to let London's poor people die and "decrease the surplus population." When someone asks us for something, we may couch our response more diplomatically, but the answer is often the same—no.

It's usually easy to come up with ten reasons to say no without even blinking. Our lives and our resources are stretched among professional, personal, and spiritual responsibilities. We say no so often that it becomes second nature: "I'm sorry, I can't, but try me again next week—maybe I'll have more time." When was the last time you said yes?

Maybe a coworker is pulling extra hours trying to complete a project by deadline. Sure, you have plenty of tasks to keep you busy, but things aren't as hectic for you now as they have been. If your colleague asks for your help, your first impulse might be to find a polite way to refuse and then use your extra time to take advantage of the beautiful weather on the golf course.

Or maybe you're driving to work and see a homeless person shivering under a newspaper on the same park bench every morning. Your eyes meet as you're stopped at the light, and you quickly look away—just like every other morning. You try to put him out of your mind or say to yourself that next month maybe you'll try to do something for the man, secretly hoping that by next month he'll have found a new post and your conscience won't be pricked so unpleasantly.

We're commanded to do good for our needy and deserving neighbors—not with lip service and not tomorrow. We're to act today. So the next time you're faced with a real, tangible need that you can do something about, fight the impulse to say no. Say yes, and make a difference in someone's life.

Pick Your Battles

Do not rebuke a mocker or he will hate you; rebuke a wise man and he will love you. PROVERBS 9:8

The workplace is made up of a variety of personality types—bold and shy, steady and impulsive, Type A and Type B, INTJ and ESFP. But the mocker, one of the more notorious characters in the Book of Proverbs, stands out in a crowd. This person is a center of negative energy who scoffs at people who try to carry out their responsibilities with honor and integrity. The mocker looks for people to share his or her nastiness in making life unpleasant for the upright.

You may have the misfortune to work over, under, or in close proximity to this kind of person. This warrants tremendous amounts of prayer and discernment. If you try to point out the error of this person's ways, you're asking for trouble—you'll just make yourself the subject of future attacks. When you're choosing your battles, choose to avoid this one, the writer of Proverbs says.

On the other hand, the wise person—the hero of Proverbs—responds to criticism with a totally different attitude. This person wants above all to do things right and welcomes any input on ways to improve his work and character. Not only that, Scripture says he will love you, so this person may seek a mentoring relationship with you. Invest in these people.

The unspoken question is, Which kind of person are you? When your boss, for example, offers constructive criticism, how do you respond? With defensiveness and even scorn? Do you gripe about him behind his back and try to get your coworkers to agree with your negative assessment? Do you—be it ever so subtly—look for ways to get even with him for upbraiding you?

Or do you swallow your injured pride and look for the truth in his words, even if they hurt? If you take the latter choice, you're on the path to greater wisdom.

Direct Flight to the Poorhouse

Lazy hands make a man poor, but diligent hands bring wealth. He who gathers crops in summer is a wise son, but he who sleeps during harvest is a disgraceful son. PROVERBS 10:4–5

Many proverbs that deal with money focus on wealth or poverty, but this one is about work ethic. Generally speaking, a man who is bent toward laziness will miss out on the fruits of the harvest, while the diligent worker collects wealth. The diligent employee—the one with the good work ethic—is wise; the lazy employee—the one with the bad work ethic—is a disgrace.

A diligent person has the initiative he needs to stay focused on his task. In this setting, for example, he knows exactly when the crops are ready to harvest, and he works long hours during the harvest to get them gathered up and stored in the barn.

The lazy employee, on the other hand, likes to sleep in. When he makes it to the office, he does his job with very little enthusiasm. He doesn't pay attention to detail. If he works hard one day, he slacks off the next. Unlike the ant in Proverbs 6:7–8, which "has no commander, no overseer or ruler, yet it stores its provisions in summer and gathers its food at harvest," the lazy employee has absolutely no idea what it means to be self-motivated. Without a boss dangling an incentive package or bonus in front of his nose, he just can't get going.

Every work setting provides ample opportunity for lazy people to survive, perhaps even to thrive. It might be a little more difficult in a smaller, entrepreneurial environment where everyone has to pull his own weight, but if given the chance, a lazy person could scheme his way out of good work there, too. In the long run, however, such a work ethic leads to only one place: the poorhouse.

Are you a diligent worker, or do you tend to be a bit on the lazy side?

Selective Confrontation

Hatred stirs up dissension, but love covers over all wrongs. PROVERBS 10:12

Accountability is a big deal in our society. It's extremely beneficial to have people in our lives who will come alongside us and call a foul a foul, friends who are courageous enough to tell us when we've done something wrong.

But there's also a place for a someone to say, "I'm not going to call you into account for every little thing. There will be times when I will have to confront you, but there will be other times when, out of love for you, I will simply cover for you."

This is a common practice at home—if you called your spouse into account for everything he or she did wrong, the confrontation would never end. It's not quite so common at work—but it should be. "Above all," writes the apostle Peter, "love each other deeply, because love covers over a multitude of sins" (1 Peter 4:8).

There are some issues in the workplace that must be dealt with—for example, if someone is stealing from the company or violating the corporate code of ethics, confrontation is necessary. But there are many other things that happen in the daily course of life—things that we might call "wrongs"—that we simply let roll off our backs. Let's say we greet someone as we walk past him in the hall, and we don't get a response. We could get offended, or we could just assume he's having a bad day and let it go. Or maybe a meeting gets heated and a coworker swears at us. We could get mad, or we could chalk it up to frustration and ignore it.

In a work setting, the ability to not take offense at every little thing makes a huge difference in our ability to get our work done and to maintain productive relationships on the job. Some wrongs need to be righted. But there also are some wrongs we need to forgive, some wrongs we need to release, and other wrongs we just need to forget.

Is there an offense at work that you need to release?

Nourishing Words

The lips of the righteous nourish many. PROVERBS 10:21

A righteous person—someone who has a personal connection to God—is a person who inherently nourishes others with his or her words.

It's easy to see the correlation between being righteous and being right, or between being righteous and being holy. But the connection between righteousness and nourishment is often overlooked, perhaps on purpose. After all, if we call ourselves believers but fail to use nourishing words, we are probably not as righteous as we think.

According to this verse, a righteous person is a source of comfort, whether she's at home, at work, or in any other setting. She's a source of good. She's a source of wisdom, encouragement, and growth. In short, she's just the kind of person we would want on our team or in our department at work.

Every year surveys are done on what really motivates people at work. A genuine opportunity to make a contribution usually ranks as the top motivating factor, followed by money in second place. The third most significant source of motivation, employees say, is recognition from a boss or supervisor that lets them know someone thinks what they do is valuable and worthwhile. Said differently, employees are motivated by nourishing words.

No matter what our position, we can do a lot to make our workplace a great environment for others simply by nourishing and encouraging them with our words. On the flip side, we can do great harm to our workplace if we *don't* nourish others with our words. If you lined up your employees or coworkers and asked them if you nourish them, what might their answers be? If they said no, what are you missing in your walk with Christ and in your desire to be righteous?

If you want to make your coworkers' lives richer, you have a ready tool at your disposal called *nourishing words*. Do your words leave others nourished or depleted?

2,100 Days and Counting

The fear of the LORD adds length to life, but the years of the wicked are cut short. PROVERBS 10:27

One of our board members opened up a meeting by stating that he makes it a practice to keep track of how many days he has left. Scripture teaches us to number our days (Psalm 90:12), he said, and having a number that he is counting down toward helps him to remain focused on the task at hand. It also reminds him to make every day count for Christ.

To begin, he looked at his family history, projected realistically how long he might live, and started counting down the days. Had he wanted to, he also could have visited various Web sites that allow users to plug in data about themselves and then tell them how long they have to live, statistically. Armed with that information, he could have programmed his computer to announce the number of days he has left when he turned it on every day.

This might sound a bit morbid, but the application is clear. We might not go to the extreme of checking off our days on a chart, but we do need to recognize our mortality. We need to acknowledge that someday we will run our last lap. And with that in mind, we need to embrace a lifestyle today that will allow us to be fulfilled and happy when we cross the finish line of life.

That lifestyle, according to Proverbs 10:27, is one that gives prominence to the fear of the Lord. This verse doesn't mean that if we love God and obey His commands, we'll all live to be one hundred years old. It does mean, however, that if we live in correct union with Him, patterning our lives after the model set forth in Scripture, we can expect to live fuller, richer lives.

Are you making the most of the days that you have left?

Prescription for a Long Life

The fear of the LORD adds length to life, but the years of the wicked are cut short. PROVERBS 10:27

Why does the fear of the Lord add length to life?

One reason has to do with stress. When I (Tom) worked as a truck driver many years ago, I drove the speed limit and all my coworkers drove very quickly. Because of their driving habits, they were always looking over their shoulders, stressed out about whether they were going to get another ticket. But I never worried about that one bit. I knew I was staying within the boundaries of the law, so I didn't have to fear when I saw a state trooper in my rearview mirror.

The fear of the Lord adds length to life because when we follow His rules, we don't have the stress of constantly looking over our shoulders. In Him, we have Someone to Whom we can go for advice; Someone Whom we acknowledge is in control of good times and bad times. We have Someone we can depend on, Someone Who nourishes us, Someone Who cleanses us. When we fear the Lord, we don't have to live a life of guilt, regret, and stress—all things that might contribute to an early demise—unless we choose to. There is a real pragmatic physical result that accrues when we fear God instead of living a life of wickedness.

But the fear of the Lord doesn't just add length to our days. It also adds depth. Jesus came so that we could have a full, or abundant, life (John 10:10). When He is our Master, we get more out of the days that we do have. Our days—both on the job and at home—are deeper and more fulfilling than they would be if He were not involved.

With a promise like that, why would you want to do anything but fear Him?

Corporate Goodness

When the righteous prosper, the city rejoices; when the wicked perish, there are shouts of joy. PROVERBS 11:10

When righteous people embody the spirit of Christ in their daily lives, they have a positive effect on their culture. Their influence is strong. Their presence is sweet.

It's like a rescue team entering a dark cave full of terrified people and turning on a bright flashlight. The impact is obvious. A sense of relief replaces the fear. A sense of hope replaces the despair. A sense of comfort replaces the confusion.

The same thing happens when truth shows up in the middle of falsehood or when kindness shows up in the middle of meanness. When you place a kindhearted person in a workplace full of meanspirited people, he might receive some abuse at first, but eventually his kindness starts to take effect. Good things start to happen. Other people will become happier, easier to deal with, nicer.

Two scenarios are mentioned in Proverbs 11:10—when the righteous prosper and when the wicked perish. Both events bring joy to the city. It's good news to the corporate whole when someone who obviously has done wrong gets caught and is taken out of commission. And it's also cause for celebration when someone who really deserves some credit is rewarded or recognized.

When the rules are confusing and employees can't really distinguish between right and wrong, good and bad, fair and unfair, over time, that corporate culture will disintegrate. It might seem to work for a while, but it's difficult to maintain any sense of order or accountability in that situation.

On the flip side, any community of workers will be much happier and more satisfied when the standard of right and wrong is clear and enforced. When goodness is elevated in a workplace, it brings a certain amount of liberation to the environment. When wrong is judged and dealt with, it ushers in a certain amount of freedom.

What sort of environment are you fostering in your workplace? Is it an environment where people rejoice when the righteous prosper? If not, what can you do to change it?

Inner Beauty

Like a gold ring in a pig's snout is a beautiful woman who shows no discretion.
PROVERBS 11:22

Society puts a great deal of value on physical beauty, especially for women. Professional women are expected to conform to certain standards of physical appearance and then are judged by how they measure up—or fail to. Entire industries have been created to nurture society's obsession with how women look: fashion, beauty products, magazines, salons, fitness, and the list goes on.

But the writer of Proverbs says that beauty, whether natural or created, is thrown away if not paired with a character that shines as brightly inside as a beautiful exterior does outside. Getting all prettied up on the outside while our insides remain ugly is like ornamenting a pig that loves to roll in the mud and eat slop from a trough with a valuable piece of jewelry. The contrast is ridiculous.

What exactly is discretion? The word literally means "taste," and it's used elsewhere in Scripture to mean both intellectual and moral perception. Abigail, David's wife, had it and was praised for it. The woman of Proverbs 31 had it. Discretion is being able to tell right from wrong, true from false, worthy from unworthy. It also means keeping a sharp eye out for opportunities to do good for other people and then following through.

What would we be able to accomplish if we spent as much time obsessing with our inner character as we did with our outward appearance? When will we learn to ignore the messages of society telling us we'll be judged by how we look and realize that it's more important what we do?

All Hat, No Cattle

Better to be a nobody and yet have a servant than to pretend to be somebody and have no food. PROVERBS 12:9

Every now and then, you meet someone who makes a really good first impression on you, but when you get to know him better, you realize that what you saw was just that—an impression. When you start to scratch beneath the surface, you are disappointed to discover that he actually is a person of very little substance.

Then every once in a while, the situation is just the opposite. You meet someone who makes a really good first impression on you. You feel an immediate affinity. You want to spend time with him, and the more time you spend together, the more depth, goodness, and wisdom you uncover. The more you scratch beneath the surface, the more substance you find.

Our society puts far more emphasis on a person's surface appearance than on his or her depth of character. But this proverb makes it clear that it's better for us to be relatively unknown and solid in whom we are than to look like a big shot with no inner substance. It emphasizes the importance of *being* somebody of significance as opposed to just *looking like* somebody of significance.

This concept is probably more applicable in a work context than it is in any other setting. As followers of Christ in the marketplace, we need to work hard to develop depth of character. We need to sharpen our skills and continually upgrade our abilities so that when we are called upon to do something, we actually have something to offer.

People of true substance don't need their own personal PR departments. They choose to leave the promotion up to God, because they recognize that in His eyes, they will always be somebody of significance.

Are you a person of substance, or are you "all hat and no cattle"?

Lifting the Load

An anxious heart weighs a man down, but a kind word cheers him up.
PROVERBS 12:25

There is nothing quite so crippling as depression brought on by fear and anxiety. We've all at one time or another carried a burden so heavy we felt physically weighed down. Every trouble seems magnified through the lens of anxiety, and at times the situation seems completely hopeless. Despair is not far away.

If we're not going through this kind of experience, we often don't want to be reminded of it by those who are, lest it affect our own good spirits. If we're in charge of a number of employees, we may become concerned that one person's black mood will bring everyone else down, lessening enthusiasm and productivity. So we may isolate that person or suggest he or she take some personal time to deal with those personal issues.

But if we ignore anxiety or try to insulate ourselves from it, we're missing an incredible opportunity for good and may even increase a person's sense of loneliness and devastation. We may mean well, but our callousness could be interpreted as rejection.

Instead, we should turn on our emotional sensors and try to tune in to a person's inner state. This comes more naturally to some people than to others, but it's something everyone can—and should—strive for. What's bothering the anxious person the most? What is the heaviest burden she is carrying? How can we help to ease it, even lift it completely? The writer of Proverbs says it takes just one word. If we communicate an expression of kindness, encouragement, or insight, we can make a tremendous impact and help bring a person's circumstances back into the proper perspective.

"Would you like to talk?" "What can I do to help?" "How can we address this together?" "Let's pray about it." Our goal should be to help create hope and confidence in place of fear and anxiety. Words are powerful instruments, and if used with care and precision, we can turn depression into rejoicing.

How many kind words have you said this week?

Let It Go

Hope deferred makes the heart sick. PROVERBS 13:12

Have you ever waited for something for a very long time, constantly hoping that it would come to fruition? Maybe you were anticipating the offer of a better job. Maybe you were hoping your boss would follow through on her promise to hire help for you. Maybe you thought you'd get a raise. Maybe you were expecting a profitable quarter, the promise of investment capital, or a turnaround in your industry.

Whatever it was, how did you feel when it didn't happen when you thought it would? Week after week, paycheck after paycheck, quarter after quarter, year after year—nothing. No change. No results. Just disappointment, again and again. If you've been there, you can surely identify with this proverb, even if you might not have thought to phrase it this way. Hope deferred made your heart sick.

What can we do to heal a sick heart? Is there any cure at all, or is it a terminal illness? If we're to maintain our sanity, there comes a time when we may simply have to put our hope away. We need to tuck it away on a shelf where it's out of sight even if it's not out of mind. We may not forget whatever it is we're hoping for, and we might even continue to pray that it will still happen. But we have to move on. We can't spend all our energy hoping that one thing will happen; if we do, we'll miss out on the blessings God has for us today.

Is there a hope in your life that you need to put on the shelf? It can be very difficult to grab a stepstool and place that dream high above your head where only God can see it. But maybe it's time to let it go and to start hoping for something else.

The Benefits of Work

All hard work brings a profit, but mere talk leads only to poverty. PROVERBS 14:23

When your alarm goes off at 6:00 on Monday morning after a hectic weekend, you may find it difficult to remember why you go to work. *Why is it,* you wonder, *that I can't stay in bed for a few more hours, then spend the day doing what I like to do?* It slowly dawns on your sleep-fogged brain: *That's right—I like being able to pay the bills. I like being able to provide for my family. And, most of the time, I even like what I do.*

The writer of Proverbs would offer a hearty affirmation. Work is a profitable way for us to spend our days. First, there are the obvious reasons. We get paid for our work, which enables us to meet our material needs and then some. Depending on our circumstances and our decisions, the material profit is lesser or greater.

But work is not only profitable because of what is produced. It is also good because of what it does for our character. The process itself is valuable. Hard work occupies our minds—it directs our energies and sharpens our faculties. It also keeps us from temptation. There's not much left over for schemes of corruption or immorality if most of our energy is funneled into work. Work gives us goals and purpose, a reason to get out of bed on Monday morning, as we look forward to the next days, weeks, months, and years. And finally, hard work is therapeutic. During times of turmoil, confusion, and loss, it gives us an outlet, a way to get away from the source of our pain and do something productive. Then, when the pain has passed or at least eased, we can look back on that difficult time and see something we've accomplished.

Without work, all we've got is talk. Proverbs doesn't say talk itself is bad, but mere talk—talk unaccompanied by action—leads to poverty. If we don't work, it isn't long before physical hardship sets upon us. And spiritual poverty is not far away, especially if we let temptations preoccupy our thinking.

Yes, work is hard. It bends our backs, roughens our hands, and taxes our minds. But it's also a blessing. The next time you have a hard time crawling out of bed to get ready for work, say to yourself, "All hard work brings a profit." It might not bring a bounce to your step and a sparkle to your eye, but it just might get you into the shower.

Deflecting Anger

A gentle answer turns away wrath, but a harsh word stirs up anger. PROVERBS 15:1

Gentleness is not a character trait our society holds in very high esteem. Instead, the forceful personalities who face down any challenge and say exactly what's on their minds are admired and looked to as role models. Can you remember the last gentle person who made the lead on the news?

Between our social conditioning and our human (read: sinful) nature, a gentle answer does not come easily. When we're insulted or when someone becomes angry with us, our first reaction is heated indignation; the need to defend ourselves and save face roars louder than any other impulse. So anger provokes anger, which provokes more anger, and soon there's an ugly scene that leaves both parties with a bitter taste in their mouths. The seeds of resentment that may take days, weeks, or even months or years to resolve.

A far better way, though not our natural way, is to respond to anger with a gentle answer. Dale Carnegie, author of the bestseller *How to Win Friends and Influence People,* based much of his philosophy on this concept. The book is full of story after story of people who tried, just once, to see what would happen if they responded to an angry person with mild words. They were usually astonished at the results—the anger melted because the person had no momentum.

So how do we teach ourselves to come up with a gentle answer? We have a perfect role model in the person of Jesus Christ. Read through one of the Gospels and make a note of the time the Pharisees or the mockers or even one of the disciples becomes angry. Though there are notable and perfectly righteous exceptions, the vast majority of the time, Christ's response is gentleness and compassion. Angry Pharisees put down their stones. Smug Sadducees become dumbfounded and walk away. People are amazed and praise God.

What results do your words produce?

Nowhere to Hide

The eyes of the LORD are everywhere, keeping watch on the wicked and the good. PROVERBS 15:3

Unlike the process in our justice system, God doesn't need to gather evidence to come to a decision about our guilt or innocence in a given circumstance. He sees every action, and He even sees our hearts as we undertake those actions. Knowledge of this aspect of God's character can be a source of great comfort or great fear.

Many passages in Scripture marvel at God's omniscience—with particular emphasis on His all-seeing eyes. While they lead us to understand God's nature better, they also give us a powerful incentive for righteous conduct.

For example, 2 Chronicles 16:9 says, "[T]he eyes of the LORD range throughout the earth to strengthen those whose hearts are fully committed to him." Likewise, David remarks that God examines the sons of men. As a result, He rains down fiery coals and sends a hot wind to the wicked, but upright men see His face (Psalm 11:4–7). And Hebrews 4:13 says, "Nothing in all creation is hidden from God's sight. Everything is uncovered and laid bare before the eyes of him to whom we must give account." Because God sees everything, He will strengthen us in our devotion, punish the wicked, allow the upright to see His face, and one day demand an account of our actions.

But perhaps the most eloquent and well-known commentary on God's omniscience is Psalm 139, in which David ends with a plea for God to search his heart and his life because nothing is hidden from Him (vv. 23–24). This reveals yet one more facet to God's penetrating vision: He sees what we are blind to in ourselves. So even if we think we're doing right, acting with integrity, and treating our fellow human beings justly, there may be pockets of offensiveness that we won't—or can't—acknowledge.

It's easy to look at our lives and become self-satisfied. We don't steal or lie; we don't cheat on our spouses; we're faithful and consistent in our work. What would happen if, like David, we asked God to test us and reveal our shortcomings—*all* of them? The result for most of us would probably not be pleasant. But only by ridding ourselves of those offensive ways will we be able to commit to Him fully.

Pass the Vegetables, Please

Better a meal of vegetables where there is love than a fattened calf with hatred.
PROVERBS 15:17

There's nothing wrong with good food—and the wealth that allows us to indulge in our favorite culinary luxury once in a while, whether it's prime rib or Häagen-Dazs. The Book of Proverbs makes it clear that wealth is desirable and honorable when attained and used in a righteous way.

But this verse reminds us that there's a negative side to wealth, a danger to watch for. Too often fortune becomes the most important thing to a family. Its members dine on the best fare (and wear the best clothes and live in the most beautiful home) but are bereft of the most valuable spiritual treasure—love. And the absence of love is the perfect environment for hatred to flourish.

In the hierarchy of God's economy, spiritual wealth is far more important than material wealth. It's so important, in fact, that it's better to have spiritual wealth and nothing else. Daniel and his friends recognized this truth when they refused to eat meat sacrificed to their captors' gods and instead ate only vegetables and water. In fact, when we sacrifice material rewards in order to preserve our spiritual health and that of our families, God often responds by providing our material needs as well, as He did for Daniel.

We're faced with decisions every day. We filter those choices through our value systems, come to a decision, and act accordingly. What is the result? If we decide to pursue a course of action that enhances our bank accounts but hurts our family lives or our relationships with God, how much damage are we really doing? Maybe not much this time, but we've reinforced a pattern that in the long term could lead to destruction. We may one day find ourselves sitting down to sumptuous meals with no appetite because we realize that love has left our houses.

Are you cultivating an environment of love in your home, no matter what your income level?

An Army of One

Plans fail for lack of counsel, but with many advisers they succeed. PROVERBS 15:22

"I can do it myself!"

Anyone who's been around a three-year-old has heard this emphatic utterance more than once—or some variation of it, such as, "No help! My do it!" We smile patiently and let the child struggle through the task he or she is trying to accomplish.

Some of us don't change much in that respect as we get older. Independent to the core, we loathe group projects in school and prefer to function as a unit of one in our careers. But Scripture says this is a bad idea and lets us know that we're setting ourselves up for trouble.

Why don't we ask others for their input when we know theoretically that we should and that there are trustworthy people who would be glad to help? The list of answers is long. We may fear that asking for help makes us seem incapable. Or we want to take all the credit for any success that comes of our plans. We may be in a crunch and simply don't have time for long discussions about the best course of action. If we're engaged in projects that are particularly close to our hearts, we may fear criticism of our plans that reflects back on our abilities. Often, especially in our individualistic society, we charge ahead on our own simply because we can. We're in positions of autonomy that don't require us to seek guidance.

A far better way, however, is to gather trusted advisers and let their insights benefit our plans. Even the wisest person is prone to errors of judgment. Even if our plans aren't fundamentally flawed, another person's experience and viewpoint can enhance our strategies to make them even more effective. Not only is success much more likely, the experience of relying on others for advice keeps us humble and fosters a healthy environment of cooperation.

So the next time your inner child says, "I can do it myself," listen instead to your grown-up self that says you need some help. The child in you may pout, but in the meantime you'll be on your way to success.

Formula for Success

Commit to the LORD whatever you do, and your plans will succeed. PROVERBS 16:3

It's not a money-back guarantee, but the general principle spelled out in this verse is one that we would all do well to practice.

So many times when we're working on a big project—an expansion of our business, a new joint venture, the development of a revolutionary product, etc.—we get so caught up in projections, schedules, and strategies that we fail to consider what God thinks of what we're doing. We forget to consult Him every step along the way; instead, we wait until something begins to go wrong to seek His guidance and His blessing.

That's not the approach we need to take if we want our plans to succeed, however. As this verse indicates, we need to commit every plan—whether it be as significant as a career change or as seemingly minor as when we take our next vacation—to the Lord, not in the middle of it or when we're almost done, but before we start.

The Hebrew word translated "commit" offers a vivid word picture of how we should handle our plans. The word actually means "roll," which indicates we should "roll over" our plans to the Lord (see also Psalm 37:5). If we roll them over to Him, the implication is that we are giving up the control. That might not appeal to the micromanagers among us, but it's actually a rather comforting thought. You see, once our plans are in the safe hands of God, they are far less burdensome to us. If God wants them to succeed, they will; if He doesn't, they won't.

Either way, we no longer have to worry about it. We just have to work hard, strive to make wise decisions, and, above all, make sure that we aren't trying to roll our plans back over into our laps. "Be satisfied with His management of your concerns," writes one commentator. "Let your heart habitually turn to the throne of grace; so that in a crisis of trouble instant faith, instant—perhaps speechless—prayer, may bring instant composure and courage."[10]

Are you the project manager of your life, or have you rolled that responsibility over to God?

The Best-Laid Plans

In his heart a man plans his course, but the LORD determines his steps. . . . The lot is cast into the lap, but its every decision is from the LORD. PROVERBS 16:9, 33

Preparation is a crucial element of any successful business endeavor. Whether we're getting ready for a big presentation to a potential client, a major renovation of our office space, a meeting with a key investor, or the final phase of an important project, we do our best to cross every "t" and dot every "i."

We put together the most highly qualified team. We do the research. We lay the groundwork. We even commit the project or meeting to the Lord and ask Him to grant us success.

We do everything we know to do. But sometimes, things don't turn out quite like we hoped or expected. The potential client chooses another company to represent her. The office renovation takes five months longer than scheduled. The investor pulls his funding. The final phase of the project turns into a logistical nightmare.

As the saying goes, even the best-laid plans go awry. But as frustrating, even as devastating, as this might be, it shouldn't surprise us. It's certainly not a new phenomenon. The writer of Proverbs was well aware that life often seems like a game of chance. As the New Living Translation so eloquently puts Proverbs 16:33, "We may throw the dice, but the Lord determines how they fall."

This thought can be very unsettling, especially for those of us who like to be in control of our lives down to the very last detail. But it also can be a source of great comfort to know that what we sometimes mistake for chance is actually divine orchestration. God knows the outcome long before we do. He sees the big picture. He's in control. So when things don't go our way, even after days, months, or even years of preparation, we can rest in the knowledge that God is still at work.

Such rest isn't easy, of course. It takes faith. It takes trust. It requires us to loosen our grip on the steering wheel. But in the end, it makes it much easier to accept the outcome, whatever it may be.

The Wise Request

How much better to get wisdom than gold. PROVERBS 16:16

What do you pray for? If you're like me, your list of requests looks something like this: God's protection of family members. Financial provision. Traveling safety. The salvation of nonbelieving friends and loved ones. Healing for a sick parent or neighbor. Strength to make it through a difficult season at work. And so on.

Those are all legitimate requests, concerns that God wants us to bring to Him. But when was the last time you prayed for something a bit deeper? When was the last time you prayed for *wisdom?*

Such a request is not as specific as, say, asking God to give you a safe, productive business trip or pleading with Him to protect your child from the chicken pox epidemic at school. But it's just as important, if not more so. We all need wisdom, no matter what we do for a living, no matter where we work or live, no matter how much money we make, no matter how smart we think we are.

But we don't just need any kind of wisdom. We need *God's* wisdom—especially at work. We need it when we're trying to come up with solutions to complex business problems. We need it when we're planning our schedules for the day, the week, and the month. We need it when we're handling sensitive personnel issues. We need it when we're dealing with difficult coworkers. We *especially* need it when we're facing ethical dilemmas or when we sense that God wants us to confront a colleague about something.

Asking God to give us wisdom on a daily basis isn't odd or self-serving. It's the wise thing to do.

Follow Solomon's example (1 Kings 3:4–15). He could have asked God for any blessing in the world—wealth, honor, victory over his enemies, a long life, etc.—and yet his only request was a wise, discerning heart. He believed that wisdom was better than gold.

What about you? Do you genuinely desire wisdom, too? More important, do your *prayers* show that you desire wisdom?

Headed for Destruction?

Pride goes before destruction. PROVERBS 16:18

What does pride look like in your life?

"Wait a minute," you might say. "I don't have a problem with pride."

No one's accusing you of having a *problem*—not exactly. But take a careful look in the mirror. View your words and your actions—all of them—through the eyes of your coworkers, your spouse, your children, your close friends. Now answer the question again: *What does pride look like in your life?*

We're not talking about that well-deserved feeling of accomplishment that sweeps over you when you complete a big project, land an important client, or close a big sale. There's nothing wrong with that, as long as it doesn't lead to a big head. But what about the subtle kind of pride that sneaks up on you and makes you do and say things you didn't even know you were doing and saying?

Have you ever jokingly put down a coworker when he wasn't there to defend himself? That was pride saying, "I'm better than he is." Have you ever made sarcastic comments about a subordinate in front of her peers? That was arrogance saying, "She's not worth much, is she?" Have you ever forced a colleague to drop what he was doing so that he could help you finish a project that you should have completed days ago? That was conceit saying, "My needs are more important than the needs of my coworkers." Have you ever gotten irritated when someone else received well-deserved praise? That was vanity saying, "I deserve some recognition, too." Do you ever act as if you're the only one in the office who knows anything or the only one who can do your job? That's self-satisfaction saying, "I'm really something, aren't I?"

What does pride look like in your life? Is it under control, or are you headed for destruction?

The Stakes Are High

There is a way that seems right to a man, but in the end it leads to death.
PROVERBS 16:25

Unless we work for an evangelistic ministry or serve on the staff of a church, we probably don't spend our days thinking about how we can do our part to spread the gospel to a lost and dying world. We're usually more concerned with deadlines, budgets, balance sheets, vendors, and clients than we are with strategizing about how to get the good news out to nonbelievers most efficiently. It's not that we don't care or that we don't intentionally look for ways to share our faith at work. It's just that we get paid to do a job, and we feel it's our God-given responsibility to do it well.

All that is as it should be. But it's difficult to read this proverb and not feel a sense of urgency about telling our friends and coworkers about Jesus. All around us are people who think they're on their way to heaven. They try hard to be good. They attend church. They're nice to their children. They recycle. They support the Salvation Army, they help out at the local soup kitchen, and they even give blood occasionally. They're doing everything they can to make sure that when they reach the end of their lives, the good that they've done will outweigh the bad and the Pearly Gates will open to them.

Unfortunately, they're wrong—dead wrong. "There is a way that seems right to a man," the writer of Proverbs says, "but in the end it leads to death" (16:25). Working for eternal life seems right. It seems logical. It seems reasonable. But it won't work.

If you are a follower of Christ, you know that. But do your coworkers know it?

Respect Your Elders

Gray hair is a crown of splendor. PROVERBS 16:31

In our youth-oriented culture, gray hair isn't considered to be desirable. When the gray strands start to outnumber the colored ones, our first inclination is to hop in the shower to "wash that gray right out of our hair." We'd rather apply chemicals to our hair than run the risk of looking old before our time, especially if we're in a profession that places a premium on youthful good looks.

In Old Testament times, however, gray hair was not something to be dreaded. In those days, people respected their elders. People naturally assumed that older people—easily identified as such by their gray "crowns of splendor"—knew more and had more wisdom than their younger counterparts.

Sadly, that is often not the case today, especially in the workplace. In a rapidly changing, extremely competitive corporate environment, it is usually the young, energetic, aggressive, innovative twenty-somethings and thirty-somethings who get noticed. They're the ones with all the potential and all the fresh, new ideas. Or are they?

While it's true that many workers in their fifties and early sixties are simply biding their time until retirement, many others have just as much to offer as their youthful colleagues. In fact, when you factor in the wisdom and knowledge that often comes with experience, the gray-haired employees might even have more to offer.

If you're in a position of leadership at your company, don't bypass someone for a promotion or key position just because he might qualify for the senior citizen's discount at Denny's. His expertise might be just what's needed to take that department or project to the next level. And if you're one of those aggressive twenty- or thirty-somethings, make it a point to seek out advice and counsel from your older coworkers. They might teach you more than you think—about work and about life.

Just What the Doctor Ordered

A cheerful heart is good medicine, but a crushed spirit dries up the bones.
PROVERBS 17:22

It's sometimes difficult to find much cheer on the job. Our work is often tedious. Coworkers can be meanspirited and crude. Unreasonable deadlines cut into our personal time. Bosses are sometimes incompetent, critical, or unfair. Budgets are tight and clients get frustrated. You get the picture.

As a result, we often walk around looking like we have a stomachache, practically champing at the bit so we can jump down the throat of the next person who asks us for something.

That, the writer of Proverbs says, is not the way it should be. Thousands of years before twentieth-century medical and mental health researchers determined that laughter played a significant role in physical well-being, Solomon had already figured out that a "cheerful heart promotes health while a dispirited one prompts illness."[11]

Ours is a health-conscious culture. We exercise. We watch our cholesterol and fat intake. We monitor our blood pressure. We try to lower the stress in our lives. We eat fruits and vegetables and take daily vitamins. But we often overlook one of the best health remedies of all—laughter.

Few things are more disheartening than to see a professed follower of Christ who walks around all day looking as if he just lost his best friend. Such a demeanor certainly does nothing to make his coworkers want to share his faith; why would they want what he has if it makes him so gloomy? On the other hand, few things are more attractive than a believer whose face reflects the joy she feels in her heart, joy that comes solely from knowing Jesus personally.

Take a look in the mirror. Do you look like you have a perpetual stomachache? Lighten up. Laugh a little. It's just what the doctor ordered.

Think before You Speak

Even a fool is thought wise if he keeps silent, and discerning if he holds his tongue. PROVERBS 17:28

Have you ever been in a meeting with an unfamiliar coworker who insisted on asking stupid questions or making dumb, irrelevant comments? Few things are more frustrating than listening to such foolish babble, especially when you're up against a deadline and really need to be finishing a project at your desk instead of sitting in a meeting. As you left the meeting, perhaps your mind was flooded with such thoughts as, *That guy is such an idiot! Somebody really needs to teach him when to be quiet.*

Now think about what your postmeeting thoughts would have been if your coworker had sat through the meeting and not said a single word. You've never met him before, so you have no preconceived notions about what he's like. By his silence, you just might infer that he was intelligent and perceptive, only willing to speak when he had something beneficial to offer the conversation. You'd be wrong, of course, but you wouldn't know it. That's because, as Proverbs 17:28 says, "Even a fool is thought wise if he keeps silent, and discerning if he holds his tongue."

Knowing when to speak and when to be silent is a valuable (though often missing) skill in today's work settings. It's so easy to spout off facts and opinions at a moment's notice—it makes us appear intelligent, we think, and if we look smart, perhaps we'll get promoted or at least recognized by our boss. But more often than not, it's much better—for us and for everyone around us—if we just hold our tongues. As someone once quipped, "It's better to be silent and be thought a fool than to open your mouth and remove all doubt."

Don't Cut Corners

One who is slack in his work is brother to one who destroys. PROVERBS 18:9

Are you a diligent worker, or do you tend to be a slacker? Do you complete every task to the best of your ability, or do you rush through your assignments, doing just enough to get by?

We might think that slacking off occasionally is perfectly harmless; after all, we all get a little lazy every now and then, don't we? Maybe so, but that doesn't make it right. According to this proverb, in fact, shoddy work is actually destructive. Here's how one Bible scholar describes it: "Lazy people look for short cuts; they don't use the level and square as often as they should and don't tighten bolts as much as they should. The end product is not only inferior but potentially dangerous; think of a car with faulty brakes or a house with inferior wiring."[12]

That puts it in a whole different light, doesn't it? We could easily expand the list: Think of a badly designed bridge, a carelessly done surgical procedure, or a flaw in a pharmaceutical formula.

The shortcuts we take at work might not lead to an automobile accident, a raging house fire, or other kind of tragedy, but they can still have a negative effect. As far as the bottom line is concerned, cutting corners in a proposal might make our company miss out on a potential sale, and shoddy work on a project could lead an existing client to take his business elsewhere. From a relational standpoint, when we fail to carry our load, we're usually creating more work for someone else, which usually doesn't do much for our relationships at work.

How much time do you spend hanging around other people's work areas, lingering by the snack machine, or doing nonwork-related things at your desk? Do your answers indicate that you might be a slacker? If so, make it a point to be more focused at work. Pay attention to the details. Measure twice; cut once. Reread the directions. Be conscientious.

In other words, make Ecclesiastes 9:10 your motto: "Whatever your hand finds to do, do it with all your might."

Don't Talk, Listen

He who answers before listening—that is his folly and his shame. PROVERBS 18:13

None of us likes to be interrupted, nor do we appreciate being given advice before we've had a chance to explain the whole problem. And yet so many times, that is exactly what happens.

We begin telling a coworker about a sticky client issue only to have him immediately launch into an elaborate dissertation about how to fix it. Or we start telling a friend about the horrible date we had only to have her interrupt us with her own woeful weekend tale. Such responses are frustrating, annoying, and downright rude.

But we're all guilty in this area. We're so anxious to impart our knowledge and share our experiences that we fail to listen carefully to what's being said. In doing so, we often ignore key points. We overlook subtle inferences. We miss hidden meanings.

And on top of all that, we show disrespect. Nothing screams, "I don't care about you or about what you're saying" louder than a rude interruption. By acting as if we have all the answers, or, worse, by behaving as if we don't have time to listen to the whole story, we are basically blowing someone off. Such a response, Proverbs says, is shameful.

How do you respond in conversations with your coworkers and employees? Do you wait until they're finished speaking before you open your mouth? Do you listen carefully, making eye contact to show you're really interested? Or do you interrupt frequently, tap your fingers, focus on other activity in the office, or mess with your Palm Pilot when someone is trying to explain something to you?

Think about how *you* like to be treated. Then treat your coworkers the same way.

Two Sides

The first to present his case seems right, till another comes forward and questions him. PROVERBS 18:17

There are two sides to every story.

It's an unspoken motto of every wise parent, every discerning judge, every smart teacher, and every diligent boss. There's no way to accurately assess a fight between siblings, a difficult court case, a squabble among classmates, or a conflict between coworkers without hearing from *all* the parties involved. Each person tries to present his case in the best possible light; it's only as all sides are heard that the inconsistencies are revealed and the truth begins to emerge.

We may not be in a position to hear cases or settle disputes at work, but if we practice the principle spelled out in this verse, we could save ourselves a lot of grief and stress. How many times do we jump to conclusions about something our companies, our bosses, or coworkers are doing without finding out all the facts first? We might hear that the CEO has been meeting with all the department heads, and the next thing we know, the rumor mill is grinding out speculation about an impending layoff.

When that happens, we have two choices: We can start losing sleep over the fact that our job might be in jeopardy, or we can ask our boss what's really going on. The truth may hurt, but at least we'll know it's the truth.

On a more personal level, think about what would happen if one coworker told you that another coworker—one whom you like and respect—had been critical of your work. Your first reaction might be to get angry and start gossiping about the other person, but if you follow the advice in this verse, you'd check your anger and find out the rest of the story. It may well be that the coworker you trust actually did say something about you, but your other coworker may have taken it completely out of context.

Are you willing to reserve judgment until you have heard all sides? If not, you're setting yourself up to be misinformed, perhaps even deceived.

Style versus Substance

It is not good to have zeal without knowledge. PROVERBS 19:2

According to Aristotle, men who want to be persuasive but don't really have anything to say simply speak louder. That makes us chuckle, but we only chuckle because we know it's true. Ours is a world of loud talkers—salesmen who promise one thing but deliver another, companies that offer great jobs to prospective employees but fail to follow through, and people who project one image on a résumé but fail to live up to the picture they paint of themselves.

Our culture platforms the extroverted, Type A, charismatic types, but many times, those people are all style and no substance. They can talk a good line and make others laugh, but when it comes down to getting things done, they're practically useless.

Proverbs 19:2 reveals that the most effective persuader is a person who has enthusiasm plus content. Rather than being a bunch of hot air, he or she is someone with passion and energy that is woven around a core of substance and knowledge. As a matter of fact, that's also a really good formula for business success. A company with good intellectual property *and* a capable sales and marketing engine is a company that probably will fare very well.

Enthusiasm by itself doesn't get the job done. It only takes emotional hype to have zeal, but it takes energy, hard work, and time to build a base of knowledge. Zeal will carry you along for a ways, and, for a short time, it might even seem more impressive. But if you want long-term results and long-term success, there's no substitute for knowledge. In order to excel at work, we need substance first. Any style that comes along later is just the icing on the cake.

Do you deliver what you promise, or are you all hype and no substance?

Lifelong Learning

Stop listening to instruction, my son, and you will stray from the words of knowledge. PROVERBS 19:27

We will never reach a point at which we know everything there is to know about life, about our spouses, about our professions, or about anything else. But we do sometimes run into the danger of thinking we know *enough*. Enough to get by. Enough to stay on course. Enough to maintain the status quo.

Not so, says Solomon. When we stop listening to instruction, we stray from the truth. That applies whether we're talking about the truth of Scripture or the truth about the latest breakthroughs and thinking in our professions or industries.

The Hebrew word translated "stop" in this verse is "actually a rhetorical device designed to say just the opposite, 'do *not* stop learning.'" In other words, learning is an ongoing, intentional discipline. We might grow tired of studying and reading, but Solomon's admonition is for our own good. After all, "constant energy is needed to resist ignorance and all its associated vices."[13]

How do you respond when your boss sends around a memo outlining the required continuing education classes for the year? Do you grumble and moan, or do you look at it as an opportunity to stretch yourself and expand your horizons? What about when you're given a list of supplemental reading materials in your Bible study class at church? Do you promptly throw it away, or do you try to locate the books and spend a little time each week absorbing the information?

Don't settle for the status quo. Don't stop developing the brain God gave you. The more you learn, the more you'll discover that you don't know. But that's OK. That will keep you from getting a big head about all your newfound knowledge.

Actions Speak Louder Than Words

Even a child is known by his actions, by whether his conduct is pure and right.
PROVERBS 20:11

"What you're doing speaks so loudly I can't hear what you're saying."
"He's all talk and no action."
"Actions speak louder than words."

We could continue with this list of clichés, but the point is clear: What we *do* says far more about us than the words that actually come out of our mouths. That can be a scary thought, especially for followers of Christ. It's easy to quote Bible verses and sprinkle our conversations with religious jargon. We're letting our light shine, we think, as we offer to pray for coworkers who are going through tough times.

But what are we telling that coworker about our faith when, five minutes later, we start chewing out customers on the phone? How are we affecting their opinion of Christianity when we lie to our bosses about our progress on a project or engage in nasty gossip about another employee?

Don't be fooled. If people know you're a Christian, they *will* be watching to see if your words are congruent with your actions. If what you do matches what you say, the people around you may or may not connect that to your relationship with Jesus. But if your words *don't* match your deeds, you can be sure that you're not helping the cause of Christ. In fact, you might be the stumbling block that keeps someone else from wanting to know Jesus.

It's a sobering thought, one that should make you think twice before you bring God into a conversation with a coworker. Do your actions and attitudes on the job honor Christ? If not, keep your mouth shut until you change your actions and adjust your attitudes. Don't let anyone accuse you of being all talk and no action.

Biblical Negotiating

"It's no good, it's no good!" says the buyer; then off he goes and boasts about his purchase. PROVERBS 20:14

Anyone who has ever haggled over the price of something—perhaps at a car lot or antique shop—can relate to the humorous exchange recorded in this verse. A buyer demeans the very thing he wants to buy at the store, desperately hoping to push the price down. But as soon as the cash register rings the final sale, he goes off and brags about his new purchase to all his friends.

This passage specifically addresses a retail transaction, but the principle behind it applies to any kind of negotiation. Ideally, both parties involved in a negotiation come away as winners. In reality, however, one party often wins and the other often loses. Sometimes it just works out that way; one side's case is just much stronger than the other side's. But sometimes, the parties use less-than-acceptable means to get what they want at the negotiating table. They may shade the truth, doctor the books, or conceal important information.

This is not an option for followers of Christ who want to practice biblical principles in their business dealings. We must avoid even the hint of dishonesty or deception. That, of course, pushes negotiation to a new level. Rather than looking out solely for our own interests, we must figure out ways to win our cases without leaving the person across the table in total despair. If we lie to win arguments or close a deal, or if we practice deception to hire or retain employees, secure capitalization, or make our stock price go up, we are employing tools that God has condemned. If we want to glorify Him in our work, we must figure out how to negotiate and win without being deceptive and dishonest.

Do your negotiating techniques meet biblical standards of fairness, honesty, and compassion?

Your Secret's (Not) Safe with Me

A gossip betrays a confidence; so avoid a man who talks too much. PROVERBS 20:19

There's nothing wrong with developing friendships with the people with whom we work. Spending eight, nine, or more hours a day with someone builds camaraderie and reveals common interests, and friendship is a natural outcome.

According to this verse, however, we shouldn't get too comfortable around people who talk too much, regardless of how much we have in common with them. We might feel sure that a coworker's chatter—whether verbal or, in this electronic age, through the company e-mail system—is harmless. But we never know when something we share is going to get passed on to someone else. So unless we want the entire company to know that we dislike our new boss, that we're hoping for promotions, or that we're having problems with our children, we'd best keep our mouths shut when we're around that person.

And then there are those coworkers who are always ready and willing to share information about other people. Be doubly careful around them. If they're telling you stories about others, there's a good chance that they're telling other people stories about you. So don't listen to their gossip, and don't tell them anything confidential.

Better yet, stay away from them. These people—the King James Version calls them "talebearers"—have a way of working secrets out of people. They prod and pry and flatter and tease, and before you know it, you've spilled an entire story that you had no intention of even bringing up. And once that information is elicited, there's no telling what form it will take—or how it will hurt you—when it's passed on to the next person.

Are your secrets safe? More important, are the secrets that have been entrusted to you safe? Make sure they stay that way, lest you earn the title of "talebearer."

What's in Your Name?

A good name is more desirable than great riches; to be esteemed is better than silver or gold. PROVERBS 22:1

"What's in a name?" This oft-quoted line from Shakespeare's *Romeo and Juliet* was uttered in a passionate conversation between lovers, but it is a question that bears asking in the twenty-first-century marketplace.

The "good name" in Proverbs 22:1 has nothing to do with someone's first or last name. Rather, it has to do with his personal honor or reputation. His name represented who he was—the kind of character he possessed, the kind of heart he had. According to this verse, it's far better to have a good name than it is to have a hefty bank account, and it's much better to be held in high esteem by the people who know you than it is to have a huge stock portfolio.

It's important to point out that a good name is not an end in itself; that is, we should not do work hard, help others, or give generously just so others will hold us in high regard. Rather, we do these things out of love for God, and whatever good effect they may have on our reputation is merely a nice by-product.

Even so, we do need to be aware of how our actions and words might affect our reputations. We are, after all, ambassadors of Christ, and any behavior that makes us look bad is a poor reflection of Him to those around us.

Do you have a good name? Is your focus on maintaining that good name, or are you more interested in pursuing wealth and material things? Take a moment to evaluate your reputation, your "name." Does it honor God? Or do you need to make some adjustments in your life that will enable you to start protecting your name?

Our Work Matters to God

Do you see a man skilled in his work? He will serve before kings; he will not serve before obscure men. PROVERBS 22:29

Although slick talk and big promises might turn heads at first, the best way to impress an employer is to do a good job. If we hone our skills and take great care to complete every project to the best of our abilities, there's a good chance we'll be noticed—by the boss, the division president, or the CEO. And if we're really good at what we do, we might even be called to serve outside our company or even our industry.

Although such recognition is rewarding, it should not be the driving force behind us as we develop our abilities, however. No matter what we do, whether it's driving a bus, teaching kindergarten, running a small business, designing bridges, or operating a manufacturing plant, we need to demonstrate skill in our work because our work is important to God. He gave us the gifts and talents we use every day, and when we perfect them and use them diligently, He is honored.

It's a thought that can revolutionize our work lives. If we view the completion of every assignment, every project, and every task as an act of worship to God, we will be much more likely to give it our best. We will be much more likely to treat the people we're working with on the project with respect and consideration. And we will be much more likely to give Him the glory when the assignment is done, rather than accepting all the credit for ourselves.

One of the best ways to show coworkers and employers that we are followers of Jesus is by excelling in our work. They might not realize it at first, but when they start asking why we're so diligent, why we care so much about what we're doing, or why we refuse to cut corners, we have an open door to share our faith with them.

What are you doing to develop your skills to their fullest potential? What is your motivation? Are you doing it because you want to go places and be somebody, or are you doing it because you want to glorify God in your work?

Guarding Your Heart

Listen, my son, and be wise, and keep your heart on the right path. PROVERBS 23:19

The workplace is fraught with obstacles that can knock our hearts off the right path.

There are opportunities to covet our coworkers' positions and envy their possessions. There are opportunities to flirt with or engage in sexual immorality. There are opportunities to fudge numbers, cut corners, and hide the truth from vendors or clients. There are opportunities to gossip, belittle our colleagues, and stab our coworkers in the back. And the list goes on. So how do we keep ourselves from falling prey to any of these temptations?

By guarding our hearts.

Charles Swindoll puts it this way: "The quest for character requires that certain things be kept *in* the heart as well as kept *from* the heart. An unguarded heart spells disaster. A well-guarded heart means survival."[14]

It's not difficult to determine what to keep *out* of our hearts—we can start by not lingering on any of the temptations listed above. But what do we have to keep *in* our hearts if we want to survive? Philippians 4:8 holds a key: "[W]hatever is true, whatever is noble, whatever is right, whatever is pure, whatever is lovely, whatever is admirable—if anything is excellent or praiseworthy—think about such things."

How well are you guarding your heart? Are you taking intentional steps to avoid the danger zones? Are you staying out of places that might invite you to succumb to temptation? Are you actively filling your mind with Scripture on a daily basis? Are you making it a habit to focus on things that are true, lovely, and pure? Your answers will determine the kind of protection your heart is getting.

No Gloating Allowed

Do not gloat when your enemy falls; when he stumbles, do not let your heart rejoice. PROVERBS 24:17

What do you do when someone who has long been a thorn in your side gets laid off, fired, demoted, or reprimanded? Do you get satisfaction from knowing that he finally got what he had coming to him? Do you delight in the fact that he is probably hurting, financially or otherwise? Do you rejoice that he's out of your life for good?

Such feelings are natural, especially if the person has been particularly troublesome. But be careful. Before you hold a party to celebrate his absence, read on in Proverbs to find out what might happen: "[T]he LORD will see [your rejoicing] and disapprove and turn his wrath away from [your rival]" (Proverbs 24:18).

Ouch. That kind of puts a damper on things, doesn't it?

Now let's say you continually checked your heart and your motives regarding this coworker and could honestly say that the problem was entirely with him. And let's say that you were faithful in praying for him and in asking God to help you deal with the situation. Does this passage mean that you can't be thankful that he's no longer around?

No, of course not. You did what you were supposed to do, and God took care of the rest. But any rejoicing you do should be in God's faithfulness, rather than in your former coworker's demise. Remember what God said: "It is mine to avenge; I will repay" (Deuteronomy 32:35).

Proverbs makes it clear that refraining from gloating when our enemies fall isn't always easy. The very wording of Proverbs 24:17—"do not *let* your heart rejoice"— indicates that it takes intentional discipline. What are you doing to develop that kind of discipline in your life?

Well Said

A word aptly spoken is like apples of gold in settings of silver. PROVERBS 25:11

Have you ever thought that your words could be like precious metals that have been skillfully fashioned into a beautiful piece of art?

Most of us don't think of our speech in such lofty terms, but that is exactly the picture that this verse portrays. When we say just the right thing at exactly the right time in just the right way, our words are like "apples of gold in settings of silver" (Proverbs 25:11).

In practical terms, what kind of words could be elevated to such status? We know right away that that these words are not flippant or hasty. And it's not necessarily the content of the words that makes them fit this description—they might be healing phrases that are as refreshing to the listener as a cold drink in a hot desert, but they could just as easily be painful words that pierce the very soul of the hearer. The difference lies in the thought that goes into the words, the timing of the delivery, and the way they are said.

These words are meticulously crafted. Each one is considered carefully and either accepted or rejected based on its appropriateness for the discussion. They are spoken when the listener is ready and willing to hear them, not blurted out at the first break in the conversation. And regardless of whether they are meant to confront or encourage, they are spoken in a spirit of kindness, gentleness, humility, and love.

Do you take this kind of care with your speech? Many of the conversations we participate in throughout the day don't require such contemplative speech, but there are times when such carefully crafted words are helpful, sometimes even necessary. We can prepare for those times by monitoring *everything* we say a little more closely. That way, when the occasion warrants a verbal masterpiece, we'll be ready and able to deliver one.

Retaliate with Love (Part One)

If your enemy is hungry, give him food to eat; if he is thirsty, give him water to drink. In doing this, you will heap burning coals on his head, and the LORD will reward you. PROVERBS 25:21–22

When someone hurts us, our initial reaction usually does not involve coming up with a list of ways we can help that person. Instead, we're more inclined to come up with a plan to get him back, to seek revenge, to retaliate.

Such feelings are natural, but if we act on them, we only end up hurting ourselves even more. Proverbs 25:21–22 offers an amazing alternative—retaliate with love. "If your enemy is hungry, give him food to eat; if he is thirsty, give him water to drink" (vv. 21). It's not exactly the kind of advice you'd expect to find in a book on how to get ahead in today's cutthroat workplace, but that doesn't make it any less relevant.

So how does such guidance translate into the modern work environment? Try these on for size. If a team member who stole your idea gets caught in a deadline crunch, help him finish the project. If a colleague who constantly puts down your work has a bad day, praise her in front of your boss. If a coworker who ridicules you for going to church has a family crisis, offer to pray for him. You get the picture?

Nobody said such action would be easy. It forces us to swallow our egos, our pride, and even our hurt feelings. It might make our other coworkers question our sanity. And it may not cause any change in our enemy's behavior, at least not at first. But it is the right approach because it is God's approach. Jesus made that clear in the Sermon on the Mount when He said, "Love your enemies and pray for those who persecute you" (Matthew 5:44).

It was a new way of thinking then, and it is just as unusual in today's culture. But as we will see tomorrow, it's worth any trouble or discomfort it may cause us.

Retaliate with Love (Part Two)

If your enemy is hungry, give him food to eat; if he is thirsty, give him water to drink. In doing this, you will heap burning coals on his head, and the LORD will reward you. PROVERBS 25:21–22

Before you start looking for ways you can help that guy at work who stole your great marketing idea, let's look at what the result of such action might be. If you feed your enemy when he's hungry or give him water when he's thirsty, you will "heap burning coals on his head" (Proverbs. 25:22).

All right, you might be thinking. *I don't know how this works, but that'll show him. That will make him feel as much pain as he's caused me.*

But wait. You're missing the point. This reference to coals of fire doesn't have anything to do with hurting someone by burning him. Rather, it has to do with the smelting of iron ore. As such, the coals are not used to inflict painful punishment on the person who has wronged you; they are used to soften his heart and remove the dross from his character. Stated another way, "Love poured out in return for hatred will be what the burning coals are to the ore: it will melt and purify."[15]

How does this happen? When we are kind to people who mistreat us, we shock them into seeing their own shame. We teach them a lesson that could never be achieved if we had tried to seek revenge. "Such action is the noblest of all because it succeeds in saving the enemy while it destroys his enmity."[16]

Our action may not achieve results overnight. Things may get worse before they get better. In fact, there's no 100-percent guarantee that the situation may change at all. But *we* will change. Love and hatred cannot coexist. If we are actively seeking to show love to someone, there will be no room in our hearts for the bitterness and resentment we felt toward him previously. On top of that, God will reward us for our efforts (vv. 22). What more could we want?

Learn from Your Mistakes

As a dog returns to its vomit, so a fool repeats his folly. PROVERBS 26:11

The picture of a dog returning to its vomit is a disgusting image, to be sure. But, according to Solomon, a person who continues to repeat mistakes and refuses to give up bad habits is just as disgusting.

When you mess up, do you analyze what you did wrong and do everything you can to avoid doing it again? Or do you carelessly continue doing what you've always done, only to end up in the same exact predicament time and time again? The old saying goes, "He who does not learn from his mistakes is doomed to repeat them." But why take that chance? Why would you want to repeat bad behavior if you know good and well it will only get you into trouble?

Maybe it's a work issue. Perhaps you consistently make the same mistake on the job. You've done it so often that your boss no longer even mentions it to you; he just corrects it before sending it on. That might work now, but what happens when you get a new boss? She might be less tolerant of repeated error, and out the door you'll go.

Or perhaps it's an ethical failing, a moral failing, or a spiritual failing. You know what will happen when you do it—nothing good *ever* comes of it—and yet for some reason, you do it anyway. Maybe you like how it feels. Maybe you're addicted to it. Maybe you don't have the courage to say no. Maybe you're just unwise. Whatever the reason, you continue to revisit your sin over and over and over again, just like a dog that returns to its vomit.

Do you really want to engage in such disgusting behavior? Stop the pattern today. Learn from your mistakes. If you don't, they *will* lead to your downfall.

Don't Be a Busybody

Like one who seizes a dog by the ears is a passer-by who meddles in a quarrel not his own. PROVERBS 26:17

Only an idiot would grab a dog by the ears or the tail. Such stupidity can only lead to trouble, usually in the form of painful bites from sharp canine teeth.

The bystander who interferes in someone else's argument is just like that idiot, Solomon says. Uninvited meddling seldom helps the quarreling parties. At the least, it draws another person into the quagmire; at the worst, it might make the original combatants turn on the third person like a couple of angry dogs. Nothing good can come of it.

It's very easy to get involved in workplace disagreements that don't concern us. It doesn't matter what the argument is about—the CEO's speech at the staff meeting, a difficult deadline, a product development strategy, or the behavior of another employee—we all love to make our opinions known. But just because we happen to overhear a couple of people quarreling in the next cubicle does not mean we have to join in. Unless the discussion is about something that concerns us directly, we're better off just ignoring it.

We might be tempted to think that butting in where we don't belong really isn't that big of a deal. There are much worse things we could be doing, right? That's certainly true, but before we let ourselves off the hook, let's see how the apostle Peter categorized busybodies: "If you suffer," he wrote, "it should not be as a murderer or thief or any other kind of criminal, *or even as a meddler*" (1 Peter 4:15, emphasis added).

That's some pretty tough company, isn't it? Keep that in mind next time you get the urge to interfere. Remember Solomon's words. If it doesn't concern you, stay neutral.

Put Your Horn Away

Let another praise you, and not your own mouth; someone else, and not your own lips. PROVERBS 27:2

Praise is a wonderful thing. It can lift us up when we're discouraged. It can motivate us when we're struggling. It can make us feel loved, valuable, and respected.

But to do all that, praise must come from someone else. When it comes from within, it's really just pride.

Few things are more unattractive than a person who toots his own horn. We all know people like this—whenever they accomplish something, we fear they might break their arms patting themselves on the back. But self-praise often is much more subtle than that. It doesn't just involve saying things such as, "Boy, didn't I do a good job with this?" or "Can you believe I thought of that?" It also manifests itself in sly references to whom we know, where we've been, or what we have.

When was the last time you dropped a name or two in a staff meeting? Were you trying to build yourself up—to praise yourself—by letting your coworkers know about the elite circles that you run in? When you're standing around the water cooler talking about your recent vacation, are you sure to mention the number of stars your hotel had or the fact that you spent four hundred dollars on a meal for you and your spouse? What did you hope to accomplish by revealing those facts?

Think about your motives before you spout off such information. And do the same before you toot your own horn. Don't put yourself in the spotlight; instead, focus on complimenting others. If your work is worthy of commendation, it will be noticed eventually. And when the praise comes from someone else, it's much, much sweeter.

Structuring for Success

As iron sharpens iron, so one man sharpens another. PROVERBS 27:17

Everybody wants success in life, but few people structure for it. They want all the benefits and trappings of success, but they're not always willing to do the hard work necessary to achieve success.

In this verse, the writer of Proverbs rolls out a model for achieving success: having an iron-on-iron relationship with a peer that involves all of life, or at least enough facets of life to drive someone to authenticity.

In the world of teams and partners, we have more iron-on-feather, iron-on-wood, and iron-on-rubber associations than we have iron-on-iron relationships. Rather than being a mutual admiration society or collaboration between a leader and a follower, an iron-on-iron partnership results when two peers—two equals—develop a genuine, Christ-centered relationship. As a general rule, they don't look up or down on each other. They have admiration, respect, and a healthy sense of fear and accountability for each other. And because of that, a sharp, chiseling effect happens over time that produces improvement and progress.

An iron-on-iron partnership is easy to define, but it's hard to achieve. In order to work, it requires mutual transparency, accountability, support, correction, and friendship. Despite the effort needed, we can have these relationships in any season of life. They're best if they're between people whose lives overlap in several areas. For example, an iron-on-iron relationship with a friend from church who doesn't know your family and doesn't understand your work is OK, but it's not as good as one with someone who attends your church, knows your spouse and children, and works in a similar position.

In other words, a friendship with a peer who sees you across the different categories of life and is willing to give you advice and correction across those categories is the most preferable kind of iron-on-iron relationship. It forces you to open yourself up to another person in a way that makes you very vulnerable. But according to Proverbs, it's one of the best prescriptions for success in life.

What can you do to establish an iron-on-iron relationship with someone in your life?

Playing Favorites

To show partiality is not good. PROVERBS 28:21

It's one of the cornerstones of good parenting—don't play favorites with your children. Nothing ever good comes of favoritism; it can only lead to resentment, bitterness, jealousy, discouragement, and a host of other negative attitudes and feelings among siblings.

The same principle applies at work. Playing favorites with employees is bad for business. It dampens morale. It stirs up discord and resentment among the other workers. It forces employees to take sides, which hurts productivity. It also could harm the "favored" employee's relationships with her coworkers, especially if she is uncomfortable being put in the position of "favorite" or "golden child."

To avoid showing partiality doesn't mean employees who perform well shouldn't be rewarded. Nor does it mean a boss can't have a closer relationship with one associate than with another. Not all personality types mesh, and no one can be best buddies with everyone. It does mean, however, that regardless of the level of friendship that exists between a supervisor and his team, all employees deserve to be treated equally and with respect.

This means that "reverse favoritism" also must be avoided. Most of us enjoy being around people with certain personality types, and there are other personality types that we tend not to prefer. In other words, there are people we like and people we don't like. That's to be expected. But if our dislike of a subordinate or coworker causes us to treat her unfairly, to be unkind to her, or to pass her over for a promotion or enviable assignment even though she's the most qualified person for the job, then we're practicing reverse favoritism.

Think about how you treat your coworkers and employees. Are you guilty of showing partiality? As the writer of Proverbs says, that's not good. So what are you going to do about it?

Visionary Leadership

Where there is *no vision, the people perish.* PROVERBS 29:18 (KJV)

Vision is the ability to see something bigger than the current reality. It's being able to peer around the corner, onto the next page or chapter, or down the road a few miles and see what *could be,* rather than what *is.*

Before we delve into a discussion about vision, a disclaimer is in order. When properly translated, Proverbs 29:18 actually does not refer to "one's ability to formulate goals and work toward them, nor does it mean eyesight or the ability to understand."[17] Rather, "it is a synonym for what a prophet does,"[18] which makes the New International Version's rendition—"Where there is no revelation, the people cast off restraint"—much more accurate than the wording in the King James Version.

That said, there's no disputing the fact that vision—the ability to see that today's reality is not the end of the story—is a very biblical component of life. It drove the Old Testament patriarchs and prophets as well as the New Testament disciples.

It was vision that helped the people of Israel move from Egypt to the Promised Land. It was vision that helped David slay Goliath. It was vision that helped the prophets proclaim their message of hope to the very end. It was vision that propelled the disciples to leave their nets and tax bags to follow Jesus. It was vision that drove the early church planters to spread the gospel across the globe.

From a business standpoint, vision is what sends an organization toward the future in an integrated way. Vision is a key part of leadership because people often need to see a compelling picture of what they're working toward before they can do their best work. If the leader of an organization doesn't supply a vision, the people will often come up with their own. This can result in competing visions, which leads to competing agendas. And when there are competing agendas, people will be at odds with each other about where they're going. Any way you look at it, it's not a pretty picture.

Are you in a position that requires you to provide visionary leadership? Are you taking that responsibility seriously, or are you waiting for someone else to do it? If the latter scenario is true, perhaps you need to reread Proverbs 29:18. You don't really want your people to "perish," do you?

Whom Do You Fear?

Fear of man will prove to be a snare, but whoever trusts in the LORD is kept safe. PROVERBS 29:25

Most of us would have to admit that we probably care a bit too much about what other people think of us. But an occasional self-image crisis isn't the same as living in constant fear of others' opinions. It's natural to wonder what a coworker might think of a decision you made or an assignment you completed. But if you are confident in your abilities and, ultimately, in your worth in Christ, such thoughts usually are temporary.

It's an entirely different story, however, to second-guess everything you do for fear that your colleagues and supervisors will think you aren't good enough. Such behavior is unhealthy. It's unproductive. It's crippling. As Proverbs says, it's a snare.

This doesn't mean that you can disregard your boss's directions or the constructive criticism of a coworker. Nor does it mean that you should care *nothing* of what others think about your work, especially if what you do is critical to the success of a particular project or to the overall well-being of your company. But it does mean that if you are overly concerned about what others think—to the detriment of your own emotional, mental, and spiritual health—you need to do something about it.

It may be that the root of the problem lies with an overly demanding boss. It's extremely stressful to work for a supervisor who constantly and unnecessarily berates you and your work. If such a situation has turned you from a confident, productive employee into a fearful, anxious worker, it might be time to change your environment.

But it also might be that the problem is with you. You might be so concerned with what others think of you that you have allowed your focus to move away from being like Jesus in every aspect of your life. Instead, you spend your days comparing yourself to other people, trying to live up to their expectations, and dreading their negative feedback.

If this describes you, it's time to stop the cycle. It's time to put other people and their expectations and opinions—unrealistic or not—aside and start trusting God. Only with Him will you find peace, safety, and freedom from the crippling fear of man.

Moderation Is the Key

Two things I ask of you, O LORD; do not refuse me before I die: Keep falsehood and lies far from me; give me neither poverty nor riches, but give me only my daily bread. Otherwise, I may have too much and disown you and say, "Who is the LORD?" Or I may become poor and steal, and so dishonor the name of my God. PROVERBS 30:7–9

It's not a prayer most of us are prone to pray: *Lord, please don't give me too much. Just cover my basic needs.*

Praying to be kept from poverty—now, that's another story. None of us wants to be poor, and we're not shy about letting God know about it.

But, as the writer of Proverbs says, it's a good idea to pray *both* prayers if we care about the health of our relationship with Jesus. Call it preventative praying: *Don't give me too much, lest I get too comfortable and forget about You. But don't give me too little, either; otherwise I might have to resort to stealing, and that also wouldn't honor You.*

Agur, the originator of this proverb, had keen insight into the foibles of human nature. He knew himself well enough to know what would happen if he was pushed too far in either extreme. He understood that moderation was the key to godly living.

In our success-oriented culture, such a prayer doesn't make any sense. We are programmed to want it all—a house in a prestigious neighborhood, a luxury car, a vacation home, a hugely profitable business, prestige, power, and so on. These things are not wrong in and of themselves, but as we acquire them, they can begin to have a detrimental effect on us. Pretty soon, we're not praying as much. Our Bibles remain unopened for days, maybe even for weeks. We're spending more and more time at the office and less and less time at home and church. Our attitudes and actions begin to scream out, "Who is the Lord?"

Perhaps it's time we need to evaluate our lives, adjust our priorities, and start praying Agur's prayer: "Give me neither poverty nor riches, but give me only my daily bread."

Small but Wise

Four things on earth are small, yet they are extremely wise: Ants are creatures of little strength, yet they store up their food in the summer; coneys are creatures of little power, yet they make their home in the crags; locusts have no king, yet they advance together in ranks; a lizard can be caught with the hand, yet it is found in kings' palaces. PROVERBS 30:24–28

Just because someone is small or seemingly insignificant doesn't mean that he cannot have an enormous impact in his world. Ants, coneys (or rock badgers), locusts, and lizards are practically invisible next to a majestic lion or a great bear. But they know how to function skillfully in their environment, and as a result, they are able to survive and thrive.

Ants aren't strong, but they demonstrate incredible foresight by storing up food for winter. Rock badgers don't have much power, but they are able to function and live in the most formidable of places—in inaccessible rocks. Locusts have no leader, but their unity allows them to mobilize, march, and conquer. And lizards, though small enough to be caught by someone's hand, can slip easily into a place most of us will never enter—the palace of a king.

So what workplace encouragement can we find in the behavior of these tiny creatures? For starters, when you start feeling bad because your résumé isn't very impressive, persevere. Just as the ant faithfully prepares for winter, the work you're doing now is setting the groundwork for your future roles.

When you find yourself powerless in an impossible situation, improvise. Like the rock badger, you also can survive under such circumstances.

When your department head abdicates her leadership responsibilities, encourage your coworkers to work together. Like the locusts, your group also can get things done without a leader.

Finally, next time you wonder if your efforts to stay out of the spotlight and not seek social acclaim are worth it, think of the lizard. Like him, you, too, may end up in the palace of a king (or in the corner office, or maybe even the Oval Office) someday.

Queen of Organization

She gets up while it is still dark; she provides food for her family and portions for her servant girls. . . . She watches over the affairs of her household and does not eat the bread of idleness. PROVERBS 31:15, 27

When you read about the woman in Proverbs 31, the one often described as the "wife of noble character" or the "virtuous woman," you get the distinct impression that she was the epitome of the word *organized*.

There is absolutely no way in the world that she could have taken care of everything in her life—her husband, her business, her investments, her employees, her children, her philanthropic interests, her health, and her community responsibilities—if she did not possess the ability to juggle numerous balls in a highly efficient manner.

We may not have as many responsibilities as she did, and it may not even be realistic to expect us to handle the ones we do have with such grace. We can, however, learn a couple of very valuable lessons from these verses that will help us juggle all the balls in our lives a little better.

First, she did not waste time. She got up early, stayed up late, and she didn't participate in any nonproductive, brainless activities. This was not a woman who spent several hours—or even one hour—a day watching soap operas. She didn't flip on the TV at night and spend the evening watching mindless sitcoms with her children.

Second, she anticipated the needs of the people in her life. As a result, she didn't have to spend her days rushing around, frantically trying to get things done at the last minute. She watched over the affairs of her household closely enough to know when supplies were running low and when tensions were beginning to escalate, and she was able to take steps to fix problems before they escalated into full-blown crises.

You may not have the organizational gifts that the Proverbs 31 woman had. But you will be much more effective—both at home and at work—if you intentionally stopped engaging in nonproductive activities and started anticipating the needs of the people around you a little better. Try it—the results might surprise you!

Physically Prepared (Part One)

She sets about her work vigorously; her arms are strong for her tasks. PROVERBS 31:17

The last thing you might expect to find in a devotional book is a lecture about physical fitness. But don't go turning the page in hopes of finding something a bit more "spiritual" just yet.

If you're a woman, you might tend to get a bit discouraged when you read Proverbs 31. *That gal is superwoman; there's no way I could ever measure up to her,* you might think. If you're a man, you might be tempted to ignore this portion of Scripture because you think it's totally irrelevant to your life. But both men and women can learn a great deal from this lady's life, particularly when it comes to the all-important area of health.

Proverbs 31:17 says that the woman "sets about her work *vigorously*" and that her arms are "*strong* for her tasks" (emphasis added). In other words, this woman is in top physical shape. She might not be able to run a marathon, but she has the energy and stamina she needs to care for her household, her family, her business interests, and herself. Although the Scripture doesn't specifically say it, it stands to reason that there's no way she would have that much energy and stamina if she didn't engage in the discipline of regular exercise. She might be able to maintain a schedule like that for a week without exercise, but not over the course of several months or years.

So what does this mean for us today? Quite simply, that if we want to be as fruitful in all aspects of life as this woman was, we need to make sure our bodies are "strong for our tasks." In other words, we must make exercise a regular part of our lives.

Is exercise a priority in your life? If not, you're probably not as productive as you could be.

Physically Prepared (Part Two)

She sets about her work vigorously; her arms are strong for her tasks. PROVERBS 31:17

*P*hew, you might be thinking. *That lecture wasn't as bad as I thought it was going to be. I felt a little guilty, but now I can move on to something else.*

Think again. The whole subject of physical preparedness is too important to pass over so lightly. "Do you not know that your body is a temple of the Holy Spirit, who is in you, whom you have received from God?" Paul writes in 1 Corinthians 6:19–20. "You are not your own; you were bought at a price. Therefore honor God with your body." Although Paul was specifically addressing sexual immorality in this passage, the application extends much further. Do you want the Holy Spirit to have to make His home in a flabby, out-of-shape, heart-attack-prone, tired-out temple? Those are the accommodations you're providing Him if you don't make physical fitness a priority.

"You just don't understand the demands on my time," you might say. "By the time I work ten hours a day, get supper on the table, do the laundry, spend time with the kids, and squeeze in a few minutes of Bible reading and prayer, there's just no time for the treadmill."

That's understandable—we're all busy these days. That's where good old-fashioned discipline—plus a little bit of creativity—comes into play. How can you make your time stretch? Maybe you could get up a half-hour earlier—just the amount of time you need to get a vigorous workout on that treadmill. Perhaps you could give up watching one of your favorite sitcoms or news shows and devote that time to exercise. Or maybe you could combine working out with your prayer time—instead of watching television while you jog in place, pray. If you stay focused, you'll be amazed at how much ground you can cover with God during a twenty-five-minute stint on an exercise machine.

Don't lose sight of your ultimate goal: providing a healthy home for the Holy Spirit. All the other results—increased productivity and energy at work, better health, a stronger body, etc.—are all fringe benefits.

Ready for Anything

She is clothed with strength and dignity; she can laugh at the days to come.
PROVERBS 31:25

Although the woman in Proverbs 31 is obviously quite well-to-do, we get the distinct impression, particularly from this verse, that she hasn't placed all her hope and security in her stock portfolio and business holdings.

She can "laugh at the days to come," meaning she doesn't fear the problems or disasters that tomorrow may bring, because she is "clothed with strength and dignity" (v. 25). She doesn't spend her days worrying about the future; instead, using her God-given wisdom and talents, she takes all the necessary steps to ensure that her loved ones are well-clothed, well-fed, and well-cared-for in the future. Even then, her ultimate confidence does not lie in herself and her activities; it lies in her fear of the Lord (v. 30). As a result, she truly is ready for anything.

Does the future make you nervous? Scared? Anxious? Or are you looking forward to it with great excitement and anticipation, knowing that you've done everything you can to prepare for it, and resting in the knowledge that no matter what happens, God will be with you?

A person who can "laugh at the days to come"—not in an arrogant, "My-wealth-will-take-care-of-me" way, but in a confident, "God-will-take-care-of-me" manner—really sticks out in our culture. A person who is clothed with strength and dignity sticks out because he or she radiates a faith and hope in Jesus that nonbelieving onlookers can't help but be intrigued by.

Are there people in your office who seem scared of the future? By your attitudes and actions—by your spiritual "clothing"—you can show them a better way.

Don't Judge a Book by Its Cover

Charm is deceptive, and beauty is fleeting; but a woman who fears the LORD is to be praised. PROVERBS 31:30

Appearances can be deceiving. The attractive, trim, sharply dressed man might look like the ideal executive, but he could actually be the worst manager who ever walked in the door. The balding, somewhat dumpy fellow in the outdated suit might look like a social outcast, but he might be the most effective leader in the company. You just never know.

That's why looks should never be the measuring stick that is used to determine someone's potential, effectiveness, or worth. It's not that we shouldn't try to look nice and present ourselves in a pleasant manner, but it really is what's inside that matters. A person's character certainly matters to God, and it should matter to us.

The people in the Proverbs 31 woman's sphere of influence understood this. We don't know whether this lady could have won a beauty pageant; the Scriptures don't describe her outward appearance other than to say that her arms were strong (v. 17) and that she was well-dressed (v. 22). It does say that she feared the Lord, and for that she was praised. She wasn't praised for any charm she might have possessed—that is deceitful. She wasn't praised for any beauty she had—that is fleeting. She was praised for her relationship with God—the only method of measurement that carries any eternal weight.

How do you judge the people with whom you work? When a new person joins your team, do you formulate opinions about him based on the way he dresses? When you get a new boss, do you base your respect for her on her level of attractiveness? When you interview people for a position in your department, do you choose the more charming of two equally qualified candidates? Perhaps you should start looking beneath the surface to what these people are really like. Their outward appearance may reveal a few things, but it doesn't tell the whole story. Remember— charm is deceitful, and beauty is vain.

4

Ecclesiastes

Pondering the Nagging Inconsistencies of Life

Introduction to Ecclesiastes

King Solomon received the gift of wisdom at the beginning of his reign (see 2 Chronicles 1:7–12). But while he certainly used the wisdom God gave him, he pursued—with focused passion—everything *but* that God-given wisdom. He went after pleasure, knowledge, great projects, wealth, fame, and whatever else his heart desired. He could afford anything, and he denied himself nothing.

Near the end of his life, however, Solomon turned his attention back to the God-centered priorities he had focused on decades earlier. In the process, he wrote the Book of Ecclesiastes to help young leaders coming after him to stay centered on the kind of thinking that a God-life entails. The book covers a wide range of subjects, all relating to the uncompromising pursuit of a complete and meaningful life. Topics include ambition, accomplishments, the mundane routine of life, pleasure, wisdom, work, wealth, and the place of God in it all.

Solomon is a deep thinker with a philosophic bent who addresses with enthusiasm the hard topics of life that other authors often shy away from, such as, "Why do people who are unjust continue to flourish?" or, "If God's in charge, why are people still oppressed?" Because he takes this approach, however, his content in Ecclesiastes is sometimes misunderstood. Some people come away with the impression that he's just a cynical person who's out to prove that nothing really makes sense.

It's easy to think that way. Two verses into the book, he proclaims, "Meaningless! Meaningless! . . . Utterly meaningless! Everything is meaningless" (Ecclesiastes 1:2). But although Solomon sometimes comes across as having a dark, fatalistic view of life, he really doesn't. He is simply brutally realistic and honest. That's a good thing because he's talking to leaders who, by their very nature, want to fix things. Unfortunately, as he points out time and time again, many things—such as corruption, bribery, and evil—simply can't be fixed. No matter who you are or where you are, you'll never solve these issues. The only solution, he ultimately asserts, is to trust that God knows and will take care of them eventually.

In order to understand the content of Ecclesiastes properly, we must understand its structure. It is comprised of four sections, and the key to understanding each one comes at the end of each of the sections, not at the beginning. The first section, Ecclesiastes 1:1–2:26, covers reality checks and concluding options. The second section, Ecclesiastes 3:1–5:30, discusses God's presence in all details of life. The third section, Ecclesiastes 6:1–8:15, addresses evaluating appearances, judging character, and affirming government. And the final section, Ecclesiastes 8:16–12:14, ties up the loose ends.

The first three sections end with the refrain that we are to eat, drink, and find satisfaction in our work because it is a gift from God (See Ecclesiastes 2:24; 5:18; 8:15). The fourth section in Ecclesiastes 12:13–14 ends with Solomon's overall conclusion: "Fear God and keep his commandments, for this is the whole duty of man. For God will bring every deed into judgment, including every hidden thing, whether it is good or evil." To keep yourself from getting confused or disillusioned as you read Ecclesiastes, it might be helpful to read the end of each section before you dive into the book and to keep reminding yourself of those conclusions as you work through each chapter.

Perhaps more than any other book in the Bible, Ecclesiastes addresses an individual in a work context. The refrains at the end of each section clearly assert that work is a gift from God, and as Solomon addresses the young leaders in his class, he is overtly pushing a theology of integration. He is very comfortable talking about pleasure, justice, ambition, wisdom, and other parts of life that integrate with our work life.

Ecclesiastes is not a speed-read; it's a book to study for a period of time. If you roll through it quickly, you're going to come away very confused. Don't forget—you're dealing with the distilled teaching notes from a life that's been lived to the fullest, and like any rich set of teaching notes, they need to be reflected on and thought about versus quickly read and then passed by.

Making a Difference

Generations come and generations go, but the earth remains forever.
ECCLESIASTES 1:4

We like to think we are in charge, but we actually exercise absolutely no control over many aspects of our existence. We may expend an enormous amount of energy in doing our work, all the while thinking that we're making a significant difference. Let's be realistic, though.

Generations come and generations go, but the earth stays the same. No matter what we do, the sun rises and sets on its own. Whether we like it or not, the wind blows in one direction and then another. Even if we wanted to, we couldn't stop the rivers from flowing into the sea. No matter how much we accomplish, regardless of what position we attain, the changes we make in the world we work in—even over the course of a lifetime—will be minuscule compared with what God does each day.

Throughout the Book of Ecclesiastes, Solomon sizes things up and puts them in proper perspective. That's exactly what he does in this verse. He sizes up the significance of each generation and places that against the perspective of the longevity of earth itself. A single generation is insignificant when compared with earth's lifespan.

Our lives and our careers should make a difference. But it is God Who makes the ultimate difference. Solomon, a realist at heart, makes his point clear: Whatever we do in life, we must never maximize our impact while minimizing God's. His impact is forever.

Nothing New

What has been will be again . . . there is nothing new under the sun.
ECCLESIASTES 1:9

Being creative is part of what it means to be human. When we make comments such as, "I have a great idea" or, "Let's look at this problem from a different angle" or, "There's a different way to approach that," we are expressing a commonly held belief—namely, that we are creative people.

Creativity is a vital element of the human experience. When we go to work and tap into our brainpower to accomplish the task at hand, what surfaces is something that seems to us to be new and fresh. No one can convince us that our "original" thoughts are simply a rearrangement of someone else's ideas or a restatement of another's words. To our naiveté Solomon says this: What seems to be original thinking is nothing more than leftovers from an earlier time.

Throughout Ecclesiastes, Solomon occasionally slips from being a realist and turns into an unrelenting pessimist. That's what he does here. In this case, though, he is heading toward a conclusion, but he doesn't reveal his conclusion right away. Later, we'll take a look at what he concludes.

For now, Solomon is bringing reality to our thinking. We are creations of the Creator. We are not little gods walking around on earth. Our thinking and creativity is that of a creation, and it is not in the same category or of the same caliber as that of the Creator. Our creativity is often helpful, but it is not necessarily very original.

For whatever creativity we possess, we have only our Father, the Creator God, to thank. Take time to thank Him for your creativity today.

Just Who Are You?

There is no remembrance of men of old. ECCLESIASTES 1:11

We love to think big. We believe we will make a huge difference, we will offer original thinking, and we will be remembered long after we are gone. But Solomon bursts our bubble in a big way: "You are mistaken," he says. "You are only dreaming."

There's no place for false illusions here, is there? The wise sage certainly doesn't leave us much wiggle room.

Because life is so short, it would be nice to think that the legacy that we leave will last long after we draw our final breath. After all, thinking about death is depressing. Thinking that we will be forgotten soon after we die is even more depressing.

At this point, though, Solomon doesn't seem very concerned about our state of mind. He is still focusing on the issue of perspective. Do you accurately perceive who you are—not in your eyes, but from God's vantage point?

Solomon is stating unequivocally that we think far more of ourselves than we ought, that we give ourselves far more credit than we should, and that we over-estimate our contributions to society. In short, our pride far exceeds our impact, originality, and longevity. By humbling ourselves before God, we can alter that scenario. Are you willing to see yourself as God sees you?

The Bliss of Ignorance

[W]ith much wisdom comes much sorrow; the more knowledge, the more grief.
ECCLESIASTES 1:18

Life is full of things we can't control. We can't control the weather. We can't control the traffic on the way to work. We can't control our coworkers' moods. We can't control the stock market. We can't control the price of gasoline.

But instead of focusing on things over which we can exercise little management, maybe we ought to focus on things we can really get our hands around.

Perhaps, for example, we ought to leave everything else alone and focus on gaining wisdom and knowledge. After all, it follows that the more you know, the better equipped you will be to deal with whatever life throws at you.

Knowledge is power. We can use it to dominate things and people. But according to Solomon, wisdom and knowledge bring sorrow and grief. Ignorance really is bliss in some instances. The more we know, the more we realize we can't change very much. We are nevertheless left with the burden of what we have studied and what we now understand. In other words, if we are looking for wisdom and knowledge to be our salvation, we are in big trouble.

Wisdom and knowledge cannot save anyone. Wisdom and knowledge may be helpful for many things, but they are not our hope. God alone is our hope, and by seeking Him, we can draw on *His* wisdom.

When was the last time you asked God to give you His wisdom for your circumstances?

Gratuitous Pleasure

"I will test . . . pleasure. . . ." But that also proved to be meaningless.
ECCLESIASTES 2:1

If wisdom and knowledge don't give us a tremendous sense of meaning and hope, maybe we ought to pursue something that is a lot easier to acquire. Maybe, instead of trying so hard to find something that satisfies, we just ought to go directly to pleasure, laughter, and the good things of life.

Perhaps those things aren't by-products of something else; maybe they are worth pursuing all on their own. After all, in the end, we only want to be happy. What could give greater happiness than pleasure, wine, and laughter?

As he does with everything else he has talked about in Ecclesiastes 1–2, Solomon throws cold water on that great idea. So far he has checked everything off the list we have placed in front of him. It is as if he has read our minds, anticipated our thinking, and managed to checkmate us every time we moved in a different direction.

Sure, he says, pleasure feels good, comedy works for a while, and wine tastes great. But in the end those things prove to be anything but worthwhile. They don't work very well as the focus of our lives.

Have you been filling your life with temporal pleasures? How would your life be changed if you began to focus on the eternal instead?

Great Projects

I undertook great projects. ECCLESIASTES 2:4

If wisdom and pleasure don't yield the fulfillment we are looking for, then maybe what we ought to do is engage in really hard work.

If we immerse ourselves in our careers—if we launch great projects and build houses and plant fields—maybe then we will look on the work of our hands and be able to say with some degree of satisfaction that it was all worthwhile. Doing all of this takes much more effort than simply engaging in pleasure and looking for something to laugh about, but surely it will yield a greater sense of significance in the long run.

This is perfectly logical thinking, Solomon says, but as unrealistic as any other options that have been proposed. Undertaking great projects may occupy our time, and it might keep our minds from reflecting on other things, but in the end it will have no greater effect in bringing us a sense of enduring fulfillment than wisdom or knowledge or pleasure will.

So where does that leave us? If we've been paying attention, we realize it leaves us in a better position to view our work realistically. Have you been trying to silence the still, small voice of God by undertaking "great projects"? How has that worked for you?

How's Your "Stuff" Collection?

I amassed silver and gold for myself. ECCLESIASTES 2:8

Where are you on the "stuff-collection" scale? We all love having stuff, and acquiring more things can be a daily activity. Every time we go shopping or scan the newspaper for a second home or make out our Christmas list or consider what kind of furniture we should purchase or what model of car to get next, we are arranging our lives around all the stuff there is to possess.

Solomon was an expert at acquiring things. According to Ecclesiastes, he was not only the king of Israel, but he was also the king of possessions. He purchased slaves, owned herds, amassed silver and gold, bought entertainment, built palaces, and maintained a fleet of chariots and trading boats, among other things.

It's interesting that Solomon never describes the amassing of material goods as a bad thing. But in this passage and elsewhere, he does say that if we think collecting things will offer any measurable sense of fulfillment, we are seriously mistaken. If our goal is possessions—finding them, buying them, and using them—then we will be sorely disappointed in what we get in return. When Solomon surveyed all that his hands had accomplished, he discovered that "everything was meaningless, a chasing after the wind; nothing was gained under the sun" (Ecclesiastes 2:11).

What Solomon says in these verses runs counter to what most people believe. But he's insistent about it: Wisdom and knowledge aren't fulfilling, nor are pleasure and laughter. Spending a lifetime pursuing great career goals ends up being no more meaningful than amassing huge wealth and collecting material goods.

We might be tempted to dismiss a person who holds such notions as one who really doesn't understand how the world works. But it's very difficult to do that with Solomon. He could afford to explore it all, and he did. Now, at the end of his life, he has a message for us: None of those things—either separately or in combination with each other—give us what we so desperately want: satisfaction and meaning.

Where are you looking for fulfillment in your life? Is there a bit of the younger Solomon in you?

The Foolishness of Wisdom

Like the fool, the wise man too must die! ECCLESIASTES 2:16

If nothing else brings satisfaction, then let's consider something truly ridiculous. You would think that if wisdom is good and foolishness is bad, then the person who pursues wisdom has at least some measure of satisfaction in his life, while the person who pursues foolishness lives nothing but a life of grief. That seems logical. That only seems right. It certainly seems fair.

But according to Solomon, it makes no difference whether you pursue wisdom or foolishness. Why? Because the same fate overtakes the one who pursues wisdom and the one who pursues foolishness. Even though the wise man walks in some degree of light and the fool walks in complete darkness, both eventually will die. To add insult to that unfair common fate, neither the wise man nor the fool will be remembered for very long after he is gone. As Solomon says, "[I]n days to come both will be forgotten" (Ecclesiastes 2:16).

So does Solomon suggest that we all take the easier route and just live like fools? No. But like everything else he has said up to this point, he wants us to remember something very important: If we think that devoting a lifetime to acquiring wisdom will leave us better off than the person who lives his life as an undisciplined fool, then we are seriously mistaken.

Wisdom by itself yields no more satisfaction and meaning than its lack does. Sound depressing? It is, especially if you give up on Solomon at this point. Hang in there; he has much more to say about finding fulfillment in life.

Without God?

So I hated life, because the work that is done under the sun was grievous to me.
ECCLESIASTES 2:17

The opening salvo of the Book of Ecclesiastes finds Solomon lobbing his ammunition at the myriad elements of life that seem to promise happiness and satisfaction but always fail to deliver. He lists the false gods that many people believe will bring them a tremendous sense of fulfillment—wisdom, a full career, pleasure and wine, among others—and then states unequivocally that those people are dead wrong. Such things do not satisfy and, in fact, never can or will.

At first, Solomon's list is little more than a litany of depressing statements and information. He hasn't done us the favor of offering an alternative; he simply reads our minds. He defines what we think is important in life and explains how misled we are in our thinking. Finally, in Ecclesiastes 2:17–26, he offers several options—a choice of conclusions we can reach after reading all this.

The first option is a conclusion that we could label "without God." That is, if we pursue those things but do so without God as an integral part of the equation, then we will reach a bitter summary at the end of our lives. Without God, we come to hate life. Work becomes "grievous" (v. 17). Everything, in fact, becomes meaningless. Whatever we accumulate—not just material wealth, but also our bitter perspective on life—will be left to those who come after us. Is that what you want to leave behind?

According to Solomon, it gets worse before it gets better. Later, we'll look at Solomon's continuing thoughts on the futility of a life without God. And then we'll discover a better way to live.

Chasing the Wind

All his days his work is pain and grief; even at night his mind does not rest.
ECCLESIASTES 2:23

Some folks are wise, and some folks are fools. For all we know, a fool may be the one who ends up controlling all of our efforts at work. But even if we work for a wise man, the work itself can cause pain and grief and rob us of our sleep at night.

Here's what Solomon has said up to this point in this book: We have no original ideas; pleasure, knowledge, work, and amassing "stuff" are all meaningless; wise folks and foolish folks end up the same; everything we do will be left to someone else; and after we are gone, we will be forgotten.

Throughout Ecclesiastes, whenever Solomon uses the word *meaningless* or the image of chasing the wind, he is referring to a certain kind of scenario. When we try to live life without God—even though we think that what we pursue will bring us what we want—we end up with a very bitter and unsatisfactory conclusion.

Ecclesiastes is all about an old man reflecting on a long and full life then drawing conclusions that he wants to pass on to others to help them avoid making the mistakes he made. So how are you doing in arranging all of the elements of your life to include God in the equation? It isn't enough to have God in one part of our lives if He doesn't also permeate the other parts. For example, if we include God in our marriages and family lives but shut Him out of our work, the conclusion we will reach at the end of our work lives will be precisely what Solomon articulates here: Our work and careers were meaningless; they brought us no fulfillment.

Solomon's clear message is that any part of our lives that does not include God will end up being completely worthless. We can argue with Solomon about this, but we are arguing with someone who has been there, done that, and drawn some very pointed conclusions. We are arguing with an expert, one who once believed that those things would satisfy.

Have you been excluding God from any part of your life? If so, that aspect of life will lack fulfillment for you until you allow God to infuse it with meaning and significance.

Solomon's Equation

A man can do nothing better than to eat and drink and find satisfaction in his work. ECCLESIASTES 2:24

The bottom line, according to Solomon, is that God wants us to enjoy our lives and our work. He wants us to do it right now, not at some time in the distant future. This is present tense, not future.

Finally, there is some light at the end of the tunnel in all of Solomon's talk. He gives us the key that unlocks the door to happiness and meaning, the secret to life: It is impossible to enjoy our lives and our work without God. Why? Because the enjoyment of life and work is *separate* from life and work itself. You can have one without the other.

It's possible to have a life full of work and a life lacking enjoyment of that work. Most people don't understand that secret. They have one part of the equation, which is work or pleasure or laughter or wine or wisdom or knowledge or possessions. They may have these things together or separately, but they are missing the second half of the equation, which is God's gift of enjoyment of those things.

In other words, if you have a relationship with God and bring Him into all the different areas of your life, then you will live a life of joy, meaning, and fulfillment. Do you believe Solomon's equation? It took Solomon himself a long time to believe it, but in the end, he found it to be true.

Hand It Over

To the man who pleases him, God gives wisdom, knowledge and happiness.
ECCLESIASTES 2:26

Solomon says there are two conclusions at the end of life, after we have done everything we are ever going to do. The first conclusion results from doing all of those things without God. But to live life without God, he says, leads to emptiness and lack of meaning in life.

The second possible conclusion is that we allow God to permeate all the different parts of our lives. When we do that, He gives us happiness, joy, meaning, and fulfillment. But then Solomon articulates another truth: People who reject God end up losing their possessions—all the things they've worked so hard to accumulate and accomplish—to one who pleases God. In Ecclesiastes 2:26, Solomon says, "To the man who pleases him, God gives wisdom, knowledge and happiness, but to the sinner he gives the task of gathering and storing up wealth to hand it over to the one who pleases God."

Solomon, in characteristic fashion, expresses our thoughts exactly: Such an end to all our effort would really be depressing. Who wants to work hard and have the fruit of our labors end up in someone else's hands? Who wants to expend all that effort and then gain none of the pleasure—and, on top of that, end up with none of the possessions or wealth? Obviously, no one. But Solomon says that's what those who reject God can expect in the end.

Do you want to be the one who hands it over—or the one to whom it's handed?

The Rewards of Worship

To the man who pleases him, God gives wisdom, knowledge and happiness.
ECCLESIASTES 2:26

Does your work please God? Is your time at work focused on and directed toward Him in an attitude of worship? His commandment is straightforward: "[H]ave no other gods before me" (Exodus 20:3). Does He get your full attention, 24/7?

Too often worship is overlooked in our daily lives. At its best, worship is a lifestyle of devotion, reverence, and obedience; at its worst, it is mindless singing on Sunday mornings. How did we manage to rid worship of its biblical meaning? Why are we so oblivious to its rewards?

Wisdom, knowledge, and happiness wait for the one who pleases God. He is, in a sense, easy to please. God is the loving Father watching us, His children, hard at work; intently noticing the details of our actions; reveling in the joy and satisfaction we derive from a job well done; and gently correcting, instructing, and teaching us along the way.

How can we *not* worship this loving Father? We fail to worship Him because we do not know Him. We do not understand His ways; we do not know His character. We have stopped seeking Him. We have allowed other gods—the gods of work and leisure and myriad other distractions—to steal away our affections.

Worship is not thanking the "man upstairs" after we score a touchdown, receive an award, or nab the last parking spot in an overcrowded lot. Worship is the day-by-day, hour-by-hour acknowledgment of God's presence. Worship stems in part from the awareness that we labor under His watchful eye and His smiling face. Surely this labor is not in vain.

What can you do today to express your worship to God?

God at Work (Part One)

There is a time for everything, and a season for every activity under heaven.
ECCLESIASTES 3:1

The bottom line of life is simple: It belongs to God. He controls the calendar and what goes on it. It is easy to comprehend that with some things. Winter, spring, summer and fall come every year, without fail. The tides ebb and flow. People are born, they grow, and they die.

In fact, these examples, and many more like them, might lead us to the wrong conclusion that God controls the obvious routine things but that we have unilateral jurisdiction over our own lives. They might make us believe that God's agenda and timing don't extend into certain life areas. He sets the planets in motion, we might think, but beyond that the specifics of our lives are within our control. He might set the calendar, but we set our own clocks.

But Solomon could not be more specific in his disagreement of our notion of control. He enumerates the macro issues of life (a time to be born and a time to die), as well as life's small details (a time to be silent and a time to speak). In both the big things and the small ones, God has a say or a plan regarding what is appropriate. That means that in all things in life, we do what He obviously mandates, or we consult Him about the appropriate action in this case, at this time, in this context.

We are not the captains of our own ships. We are passengers on a ship that God is navigating. Solomon's advice is clear: In all aspects of life, we need to make sure that we are moving in the direction that God's wind is blowing, as opposed to charting a different course that takes us directly into that wind. God sets the agenda and timing for all of life. No part of our days or activities is outside His reach. He controls the clock. The thermostat is on His wall. His finger flips the on–off switch.

The seas of life are stormy enough by themselves, without adding additional stress of attempting to sail on those stormy seas in a direction opposite of the way God's wind is blowing.

God at Work (Part Two)

[A] time to search and a time to give up. ECCLESIASTES 3:6

A feeling of career unsettledness is a common malady in our society. *Am I doing what I am supposed to be doing, in the place where I am supposed to be doing it?* we ask ourselves. *What is my calling?*

Solomon's reminder that "there is a time for everything, and a season for every activity under heaven" (Ecclesiastes 3:1) is extremely relevant in determining where we're supposed to be *right now*.

God's calling to work tasks often has a seasonal component. For Moses, this meant that early in life he was a member of Pharaoh's household, in midlife he was a shepherd in a remote desert, and later in life he led the children of Israel out of Egypt, right to the brink of the Promised Land. Each of those seasons was clearly defined and very different than the other two.

For Peter, God's calling meant that he was a fisherman before he met Jesus and a "fisher of men" afterward. Amos was a fig picker in his career as a farmer, and then he became a prophet—at least for a period of time. Nehemiah was the chief of staff for a pagan king until God called him to the construction career that led him to rebuild the wall around the city of Jerusalem.

We could go on, but the Scriptures are clear in teaching that your calling could very well change the course of your life at work. The good news is that this is your season for something specific. Do you know what it is? Are you listening to God's voice? Are you willing to take whatever risk is necessary to step from one season into another?

This life of faith sometimes turns out to be more difficult than we thought it would be. It is easy to look back on biblical characters and see how God clearly took them from one season to another. Life always looks clearer in the rearview mirror. But don't be afraid to ask, *God, what do You have for me and my career?*

Eternity Inside

He has also set eternity in the hearts of men. ECCLESIASTES 3:11

The most cold-hearted pagan can't ignore the reality of eternity. It is a built-in component from the God factory—a sneaking suspicion, an unavoidable void, an aching hunger, a feeling that can't be outrun.

The reality of eternity often is brought to the front burner by a personal disaster: divorce, job loss, disease, retirement, or the death of a friend. You can't ignore that reality in yourself, and the people with whom you work can't ignore it in themselves. It's there even if they don't know it is there.

Sometimes it's appropriate to push the truth of eternity to the surface of a person's consciousness by prodding it with conversation or by initiating a discussion about it. But it's often better to let God do His work and then make ourselves available when the floodgates open.

In a previous career as a truck driver, the men with whom I (Tom) shared a tractor-trailer over the course of a week often declared early in a run that they had no desire to talk about spiritual things. When they made that declaration, I always honored it and never brought up the topic. I didn't have to. In the course of those long hours together, they inevitably brought it up.

There was something about rolling through the Smoky Mountains at 2:00 in the morning—with the full moon shining—that made them want to initiate a discussion about spiritual things. The eternity in their hearts needed to talk. At that point I could bring a report about the good news of Jesus. That is the kind of eternity that I am interested in. As it turns out, that is the kind of eternity everybody else is interested in, too.

(Close to) Heaven in the Real World

I know that there is nothing better for men than to be happy and do good while they live. ECCLESIASTES 3:12

Solomon could be considered the ultimate realist. The "tell-it-like-it-is" guy. He paints the world like it really is, not like an impressionist artist who uses only pastels and paints only pastoral scenes. If Solomon had been a photographer, his work would have been in stark black and white. He certainly would not have been a wedding photographer who produced soft, fuzzy shots in artificial light.

But even Solomon's stark realism couldn't keep him from an unquenchable optimism grounded in a relationship with God that permeated every corner of his life. As he points out in Ecclesiastes, this relationship with God has an especially profound impact on our work lives: "That everyone may eat and drink, and find satisfaction in all his toil—this is the gift of God." (3:13) Even amid a vivid description of the realities of life—including unfairness, corruption, and bosses who don't listen—Solomon shows that God wants us to genuinely enjoy our lives and work with enthusiasm.

And the enjoyment that he refers to is always present-tense enjoyment. Solomon is not one to put off enjoying life for some future time. In the entire Book of Ecclesiastes, he lives with one foot solidly planted in the present and one foot solidly planted in eternity. He spends very little time writing about the time period between the present and eternity. He is not one who recommends that we put off joy and satisfaction in life. Those are to be experienced today. Immediately.

To the natural optimist, he says, "Get real about life, but enjoy it." To the pessimist, he says, "I confirm the realities of life, but enjoy it anyway." To both, he says, "Enjoyment comes only from God."

Where do you rate on the "pursue-the-God-life" scale? Are you putting off enjoyment now so you can experience it later? Solomon advises you to revise that game plan. Are you attempting to enjoy life now without a vital relationship with the living God that permeates every single aspect of life? Solomon recommends that you adjust that game plan, too. Our goal should be to rank high on the "pursue-the-God-life" scale today. Can you say that today is a day permeated with the joy of life?

Making an Eternal Impact

I know that everything God does will endure forever. ECCLESIASTES 3:14

Nearly everyone wants to live a life of significance. We want to make our time count; we want our lives to be meaningful. We would like to engage in work that has some kind of lasting effect.

So how can you make sure that what you do today somehow reverberates all the way into eternity? Solomon provides the key: By keeping your life within God-ordained seasons and activities. The progression goes something like this: God sets out the framework of life (Ecclesiastes 3:1–8). "He has made everything beautiful in its time" (v. 11). "He has . . . set eternity in the hearts of men" (v. 11), and He wants everyone to find satisfaction in their work (v. 13). To what end? "[E]verything God does will endure forever." (v. 14).

If you make sure that you are doing what you are supposed to be doing—that is, if you continually align your life according to God's agenda and timing, then you start the chain reaction that will end with eternal significance. So when you ask yourself, *Will my life count?* you need to answer with another question: *Am I doing what God wants me to do in this season of my life?* If the answer to the latter is yes, then the answer to the former also is yes. If the answer to the latter is no, the answer to the former also is no.

How confident are you that what you're doing now—the way your current season of life is being played out—is precisely what God wants you to be doing? The answer to that question is the key to whether what you are doing today will have eternal impact.

Behavior and Accountability

God will bring to judgment both the righteous and the wicked. ECCLESIASTES 3:17

The good news is that God sets the agenda and timing for all of life. The bad news is that people behave as if they can do whatever they want. Folks act as if God either does not exist or is blind. They walk all over other people and engage in activities that give them an unfair advantage—or are just plain wrong.

One of Solomon's most attractive traits is that he does not sugarcoat the darker realities of life. In this case, he does not suggest that every person who does selfish things will have a conversion experience and begin living a reformed life. But he *does* contend that everything will turn out right in the end. "God will bring to judgment both the righteous and the wicked, for there will be a time for every activity, a time for every deed" (Ecclesiastes 3:17).

Men might be arrogant, but God is not ignorant. He knows, He sees, He evaluates, and He judges—both the good and the bad. People might behave today as if they can do whatever they want. But tomorrow is coming. One of the practical realities of that truth is that after we have done everything in our power to see that justice happens, we need to relax with the knowledge that God will take it from here.

We can only go so far. We can only do so much. But God certainly is capable of doing the rest. That truth helps answer the question of how we can find satisfaction in life on a daily basis when there is so much obvious injustice and oppression within our line of sight. God has that on His screen; it's on His list. Nobody escapes God's notice, and He will one day bring justice to all men.

The Reality of Mortality

Man's fate is like that of the animals; the same fate awaits them both.
ECCLESIASTES 3:19

When God created the world, He left behind clues everywhere about His identity as the Creator and our identity as the creation. Since time began, God has been concerned that we not get those identities confused. The Creator sets the agenda. The creation follows the agenda.

Man's mortality is one of the most obvious signs he is creation rather than Creator. "As for men, God tests them so that they may see that they are like the animals. . . . As one dies, so dies the other. All have the same breath" (Ecclesiastes 3:18–19). We breathe, we die, and we go to dust—just like our pet dogs.

Why do we need to understand that? Because a life of fullness and joy is inextricably connected to an understanding that we come under God's authority, agenda, and timing. It also matters because we ought to live in such a way that we, created beings, properly acknowledge our Creator. Our thinking, actions, and priorities should make it clear to anyone who observes that we are individuals under authority and that the large and small decisions of our lives are not for us to make on our own.

We might be confused about many things, but we should never be confused about the fact that we are not the Creator. Nor should we be confused about the fact that the Creator is an intelligent Being Who prefers an ordered existence. Even if we don't know Scripture, what may be known about God ought to be plain to us. Why? Because God has made it plain: "For since the creation of the world God's invisible qualities—his eternal power and divine nature—have been clearly seen, being understood from what has been made, so that men are without excuse" (Romans 1:20).

As His creation, we obey God, we love God, and we worship God, our Creator.

Green with Envy

[A]ll labor and all achievement spring from man's envy of his neighbor.
ECCLESIASTES 4:4

Keeping up with the Joneses is depressing. In fact, Solomon contends that it is meaningless and chasing after the wind. There is no redeeming quality about it.

But it's a common issue: "[A]ll labor and all achievement spring from man's envy of his neighbor" (Ecclesiastes 4:4). While it's true that Solomon is sometimes given to hyperbole, that is still a strong statement. In fact, its power keeps us from immediately deciding it does not apply to us. We must consider if it does apply, and if so, how.

The implication is clear that if we are able to disconnect our strivings from what our neighbors have, then our lives will be much healthier and happier. What criteria do we use to evaluate whether our lives are chained to theirs? Income, house size, vacations, friends, cars, status in the community, clothes, furniture, health, a second home—all the usual things.

To what extent are your life goals and priorities connected with what your neighbors have—or at least what they seem to have? When you make financial decisions, how strong is the "neighbor factor"? Does it affect your recommendation about where your children apply to college? Does it affect how much you're willing to spend on a car? The list goes on, but you get the picture.

It is interesting to note that Solomon's solution doesn't involve moving to a place with no neighbors at all. He doesn't recommend that we live in some sort of hermetically sealed bubble, or that we take up residence at a cabin in the woods with no other houses in sight and no families with whom to compare ourselves. (In fact, later in Ecclesiastes he makes it very clear that friendship is one of God's most valuable gifts.)

No, Solomon's solution is to live with other people but not be chained to them when it comes to our own material priorities. What is your plan for separating what is important to you from what is important to them? Or, to use imagery from Ecclesiastes 4:4, how do you beat the envy beast back?

Going Solo

There was a man all alone; . . . "For whom am I toiling," he asked, "and why am I depriving myself of enjoyment?" ECCLESIASTES 4:8

Some people work alone because they just don't have anyone to work with. Others work by themselves because they have a "leave-me-alone" orientation to their work. But whether by circumstance or choice, Solomon offers three possible consequences of doing life solo.

The first consequence is that you might become a workaholic. Why? Because no one else is around to share the load. You have to do it all yourself. It's tough to take a vacation. You can't seem to take Sundays completely off. You travel more than you should. Basically, you work too hard.

The second possible consequence is that you might fall into the trap of always wanting more. One of the upsides of working for yourself is the connection between effort and income. If you just get another contract, if you only work an extra day, if you are able to secure that one last meeting, then you will have that extra bump of income that will get you what you want. But the benefit of being able to earn extra cash can quickly become a liability if what you are craving always costs just a little bit more than what you have. Or if you become fixed on what your work will buy instead of what your work is accomplishing. Or if you live in a state of perpetual discontent because you want too much.

The third consequence is that you might become bitter. Someday you might wake up only to realize that you have spent a lifetime working hard and accumulating possessions only to amass a fortune that will be handed off to someone else. In fact, you have worked so hard that you have never taken time to enjoy the result of all your efforts. What's wrong with that picture? Solomon's conclusion, which comes repeatedly in Ecclesiastes, is to reconsider the priorities of life so that you can enjoy both your work *and* the result of your work. What a concept!

Joint Venture (Part One)

Two are better than one, because they have a good return for their work.
ECCLESIASTES 4:9

Partnership is such a great idea. A life at work is full of all kinds of ups and downs that are difficult to face alone. Work was God's idea all the way back in Genesis 1, but the Fall in Genesis 3 made that good idea much harder to achieve: Adam was forced to work "by the sweat of [his] brow" (Genesis 3:19).

None of us has ever met anybody at the end of a career who told us that the entire experience was like eating a great piece of cake—that it was all easy and fun, that stress was never part of the equation, and that he loved every minute of it. Give us a break! Finding someone to share the load is inherently appealing. Who wants to carry the burden alone?

Solomon interrupts his logical train of thought in this chapter to recommend a joint approach to work. He suggests that it is better to have someone who can share the load and help carry the burden, someone (or perhaps more than just one individual) who can be a sounding board in developing strategy, making difficult phone calls, getting the business, and defending against the competition.

Partnership can take on many different forms: a fifty-fifty ownership split in a business, colleagues on a work team, two friends at work who work through difficult issues together, or prayer partners who are willing to wrestle corporate issues to the mat in God's presence.

Do you have someone who shoulders the burden of work with you, someone who will be there to help you up when you fall down? According to Solomon, a life at work with someone else looks much different than a life at work by yourself.

Joint Venture (Part Two)

If one falls down, his friend can help him up. ECCLESIASTES 4:10

Partnership is a great idea—unless it doesn't work. Then it seems like a terrible idea. If you want a partner—someone to genuinely share the workload—then you can't engineer the relationship to look like two sole proprietors working in tandem. It can't be the kind of arrangement in which, despite the fact that "partnership" is the title on the front door, the individuals inside are working for themselves and simply sharing overhead.

Partnership means you have to give up certain perks of being a lone ranger in order to gain the benefits of joint synergy. Synergy is not something that comes naturally or easily. Synergy means that you share the decision-making as well as the spotlight. Partnership means that you keep your ego under control. A joint venture means that you give credit where it is due and take blame where necessary. A great working definition of a productive partnership is when all involved feel as if a burden is being jointly carried.

You know you are involved in a bad partnership when you feel as if you are doing much or all of the work, while the others involved are getting a free ride on your shoulders. A good partnership is something that you will never trade in. As Solomon says, "Though one may be overpowered, two can defend themselves. A cord of three strands is not quickly broken" (Ecclesiastes 4:12).

Would you like a little help with the part of work that causes stress and sweat? Investigate the power of partnership.

Poor and Wise or Rich and Foolish?

Better a poor but wise youth than an old but foolish king who no longer knows how to take warning. ECCLESIASTES 4:13

There is almost nothing more discouraging than working around people who don't listen, who are stubborn even when confronted with data, and who are generally unteachable. They already know all the answers. Their minds are made up. Good argument to the contrary means nothing. Even their polite nods mask a steel resolve to go their own direction.

About people like that, Solomon weighs in with strong opinion: "Better a poor but wise youth than an old but foolish king who no longer knows how to take warning" (Ecclesiastes 4:13).

No matter where these unteachable individuals reside in the corporate hierarchy, they are obstacles to be reckoned with. Anyone could fall into this category—the big boss, the building engineer, the head of the mail room, or the travel agent. But at all costs, don't let it be you.

How do you take suggestions? What do you do with evaluation and feedback? Where is your response on the defensiveness meter? When was the last time you thanked someone for giving you negative feedback? When someone comes to you with an opinion different from your own, how would they describe your response? Would they use the words love, joy, peace, patience, kindness, goodness, faithfulness, gentleness, or self-control (Galatians 5:22–23)? As Solomon reminds us, it is better to end up poor and wise than rich and foolish.

What is worse than being wrong? Being wrong and not knowing or admitting it.

Walk with Caution

Guard your steps when you go to the house of God. ECCLESIASTES 5:1

One of the evidences of wisdom is the ability to think in broad conceptual terms as well as in daily practical realities. A wise individual can traffic in the ideas of theology and philosophy, but he also can answer the constant follow-up question: *How does that philosophy or theology affect the things I do today?*

Wisdom affects our thinking and behavior simultaneously. In Ecclesiastes 5:1, Solomon gets very practical: "Guard your steps when you go to the house of God. Go near to listen rather than to offer the sacrifice of fools, who do not know that they do wrong."

When we enter any kind of worship context, there are some things we should do. We need to be constantly aware that we have entered a "God zone." We have walked into a place that is about God, not about us. Solomon seems to know us well enough to understand that we spend most of our busy lives thinking about our situations, our agendas, our to-do lists, our problems, and the myriad details that surround our life. But when we go into a God zone, our responsibility is to focus our minds in a different direction.

If it is true that there is a time and a place for everything, then entering a place of worship is time to focus on God. A mind preoccupied with personal and work issues is inappropriate and out of bounds. Our job is to focus on Him. A time of worship gives us an opportunity to allow all the aspects of life to fall into place by focusing on God, not on ourselves or our situations.

Our job also is to listen. We draw near to God so that we can hear Him speak. We are prepared to hear and accept God speaking into our lives. Unless we listen, we might never know what we are doing wrong. It's amazing what we learn about the life God wants us to live when we stop long enough to pause and hear His voice.

When was the last time you paused to draw near to God and hear His voice? Do it today!

Talk with Caution

Do not be quick with your mouth, do not be hasty in your heart to utter anything before God. ECCLESIASTES 5:2

According to the psalmist, we are to number our days (Psalm 90:12). According to Solomon, we are to number our words. There is a connection between our hearts and our mouths. A quick mouth indicates a hasty heart, while a careful mouth indicates a thoughtful heart.

When we enter a God zone, quality is far better than quantity. We might not normally associate spending time in prayer with being a fool, but according to Solomon, the more words we use when talking to God, the greater the chance we have of being unwise in the communication exchange. In fact, in Ecclesiastes 6:11, Solomon comes right out and says it: "The more the words, the less the meaning."

In other words, the more careful you are when you talk to God, the better. What are you really asking for? Have you really searched your heart for wrongdoing? Do you know of things in your life that need to be changed, things that you have been unwilling to confront? What are the obvious next steps you need to take toward maturity? Are you doing what you know you should be doing in this season of your life?

It is amazing how probing questions bring focus to our conversations with God. The words might be few, but the intensity is great and the results are clear.

We spend a tremendous amount of time and energy making sure that our words are crisp and precise when we're writing a strategic plan or composing a memo that goes out to the organization. We carefully cut out extra and ambiguous language. We make sure our thinking is clear. Solomon suggests that we do the same in conversation with God. An off-the-cuff communication style with the Almighty is probably not the strategy we want to pursue. After all, Solomon calls that the "speech of a fool" (Ecclesiastes 5:3).

How careful are you with your words when you talk to God?

Promises Made, Promises Kept

When you make a vow to God, do not delay in fulfilling it. ECCLESIASTES 5:4

It is one thing to thank God, to ask Him for something, or to praise Him for His love. Even in those times we should proceed with caution—with fewer words than with many words. But it is quite different to make a promise or a vow to God. Solomon has advice about this that can't be misunderstood: "When you make a vow to God, do not delay in fulfilling it. . . . It is better not to vow than to make a vow and not fulfill it" (Ecclesiastes 5:4–5).

Making promises to God is a good way to increase your spiritual maturity. When you tell God you will do something, you are forcing yourself to focus on the issue about which you have promised. You are throwing yourself at the mercy of the Holy Spirit to help you change something in your life that is so difficult to get a handle on that the only way to address it is in the form of a promise or a vow.

When you make a vow, however, it is best to make one that you know you can fulfill, which often means that it needs to be a short-term promise, not a long-term or even a lifelong promise. You don't want to make a vow, only to find yourself unable to complete it, or worse, forgetting that you made the promise. Even with the best intentions, Solomon says long-range vows that might not be fulfilled are best avoided entirely.

If you make a promise but end up not fulfilling it, you run the risk of making God angry: "Do not let your mouth lead you into sin. . . . Why should God be angry at what you say and destroy the work of your hands?" (Ecclesiastes 5:6). Essentially, Solomon says it would be better to have never made the vow in the first place if it isn't going to be fulfilled.

A moment of reflection is in order. What have you promised that you have been unable to fulfill? Ask God's forgiveness about these issues. Then ask yourself, *What promises do I need to make to God?*

No Awards for the Naive

If you see the poor oppressed in a district, and justice and rights denied, do not be surprised at such things. ECCLESIASTES 5:8

O ur thinking might be idealistic, but life tends to be realistic. We live on earth, not in heaven. If we expect our world to operate like a perfect place, we are simply naive: "If you see the poor oppressed . . . and justice and rights denied, do not be surprised at such things" (Ecclesiastes 5:8).

When we open our eyes in the morning, we see it in our own lives, in the newspaper, and in stories we hear from others. Injustice and wrongdoing are everywhere. But despite our normal experience, we are sometimes caught off-guard by such action because we know that it really *should* be different. To which Solomon replies, "We need to *live* our lives in the 'ought-to-be' category, but we need to *view* life in the 'really-is' category." What should be and what is are not the same. No awards will be given for being naive. If we are caught off guard by such activity, it is our fault.

Scripture calls for us to be "as shrewd as snakes and as innocent as doves" (Matthew 10:16). Most of us are "very" in one of those two categories and "sort of" in the other. We are very shrewd and sort of innocent, or we are sort of shrewd and very innocent. In this case, however, we are supposed to be "very-very," not "very-sort of." Though we should not participate in such things, we should be able to anticipate the realities of oppression, corruption, selfish motives, inappropriate financial profit, injustice, and the taking of bribes.

Solomon's point is not that we should wink at such wrongdoing, encourage it, or even accept it. But he wants us to understand that regardless of our best actions, we will never eliminate it. At the very least, we certainly should never be surprised by it.

Loving Money, Wanting More

Whoever loves money never has money enough. ECCLESIASTES 5:10

We understand that wealth can be problematic—at least we know that to be true in theory. But it is very difficult to comprehend the downside to having money. Wealth puts on a great front. It encourages the new, delivers the big, allows for the comfortable, and arranges for the convenient.

Line ten people up and pose the following questions: Would you prefer to fly first-class or coach? Could you use extra cash to upgrade the furniture at your house or office? Do you wish you had more money to invest in your retirement account? It takes little intuition to predict what the probable answers would be. Wealth sets us apart from anyone with less and bestows on us a sense of respect, status, and power. It gives us options and flexibility.

But Solomon pokes his head behind the money curtain to look around backstage, and just as with any performance backdrop, things look a little rough. He contends that the more we love money, the more we want money. It serves up an appetite that grows but never goes away. It never feels like enough. The treadmill won't stop.

Solomon ought to know. He was by far the wealthiest man alive, ruling over a kingdom in which silver was worth nothing because gold was so plentiful. In that very plentiful context, Solomon says, "Don't love money."

Money itself is not the problem. Neither is having money. Loving money, however, is the kind of appetite that, if indulged in, can end up eating us alive instead of providing us with satisfaction.

Solomon gives the strong impression that it is very difficult to have a lot of money and not end up loving it. Is that true with you?

Too Rich to Sleep

The sleep of a laborer is sweet . . . but the abundance of a rich man permits him no sleep. ECCLESIASTES 5:12

The wealthy have it tough! Not only do they have to wrestle with whether they love money, but they also must deal with two other inevitabilities of having significant amounts of money. The first issue Solomon mentions is so true it almost makes us want to laugh. The more we have, the more people there are around to consume what we have. Or, as Solomon puts it: "As goods increase, so do those who consume them" (Ecclesiastes 5:11).

Money invites its own infrastructure of people who follow that money: accountants, lawyers, the IRS, landscapers, decorators, brokers. In a sense, Solomon confirms the adage that it is more difficult to keep money than it is to make it.

That isn't the worst of it. Even more distressing is that the more money we have, the less sleep we get. Such late-night musings as, *What happens if the stock market goes through a correction?* or *Will the hurricane sweep away our place on the beach?* replace what used to be slumber. Ironically, the folks who surround us because of our wealth sleep just fine, but we are left awake.

When God gives wealth, it brings unique challenges that are only appreciated by those who have it. Money by itself is not bad, but neither is it a panacea. It requires every bit as much attention to its proper stewardship as it required in earning it.

Although Solomon doesn't say so, perhaps one of the best ways to alleviate the stress caused by having money is to give it away. Maybe then some of the people who surround us to spend it would go away, and perhaps we could finally get some sleep!

Nothing to Nothing

Naked a man comes from his mother's womb, and as he comes, so he departs.
ECCLESIASTES 5:15

From his vantage point as the wealthiest man alive, Solomon observes how other wealthy people act with their wealth. He notices, for example, that wealth that is hoarded harms its owner. But hoarding wealth also indicates a belief in something that is not true. When we hoard wealth, we act as if we will be able to take our worldly wealth with us into eternity.

Whom are we keeping it for? If we have our arms around what we have earned while simultaneously trying to push everyone else away, then apparently we have fooled ourselves into thinking that we really will be able to keep it. To that, Solomon says—without equivocation—that "[n]aked a man comes from his mother's womb, and as he comes, so he departs. He takes nothing from his labor that he can carry in his hand" (Ecclesiastes 5:15). As the saying goes, hearses don't pull U-Hauls.

When God gives the gift of wealth, we must use it within the boundaries that God draws, including the reality of death being a final bookend. This suggests the final question: How can we properly allocate our wealth while we are alive? We must either designate its actual use during our lives or designate how it will be used after we die.

Have you made proper provisions for the use of your assets? Because life is so uncertain, this is better done sooner than later.

Loving Life Today

God keeps him occupied with gladness of heart. ECCLESIASTES 5:20

Life is challenging. It is difficult. It is uncertain. It is stressful.
All of that is true, but it's not the conclusion. The summary at the end of the day, week, or year is supposed to read quite differently: "It is good and proper for a man to eat and drink, and to find satisfaction in his toilsome labor. . . . Moreover, when God gives any man wealth and possessions, and enables him to enjoy them . . . and be happy in his work—this is a gift of God" (Ecclesiastes 5:18–19).

Our relationship with God opens the door for us to enjoy our work and lives. This kind of enjoyment is not some future "retirement enjoyment." It is present tense, as in this year, this month—even today.

Solomon is absolutely focused on this throughout the Book of Ecclesiastes. He probably needs to say it over and over because we might not otherwise believe that he really means it. In the middle of all the stresses and strains of life—especially the strains and stresses in our lives at work—he says we are to experience joy, satisfaction, and fulfillment. A lack of those characteristics indicates that we lack a relationship with God. After all, such great things only come as a gift from God. Many of us don't do very well with this. It almost seems as if we didn't get the memo that declares that followers of Christ have the freedom to enjoy their work and their lives.

Of course, the enjoyment that Solomon talks about is not a Pollyanna "God-will-make-life-perfect" kind of joy. He makes it very clear that life will not be perfect. But even in the middle of corruption and oppression, a man or a woman with a relationship with God receives the unbelievable gift of enjoyment, meaning, and fulfillment in life.

So how is your day going?

The Cover versus the Book

God gives a man wealth, possessions and honor, so that he lacks nothing his heart desires, but God does not enable him to enjoy them, and a stranger enjoys them instead. ECCLESIASTES 6:2

Some folks have more wealth, honor, and possessions than we could ever imagine having. We might be tempted to ask ourselves, *How lucky can they be?* But think again. Those things are not always good. "How can wealth not be good?" we might ask. The answer is profound: when God does not enable the person who possesses them to enjoy them.

By now, we shouldn't be surprised that Solomon's answer might be something like that. We have seen it so many times in Ecclesiastes. When we see someone using possessions and wealth, we should not automatically assume that he or she is enjoying them. Solomon really goes out on a limb on this one. He concludes that to have material possessions and not enjoy them is worse than not having them at all. It would be better for that person to have never been born. Not much to envy there!

It is very easy to give deference to people with wealth. We treat them better and ask them questions that indicate they have a credibility that comes simply by having wealth. In some cases, we might even ask their opinions on issues that have nothing to do with the fact that they have wealth just so we can interact with them and show that we consider them special.

According to Solomon's teaching, we ought to show them pity and love instead. We do not want what they have; they desperately want what we have. That understanding should give us more boldness than deference. We ought to build genuine relationships with wealthy people—the kind of relationships that show them we don't want their money and we're not even impressed with it. They need to be introduced to the God we know. Only then can they can enjoy the joy He gives.

Be Careful What You Crave

All man's efforts are for his mouth, yet his appetite is never satisfied. What advantage has a wise man over a fool? What does a poor man gain by knowing how to conduct himself before others? Better what the eye sees than the roving of the appetite. This too is meaningless, a chasing after the wind. ECCLESIASTES 6:7–9

Appetites can save us and kill us. When our stomachs signal hunger, we eat. Then, when the hunger goes away, we stop eating. Health is the result. But other kinds of appetites have less healthy results.

There is much in life to envy and desire. It is inevitable that we will see things that aren't ours and that we can't have: a job, a house, a car, a travel opportunity, a position of power, or a person. Those things parade before us on an everyday basis, and it is very normal for us, every once in a while, to say, "I really wish I had that" or, "Maybe someday I will have that."

But there is a dangerous progression that we should avoid at all costs: from eye to appetite. As Solomon says, "[b]etter what the eye sees than the roving of the appetite" (Ecclesiastes 6:9).

When presented with an opportunity to envy, we can look the other way, or we can dwell on it. The problem with an appetite—which we develop by dwelling on what we see—is that it continues to grow even after the object is out of our line of sight.

Appetites are not quenched by meditating on them. Hunger does not go away until we eat food. Appetites are a call to action. They are satisfied only by moving toward the object of desire. We want what we crave.

But even if we get we want, our appetites are not satisfied. We want more. The cycle goes on—and Solomon calls that meaningless.

The solution is obvious. When we see something that we can't have or should not observe, we need to call a quick time-out. We can't let what we have just seen turn into a full-fledged desire that takes over our behavior.

A Good Name

A good name is better than fine perfume. ECCLESIASTES 7:1

After warning against all sorts of things, Solomon then asks the question, "[W]hat is good for a man?" (Ecclesiastes 6:12). A good name tops the list. It is, he says, "better than fine perfume."

Why is a good name still valuable? Almost every culture recognizes the importance and value of a good name. The Greeks had a word for developing a good name, or reputation, or credibility. They called it *ethos,* from which we derive our word *ethics.* The picture of *ethos* was of an individual who is the same on the inside as he is on the outside. In other words, he has integrity.

When a coin with integrity is cut in half, it is the same all the way through. In the same way, a person with integrity shows on the outside what he or she is on the inside. The Greeks went so far as to say that good *ethos,* or credibility, is essential to persuasion. It is, they said, impossible for us to persuade others to action if we are not believable individuals ourselves.

A good name is worth fighting to protect, although ultimately God is in charge of protecting our reputations. So much in life is dependent on having a good name. What is the current value of your name currency?

A Time for Tears

Sorrow is better than laughter, because a sad face is good for the heart.
ECCLESIASTES 7:3

Solomon, the pleasure king, gives a high endorsement to the value of mourning. "It is better to go to a house of mourning than go to a house of feasting. . . . Sorrow is better than laughter, because a sad face is good for the heart" (Ecclesiastes 7:2–3).

We don't live in a culture that gives much credence to mourning. Our TV channels are filled with comedy routines and sitcoms that measure their success in the number of laughs per minute. Solomon loves laughter, but he contends that a wise person is one who balances laughter with mourning. Fools, on the other hand, care only about laughter and pleasure. But constant comedy is less than edifying.

Why is mourning healthy for the heart? First, Solomon says it is part of the natural rhythm of life that God ordains: There's a time to weep and a time to laugh (Ecclesiastes 3:4). A balance between the two is part of the ebb and flow of life. If we only have one to the exclusion of the other, we are lopsided.

Second, according to Ecclesiastes, there is much to be sad about. Solomon spends a great deal of time documenting oppression, corruption, the taking of bribes, the selfish motives of others, etc. And while he is careful to help us understand that those things should never surprise us, he also makes it clear that they are worth being sad about. Sin and wrongdoing ought to make us feel less than gleeful.

Third, according to Matthew 5:4, people who mourn are blessed because they will be comforted. In the Beatitudes, that kind of mourning revolves not around what others have done wrong, but around what we as individuals have done wrong. In other words, our own lack of righteousness ought to cause us to mourn deeply.

The mourning that Solomon suggests is not the bitterness of unhappiness that is so evident in Ecclesiastes. The mourning that he talks about here is a genuine sense of sadness at the state of the world and the state of our hearts, both of which make God sad. That kind of mourning is healthy, especially when it's balanced against the laughter and the joy that also ought to be evident in a life with Christ.

What We Do Affects Who We Are

Extortion turns a wise man into a fool, and a bribe corrupts the heart.
ECCLESIASTES 7:7

We would like to believe that who we are is separate from actions that we undertake, that our inner being is protected even when our actions are less than perfect. But Solomon contends that what we do today will have a profound effect on the state of our hearts: "Extortion," he says, "turns a wise man into a fool, and a bribe corrupts the heart" (Ecclesiastes 7:7).

Every day, we make decisions. We decide to forgive, to cheat, to show grace, to get even, to play fair, to push our positions of power, to do things legally, or to do things unethically.

When we play in the mud, we get our clothes dirty. When we engage in wrong behavior, compromising ethics, or skewed thinking, we get our hearts dirty.

How that transformation happens is a mystery. It isn't necessarily something that we can explain. The process may happen over time. But it does happen. When we engage in bad action, the result is bad hearts.

Knowing that ahead of time allows us to avoid the trap. It also gives us a greater sense of accountability for our actions. Nobody wakes up in the morning and wants a bad heart. But one of the ways a bad heart develops is by actions that are inappropriate.

What does your heart look like? If it has become dirty through unethical practices, then confess your sin to God and let Him cleanse you from your unrighteousness (1 John 1:9).

The Present-Tense Nature of Life

Do not say, "Why were the old days better than these?" For it is not wise to ask such questions. ECCLESIASTES 7:10

Whatever happened to the good old days? We may have uttered this timeless question ourselves, and we certainly have heard old-timers ask it with a certain sense of nostalgia. But Solomon says such questions best remain unasked.

A past-tense view of life is not positive. The "good old days" only look good from a distance. It is easy to forget that stress, tension, and hard times also were present then, just as they are now. Living in the past, or with an eye directed backward, leaves less than enough energy and focus on the present and moving into the future.

The gospel is present-tense truth, not past-tense nostalgia. When we listen to the words of Jesus or read the letters of Paul, it's hard to miss the fact that the good news of Christ always centers on the present in a person's life, not on the past. Jesus tells us to take up our cross daily, today, right now (Luke 9:23). His focus is not on what we did two years ago or three weeks ago. His concern is what we are doing right now. Paul evidences the same present-tense approach to his own spiritual life. He makes it clear in Philippians that he is not looking back, but instead pressing ahead to become the person God wanted him to be (Philippians 3:12–14).

We gain very little by focusing on the past and allowing it to drag us down because it wasn't fair or to slow us down because the present just simply can't live up to what once was. The past is gone; the present is all we have.

So what good is the past? Why should we remember it at all? Throughout the Old Testament, the people of Israel were asked to remember what God did in the past. Through that lens, the past was good—not for preventing them from living in the present—but for helping them to remember how God delivered them time and time again.

By remembering what God did in our past, we can be encouraged about what He is doing now and what He will do in the future. That kind of remembering is always beneficial.

God Is in Charge

Consider what God has done: Who can straighten what he has made crooked? When times are good, be happy; but when times are bad, consider: God has made the one as well as the other. Therefore, a man cannot discover anything about his future. ECCLESIASTES 7:13–14

One of Solomon's constant themes in Ecclesiastes is that much of life is beyond our control. God has the steering wheel even when we think we do.

When we forget the truth of God's control, we take credit for what works and we blame ourselves for what does not. But in either case, we are wrong. God has engineered a path of life for us designed to bring us closer to Him. We don't get healthy by only eating ice cream. Neither do we grow and mature only by experiencing times that are positive, good, full, fruitful, and full of plenty.

A healthy diet includes peas, broccoli, and sometimes even very bitter medicine. When you look at the sweep of biblical characters from Genesis to Revelation, it is nearly impossible to find a righteous man who does not experience significant trouble. Businesses go through cycles of plenty, and they go through cycles of poor financial returns. Sometimes our personal net worth is high, and sometimes our stock portfolios hit the rocks.

We can't change what God has engineered, nor can we predict what God will do. As Solomon says, "[A] man cannot discover anything about his future" (Ecclesiastes 7:14).

Our anchor is not in our ability to control, but rather in our trust of a God Who is sovereign. In other words, our trust must not be in ourselves, it must be in Him. We need to buckle up and get ready for the ride.

Righteousness or Self-Righteousness

In this meaningless life of mine I have seen both of these: a righteous man per-
ishing in his righteousness, and a wicked man living long in his wickedness. Do
not be overrighteous, neither be overwise—why destroy yourself? Do not be
overwicked, and do not be a fool—why die before your time? It is good to grasp
the one and not let go of the other. The man who fears God will avoid all
[extremes]. ECCLESIASTES 7:15–18

If it is true that we need to be careful about drawing quick conclusions about what we observe in outward circumstances, it also is true that we should not always believe what we think we see in someone's inner character.

Outward appearances are deceiving. Some people seem rich when they're actually deeply mired in debt. Some people look very successful when they're actually on the verge of bankruptcy. And it goes both ways. The fellow who drives a battered pickup truck may in fact own a retail empire. It's easy to be fooled by outward circumstances.

In much the same way, we can be fooled by what we think about a person's inner character. When Solomon writes "do not . . . be overwise" (Ecclesiastes 7:16), he uses the reflexive form of the Hebrew verb "to be wise," which means, "Don't think your-self too wise." In other words, "Don't be self-wise and self-righteous." What looks like righteousness sometimes really is self-righteousness. What looks like wisdom is often self-wisdom. When we are righteous and wise in our own eyes, we destroy ourselves.

For some, personal wisdom and righteousness end up being false advertising. They look really good on the surface, but when you scratch below the surface, what you uncover is not very pretty. It turns out they just think they're wise and right-eous. Their egos have convinced them this is the case, but it really isn't so.

Solomon writes this for two reasons. First, he wants to make sure that we are not self-righteous or self-wise. Second, he wants to make sure that we don't follow the advice of someone who is self-righteous or self-wise. That kind of advice could well direct us right over the edge of a cliff.

A personal inventory is in order. Are you wise in your own eyes? And do you take advice from people who are wise in their own eyes?

Even the Wise Are Not Right All the Time

There is not a righteous man on earth who does what is right and never sins. Do not pay attention to every word people say, or you may hear your servant cursing you—for you know in your heart that many times you yourself have cursed others. ECCLESIASTES 7:20–22

Seeking wise council is prudent; leaving all our decision-making to others is not. Even the wisest counselors are wrong sometimes, according to Solomon, and sometimes their judgment is even clouded by sin.

Does this mean that we shouldn't ask wise counselors for their advice in situations in which we're not sure what to do? Of course not. We need people to help us discern what God is telling us, but we don't need to use them as a substitute for our own sense of what the Holy Spirit wants us to do.

Someday we will stand before God and He will ask us to account for our actions and decisions. When He asks why we did or did not do something, the right answer on our part cannot be that we simply did what wise counselors told us to do. The only correct answer is that we did what we felt God wanted us to do, and in the process of figuring that out, we consulted those who were wise. We need to take the words of others seriously but with a grain of salt.

And for sure, we need to remember that even the wisest of the wise aren't right all the time. Only God has that distinction.

The Importance of Practical Wisdom

All this I tested by wisdom and I said, "I am determined to be wise"—but this was beyond me. Whatever wisdom may be, it is far off and most profound—who can discover it? So I turned my mind to understand, to investigate and to search out wisdom and the scheme of things and to understand the stupidity of wickedness and the madness of folly. ECCLESIASTES 7:23–25

Sometimes wisdom is hard to grasp. Great philosophical thinkers leave us in the dust. We don't really understand their first argument, much less the conclusion they draw fifteen steps later. Ethical theories are complicated and don't really help us make good decisions at all.

So if we want to be wise, what should we do?

Solomon makes it clear that wisdom includes a daily and constant dose of God's Word. We're kidding ourselves if we think we will develop lives of wisdom with actions that follow if we don't understand and know God's Word.

But Solomon adds something else in this passage. He suggests that if we really want to understand wisdom, we can become students of the "scheme of things" (Ecclesiastes 7:25), or how things really work. We can study the motives behind the actions, the meaning behind the words, and the reasons for changes in direction.

When Solomon—the ultimate realist—suggests that we understand the scheme of things, he is begging us to watch the world with careful eyes and to see what goes on in our daily work context in much the same way that we would observe a case study. We should study how people get ahead. We should listen to the nuances in suggestions that are made and decisions that are announced. Our purpose is to chronicle our findings and then, over time, begin to anticipate things ahead of time.

Solomon is essentially asking us to use our experience as a way of building wisdom. What good is an experience-rich résumé if we have not turned that experience into wisdom by becoming an expert in how things really happen?

We don't live in a perfect world. We won't until Jesus comes again. But we can navigate an imperfect world, at least in part, by being observant about what goes on around us.

Coming to Grips with Authority

Who is like the wise man? Who knows the explanation of things? Wisdom brightens a man's face and changes its hard appearance. Obey the king's command, I say, because you took an oath before God. Do not be in a hurry to leave the king's presence. Do not stand up for a bad cause, for he will do whatever he pleases. Since a king's word is supreme, who can say to him, "What are you doing?" ECCLESIASTES 8:1–4

It should come as no surprise that King Solomon recommends that we pay attention to rulers and other forms of authority. As always, however, his recommendations come with a practical edge: Don't offend the person in authority unnecessarily. Be careful to disagree only when you feel it is absolutely essential. Be strategic in the way you call your boss to account.

Current best-practice business philosophy calls for us to participate in decision-making and to engage fully in discussions that affect the course of our companies or our businesses. Long gone are the times when employees simply did what they were told even if they knew that what they were doing would result in catastrophe. The wisdom of the day tells us that our jobs are to make our voices known.

Solomon might applaud that business philosophy, but he still asks us to be careful. Despite current best practices, the same general principles apply. When working with someone in authority over us, it is still best to be careful, to be strategic, and to be diplomatic—always in the context of being honest.

How well are you doing with this? Are you quick to offend or to disagree with your superiors, or have you learned to hold your tongue? Our boss might invite our input, but after all is said and done, he is still the boss.

Timing Is Everything

Whoever obeys his command will come to no harm, and the wise heart will know the proper time and procedure. For there is a proper time and procedure for every matter, though a man's misery weighs heavily upon him. ECCLESIASTES 8:5–6

So much of life comes down to timing. God sets the stage in our lives, and much of our energy goes into making sure what we do is in sync with the life context that God has laid out in front of us.

In *Experiencing God,* Henry Blackaby contends that instead of initiating action and asking God to join us, we should figure out what God is doing and join Him. Much of that comes down to timing. *When* we do what we know we are supposed to do is often as important as *what* we do.

According to Scripture, Jesus came into the world at the perfect time. He certainly was needed before He arrived. In fact, God-fearing Jews had fervently prayed for and looked forward to the coming of the Messiah for thousands of years. But His coming was perfectly aligned with a series of historical events that together set the stage for His arrival. For the first time in history, there was a common language, a road system that allowed for travel, common forms of currency, and a series of other elements that facilitated the spread of the gospel. Jesus could have come anytime, but He came at the time when the world stage was best arranged for the gospel to go out to the ends of the earth.

On a smaller scale, our lives and work often come down to a judgment regarding timing. In Acts 17:26–27, Paul says something very interesting: "From one man he made every nation of men, that they should inhabit the whole earth; and he determined the times set for them and the exact places where they should live. God did this so that men would seek him and perhaps reach out for him and find him, though he is not far from each one of us." God has set us very specifically in a particular time and a particular place. Neither is by chance.

Because God has thought so carefully about the where and when of our lives and our work, it makes sense that we ought to also be very aware of the timing of our actions to make sure that they are in exact alignment with what God has planned.

Getting What We Deserve

All this I saw, as I applied my mind to everything done under the sun. There is a time when a man lords it over others to his own hurt. Then too, I saw the wicked buried—those who used to come and go from the holy place and receive praise in the city where they did this. This too is meaningless. . . . Although a wicked man commits a hundred crimes and still lives a long time, I know that it will go better with God-fearing men, who are reverent before God. Yet because the wicked do not fear God, it will not go well with them, and their days will not lengthen like a shadow. ECCLESIASTES 8:9–13

When we look around at people of influence and in positions of leadership, it is easy to find things that just aren't right. Some folks are held in high regard even though they are quite evil. Other leaders gained their leadership by stepping all over people on their way to the top.

Why are these people given such credibility and held in such high esteem? They certainly don't deserve it. It just doesn't make sense.

Solomon doesn't try to answer the question. Part of his pragmatic mind-set, which we see throughout the Book of Ecclesiastes, includes making observations about the inequities of life without trying to come up with a satisfying answer. But neither does he simply pose problems without any sense of a solution. And in this case, the solution is for us to take the long perspective.

What kind of long perspective? Unfortunately, as Solomon indicates, bad people seem to get away with doing bad things. But God knows who does what. And He will settle the score on an individual basis. Specifically, "Because the wicked do not fear God, it will not go well with them" (Ecclesiastes 8:13).

So what about somebody who does the right thing but may not get the headlines or the credit? Solomon says, "I know that it will go better with God-fearing men, who are reverent before God" (v. 12). Their days, he implies, will lengthen like a shadow.

Are you tired of keeping your integrity but remaining in the background? Take heart; your days will be lengthened, and God will bless you for it.

Guaranteed Results

There is something else meaningless that occurs on earth: righteous men who get what the wicked deserve, and wicked men who get what the righteous deserve. ECCLESIASTES 8:14

We need to guard against developing a personal sense of manifest destiny, the assurance that certain outcomes are inevitable. Salvation is not a promissory note for health, wealth, and success. Just ask Job or Joseph or David—or for that matter, any man or woman who has walked with God for any length of time. The life of faith is not walked on an easy road.

We can try all we want, but we cannot manipulate the results of the actions we take. Yes, we can plan in a way that is intended to achieve good results. At times we can manage to get good results from other people. We can even hand out rewards based on results. But ultimately, we are not in control of results. And we were never meant to be.

Results are hidden in the hands of God. We cannot see them in advance. He dispenses them in His timing and according to His will. Understanding this is fundamental not only to our faith, but also to our state of mind. We may fight to impose our will on God, but we will always lose. God wants obedient sons and daughters, not prima donnas who whine because they did not get what they wanted.

Does this mean that we shouldn't be results-oriented? Of course not. In today's economy, businesses, organizations, and markets live and die by results. But even they can't control the results, despite the millions of dollars they spend trying. Focusing on results may improve our odds of success, and we should make every effort to excel in what we do. But favorable results are never guaranteed. The only true guarantee comes from our heavenly Father, the One Who promises that "in all things God works for the good of those who love Him" (Romans 8:28).

Some Mysteries Remain Unsolved

So I reflected on all this and concluded that the righteous and the wise and what they do are in God's hands, but no man knows whether love or hate awaits him. All share a common destiny. . . . As it is with the good man, so with the sinner; as it is with those who take oaths, so with those who are afraid to take them. ECCLESIASTES 9:1–3

Solomon is certainly never one to shy away from a hard question. Why is it, he asks, that whether we are wicked or righteous, we still don't know if life will treat us poorly or well? Why is it that whether we're righteous or wicked, we all share the same destiny—death? What kind of sense does that make? More significant, what are we supposed to do about those obvious inequities?

No matter how hard we try, it will be impossible to completely solve all the puzzles of life. Why does it seem as if life looks much the same for bad people as it does for good people? How can it be fair that people who arrange their lives in a godly way seem to suffer the same end as those folks who are authentically evil? Great question. Only God knows. Literally.

If we have a philosophic bent or a reflective mind-set, such questions can stop us in our tracks. Some of us may find it necessary to know the answers before we can proceed with a productive relationship with the God of heaven Who is supposed to be in control of all of those things.

But Ecclesiastes does not encourage us to spend very much time figuring out the ultimate answers to those tough questions. Some questions, Solomon says, simply cannot and will not be solved this side of heaven. He raises the questions because he knows that we ask them. But his answer is not a long philosophic treatise; it is simply to acknowledge that there are many mysteries in life that we won't ever solve.

Life is not like an Agatha Christie novel or a detective story that we read to the end to figure out what happened and why. It is much more complex than that, and it involves a transcendent God Who doesn't always tell us what He's thinking. It must be enough that we know the God Who does the thinking, rather the substance of all of His infinite thought.

Live in Joy without Apology

Go, eat your food with gladness, and drink your wine with a joyful heart, for it is now that God favors what you do. Always be clothed in white, and always anoint your head with oil. Enjoy life with your wife, whom you love, all the days of this meaningless life that God has given you under the sun—all your meaningless days. For this is your lot in life and in your toilsome labor under the sun. ECCLESIASTES 9:7–9

If life is full of mysteries that can't be solved, and if our rational mind-set is simply to trust that God understands what's going on and that He has a solution to what seems like a gross inequity, then how should we act?

We now know that we're not supposed to allow those conundrums to prevent us from moving forward in life and in a relationship with God. But in the face of those realities, what should our perspective on life be? The answer to that question is crystal-clear: Don't let the lack of an obvious answer to those mysteries prevent you from genuinely enjoying the best of life.

The things we can't possibly solve are better left to God. He will figure them out in His time and in His way. Our job is to eat the food and drink the wine He provides. It is to keep a joyful heart and enjoy the love of a spouse. In a way that allows very little wiggle room, Solomon tells us to have fun, eat well, and revel in a great marriage relationship. He even suggests that we wear clothes that show a freshness to life.

But how does this all fit together? How can we look at the darkness around us and yet respond to life with such abandoned enthusiasm? We know Solomon well enough to understand that he's not suggesting that we simply ignore the darkness in order to revel in the light. His purpose is not to make us forget that bad things go on, but to acknowledge that after we have done everything we can in our power to make things right, the rest is up to God. He wants to remind us that the darkness caused by others must not take away the joy that God wants us to experience.

Are you experiencing joy despite the difficulties and inequities that you see and experience at work?

Work Hard While You Can

Whatever your hand finds to do, do it with all your might, for in the grave,
where you are going, there is neither working nor planning nor knowledge nor
wisdom. ECCLESIASTES 9:10

"Life is short; play hard." So the saying goes. That is actually not bad advice
from Ecclesiastes. But Solomon adds another phrase to complement the first
one: "Life is short; work hard."

Our work lives have their ups and its downs. We enjoy some of what we do,
while other tasks are less pleasant. We look forward to Fridays and don't always rel-
ish the coming of Mondays.

Sometimes, work gets a bad rap because of bad theology. Work was designed by
God, given to Adam and Eve in the Garden of Eden before the Fall. But we sometimes think that work is a bad deal because it is talked about as part of the aftermath
of the sin in which Adam and Eve engaged. That is, we think that work is a result of
the curse. But although our jobs sometimes reinforce that idea, it's not biblical.

According to Genesis 3:17–19, the work that God ordained in Genesis 1 and 2
became much more difficult because of the Fall. Just as childbearing—also ordained
by God in the opening two chapters—became much more difficult and painful, so
work would only be accomplished by the sweat of the brow and lots of hard labor.
In other words, what was easy became difficult. But work still was as ordained by
God and blessed by God *after* the Fall as it was *before* the Fall.

So what perspective does Solomon have on work? "Whatever your hand finds to
do, do it with all your might," he writes, "for in the grave, where you are going, there
is neither working nor planning nor knowledge nor wisdom" (Ecclesiastes 9:10).
Essentially, he is suggesting that we enjoy the work we're doing now, while we can still
work, because the day will come when we look back with nostalgia on all of that planning, strategizing, and thinking that we were able to engage in during our careers.

Work is not a curse. It is a gift from God, a calling. Work hard while you can,
because you don't know what the future holds.

Work with Your Head, Not Just Your Strength

I also saw under the sun this example of wisdom that greatly impressed me: There was once a small city with only a few people in it. And a powerful king came against it, surrounded it and built huge siegeworks against it. Now there lived in that city a man poor but wise, and he saved the city by his wisdom. . . . The quiet words of the wise are more to be heeded than the shouts of a ruler of fools.
ECCLESIASTES 9:13–15, 17

In the business world, it used to be that the big ate the small. Now, the fast eat the slow.

Here, Solomon suggests yet another scenario: the wise eat the fools. Once upon a time, he says, there was a great king with real strength who decided to conquer a small city with few people. Nobody seriously questioned the outcome; after all, who could go up against this king and his mighty army?

But hold on! One resident of the city was very poor yet very wise. He came up with a solution for conquering the great king and his strong army. His suggestion worked, and the king had to find another city to conquer.

The moral of the story is this: Wisdom is always in style, even when we don't have very much power or authority. People generally feel as if they have less authority or power than they need to push a solution through to completion. That applies to CEOs as well as to people lower in the organizational hierarchy. Yet Solomon suggests that working with our heads just might be more effective than tapping into the power grid.

In his story, an unlikely individual came up with a solution that saved the town. He certainly didn't have positional authority, and we're not even sure anybody asked his opinion. He simply offered what turned out to be very wise advice, and everybody was pleased with the result (except for the king who had to find another town to conquer).

So Solomon concludes, "The quiet words of the wise are more to be heeded than the shouts of a ruler of fools." Sometimes it's better to sit back, close our eyes, and think than it is to rush.

Wise Action versus Impulsive Action

If a ruler's anger rises against you, do not leave your post; calmness can lay great errors to rest. ECCLESIASTES 10:4

Sooner or later in any work context, something is going to make us really mad. It might be a misunderstanding. It could be an injustice. Or it might be some kind of strong disagreement. Regardless of the actual issue, the result might be to make us so angry that we just simply throw in the towel and walk out the door. "I'm not taking this anymore!" we fume. "I can't work with a person who does that! I'm out of here!"

Even though our frustration might be completely justified, Solomon advises us to slow down and refrain from taking impulsive action. "If a ruler's anger rises against you," he says, "do not leave your post; calmness can lay great errors to rest." In other words, continue on in your responsibility. Show a level of maturity that may be difficult but in the long run might serve as a stabilizing factor.

Obviously there are times when we need to walk off the job and never look back. But Solomon seems to be saying that those times may be fewer than we might think. More often than not, we simply need to grit our teeth, control our tongues, mask our reactions, and simply keep on working. That does not prevent us from walking off the job after we've had more time to think about it and reflect. But that should not be our first response.

How do you respond when your boss makes you mad? Do you take a deep breath and try to evaluate the situation objectively, or do you act impulsively? Be mature. Follow Solomon's example.

Get in the Game

Whoever digs a pit may fall into it . . . whoever splits logs may be endangered by them. ECCLESIASTES 10:8, 9

Everything we do in life has some element of risk. Every day we face risks—in relationships, in the stock market, in our next big decisions. Sometimes we face these risks with fierce tenacity; other times we cower in fear.

What causes some of us to be more adept at taking risks than others? Is it our confidence in our decision-making prowess? Is it that we don't care about the results? Not usually. Some people see risks as opportunities. They ask themselves, *What's the worst thing that can happen?* and then they proceed to take the chance. Other people agonize day and night over risk-taking decisions until they either give themselves ulcers or the opportunity passes them by.

No matter how large or small your risk-taking muscles might be, God wants you to trust Him. He wants you to exercise faith that overcomes fear daily. Don't stay on the sidelines. Engage. Struggle. Fail. Trust. Be courageous. Don't become like the sluggard in Proverbs 22:13 who never takes a chance because he says, "There is a lion outside!" or, "I will be murdered in the streets!"

When's the last time you took a risk so big that if God didn't come through, you'd look like an absolute fool? Take a risk on God; He's already taken a risk on you. He demonstrated His own love for you before you even knew Him (Romans 5:8). You could have rejected Him, but He took the risk.

Why are you holding back? Are you afraid of losing your status or power? Of being known as a Christian? Of sharing your faith with your friend? Go ahead—take a chance. Don't give up on God; He hasn't given up on you.

Wise Words

Words from a wise man's mouth are gracious, but a fool is consumed by his own lips. At the beginning his words are folly; at the end they are wicked madness—and the fool multiplies words. ECCLESIASTES 10:12–14

It is amazing how much people love to talk about themselves. Sit next to the typical person at a business lunch or around the conference table before a meeting starts, and he will almost always direct conversation to what he thinks, what he likes, what he did, or what he accomplished. Seldom does anyone show any interest in asking about you. In fact, sometimes the conversations are so one-sided they are almost comical. It doesn't matter how long the two of you talk—you get the feeling that if you extended the conversation another four days, the topic would never change.

One of the things that distinguish a wise person from a foolish person is the extent to which he talks about himself and whether his conversations have substance. Solomon says that "the fool multiplies words" (Ecclesiastes 10:14). In other words, foolish individuals talk a lot but don't necessarily say very much in the process. They offer long explanations without answering any questions. They sometimes talk just for the sake of speaking. While their words might be eloquent, when the whole conversation is over and you have time to reflect, you're really not sure that they said anything of substance.

In contrast, words that come from a wise man are gracious words. They are courteous and thoughtful. They are logical and shed light on a situation. A wise man may not speak as often or use as many words as someone else, but the words he does say have real impact. People can't deny their power and the advice that they represent. It takes very few wise words to completely silence the many words of a fool.

Don't Always Say What You Think

Do not revile the king even in your thoughts, or curse the rich in your bedroom, because a bird of the air may carry your words, and a bird on the wing may report what you say. ECCLESIASTES 10:20

We've all had experiences in which we said something we really felt, only to find out later that it was passed on to someone we never intended to hear it. It's an entirely natural impulse to give voice to our thoughts about other people and their actions. Something in us wants our thoughts to have verbal expression. We simply enjoy talking about our opinions of other people.

The only trouble is that sometimes when we express our opinions, the expression does not end when we stop talking. In one form or another, it gets passed on to someone else. This is a great risk, especially with our growing dependence on e-mail and other forms of electronic communication.

But this problem isn't new. It didn't just surface with the new economy. According to Solomon, we need to be careful to not revile our leaders or curse the rich because a "bird of the air may carry your words, and a bird on the wing may report what you say" (Ecclesiastes 10:20). Even when we think we are being especially careful, our opinions may find expression in ways that would horrify us. We say in retrospect, "I never would have said that if I had any idea that person would find out what I was thinking."

For Solomon, keeping quiet is another manifestation of someone who is wise. If the fool multiplies his words (Ecclesiastes 10:14), then the wise man watches his very carefully. In this case, when the words you want to say involve someone who is not in the room and whose presence would cause you not to say what you're thinking, then it's best to simply keep your mouth shut. In fact, Solomon says that we shouldn't even *think* such thoughts. And if we shouldn't think them, we certainly should be very careful about saying them. You just never know when and where that information will resurface.

Don't Be Swayed by Circumstances

If clouds are full of water, they pour rain upon the earth. Whether a tree falls to the south or to the north, in the place where it falls, there will it lie. Whoever watches the wind will not plant; whoever looks at the clouds will not reap.
ECCLESIASTES 11:3–4

Stuff happens, or so the saying goes. Sometimes the stuff that happens is profound and full of meaning. Other times it's just another tree falling in another forest. But regardless of its meaning or significance, stuff does happen. The real question is this: What are you going to do about it? This question is easy to answer when the situation is clear and the direction unequivocal. But what about other times—when the sky grows dim and the winds swirl, when the signals are mixed and the outcome is ambiguous?

The wrong time to shore up your foundation is after the storm hits. That's the time to hunker down, focus in, and wait it out.

There is work to be done while the sun is shining. Are you making preparations? *Preparations for what?* you ask. For the storm. Calm days provide the best time to dig deeper, to reinforce the walls, and to repair the cracks in the foundation. Are you anchoring your heart in God? Are you fine-tuning your ears to hear Him better? Are you learning—studying—the sound of His voice? There will come a day when the wind will blow so strong that you cannot hear yourself think, let alone discern His voice.

If we do not know our course, our direction, or our instructions, we will be tossed about on the waves like a ship without a rudder. But if we are secure in Him, then we can ride out any storm of circumstance in peace and assurance.

Live Joyfully, but Don't Forget the Times of Trial

However many years a man may live, let him enjoy them all. But let him remember the days of darkness, for they will be many. Everything to come is meaningless. ECCLESIASTES 11:8

One of the most unusual aspects about Ecclesiastes is Solomon's constant admonition to live in joy while not forgetting parts of life that are less pleasant. He does that again in these verses. "Enjoy all the years you have left," he says, "but not without stopping every now and then to remember the hard times you've been through in your life."

Ecclesiastes is a present-tense book. Solomon constantly asks us to enjoy the current season of life we're in and the current job we have because, as he points out again and again, we just don't know what tomorrow may hold. In saying that, Solomon does not ignore the future, nor does he discount the past. He simply makes it clear that our goal in life is to enjoy the present. What's done is done. What's to come will come soon enough, and it may be more pleasant or less pleasant than what we're currently experiencing. But in either case, the focus of our time is now.

That in no way means that we should forget the past—if we did that, we'd miss out on valuable lessons we learned during difficult times. Nor does it mean that we should not have an eye toward the future. Solomon frequently says that what we do today will be looked at by God in the future. Therefore, we have to make sure that our current activity aligns with His plan and His thinking.

The New Testament states that we shouldn't worry about tomorrow because it has enough troubles of its own (Matthew 6:34). In other words, we don't need to live in the future or in the past.

Have you been living in the past? Then begin to live in the present and learn to enjoy life today.

Live Adventure

Be happy, young man, while you are young, and let your heart give you joy in the days of your youth. Follow the ways of your heart and whatever your eyes see, but know that for all these things God will bring you to judgment. So then, banish anxiety from your heart and cast off the troubles of your body, for youth and vigor are meaningless. ECCLESIASTES 11:9–10

The evidence indicates that Solomon probably addressed the Book of Ecclesiastes to up-and-coming leaders near the beginning of their careers. In that context, he has a simple suggestion: "Follow the ways of your heart and whatever your eyes see, but know that for all these things God will bring you to judgment" (Ecclesiastes 11:9).

In our culture, an unsettledness regarding career options is prevalent. People often look around and ask the question, "What should I be doing?" They're constantly questioning their calling and wondering if they should change jobs. Such concerns frequently arise among professionals in certain age groups, particularly those who are just beginning their careers and those who are in the middle of their careers.

These questions are never articulated by people who feel they are following their dreams. Rather, they are asked by those who are in one career context but would rather be doing something else. *Should I begin my own business? Should I switch to a nonprofit? Should I move over to that corporation where I could occupy that position? If I move from here to there, I will take on more risk. The results will be more uncertain. What should I do?*

Solomon's advice? Live the adventure and do what your heart desires. Simply remember in the process that whatever you do will be evaluated by God. So make sure that the choices you make regarding your career are honoring to Him. Would you feel good about standing before God and explaining your rationale for what you are thinking of doing? If the answer is yes, don't hesitate to pursue it. If the answer is no, put it out of your mind immediately.

Life is a fantastic adventure. Enjoy every hour of it. Take risks. Follow your heart. Let your creativity take over. Just make sure in everything you do to stay inside God's boundaries. Someday you'll have the opportunity to explain things to Him face to face.

The Sooner the Better

Remember your Creator in the days of your youth, before the days of trouble come and the years approach when you will say, "I find no pleasure in them." . . . *Remember him—before the silver cord is severed, or the golden bowl is broken . . . and the dust returns to the ground it came from, and the spirit returns to God who gave it.* ECCLESIASTES 12:1; 6–7

Solomon begins the final chapter of Ecclesiastes by telling us to remember our Creator in the days of our youth—before our lives become complicated, before we experience great amounts of trouble, before our bodies wear out, before we die.

In a nutshell, this is a purpose statement for the first half of life. Remember God now. Don't wait until you're calloused and cynical about life. Don't wait until your teeth fall out and your eyes grow dim. Do it now.

Solomon seems to imply that as we get older, we get distracted by other things. Growing a career, starting a family, building a business, dealing with the trials of life—all of these can consume our attention to a degree that makes it difficult to remember our Creator like we could when we were younger.

At the same time, the older we get, the more we begin to experience a lack of fulfillment from all the things life has to offer. The older we get, the more we begin to realize that wealth, wine, pleasure—everything Solomon talks about in Ecclesiastes—will not satisfy. Whether we ever realize it or not, the only way we can find true fulfillment is through a genuine, vibrant relationship with our Creator.

What if the prime of my youth is long past? you might be thinking. *Is it too late for me to remember my Creator?* No, as long as you're still alive, it's never too late. But don't put it off any longer because you never know when the silver cord of your life will be severed.

It All Comes Back to God

Now all has been heard; here is the conclusion of the matter: Fear God and keep his commandments, for this is the whole [duty] of man. ECCLESIASTES 12:13

Solomon has just written a book that is chock-full of weighty, often confusing information. He poses tough questions: Why is there corruption in the world? How can God allow evil? What should I do when there's oppression? And he doesn't provide many answers, except to say that God knows what's going on and sooner or later, whoever does bad things is going to be called into account.

But in the end, Solomon does what any good teacher would do after a confusing, thought-provoking lecture—he sums it all up with one succinct statement. "In case you didn't get it the first time," he says, "here's the essence: Fear God, and keep His commands. If you do that, you've done everything."

If we're wondering what to do with all the information we've absorbed as we've read Ecclesiastes, this passage leaves no doubt. We are to focus on the person of God and on the content of His Word. That is our whole duty. It's not part of the answer. It *is* the answer. These words and God's person give us the answer to the meaning of life and the context in which to understand what happens in life.

One of Stephen Covey's "seven habits for highly effective people" is to "start with the end in mind." The Book of Ecclesiastes might have looked very different if Solomon had done that. Since he didn't, he resorts to warning us not to make the same mistake. Our duty, he tells us, is to start with the end in mind. Don't do everything else and then realize you need to fear God. Fear God, and then everything else will fall into place.

Or are you making the same mistake Solomon made? If so, reverse your course today. Do your God-ordained duty: Fear Him and keep His commandments.

The Inevitability of Accountability

For God will bring every deed into judgment, including every hidden thing, whether it is good or evil. ECCLESIASTES 12:14

Although we often think otherwise, there is no secret sin. On the flip side, neither does any good deed go unnoticed. We may rejoice in the erroneous assumption that nobody knows about our sinful attitudes and actions, and we may bemoan the fact that so many of the good things we do seem to be overlooked by others. But as Solomon concludes at the end of Ecclesiastes, God will judge every hidden deed—whether it's good or evil.

In essence, there's a good-news/bad-news aspect to every action we take. If it's a good action, God notices and remembers, and someday we will be commended for it. If it's a bad action, attitude, or behavior, He notices that, too, and someday, He will call us into account for it. As 2 Corinthians 5:10 says, "we [believers] must all appear before the judgment seat of Christ, that each one may receive what is due him for the things done while in the body, whether good or bad."

The typical work environment offers plenty of opportunities for us to take advantage of the system or to compromise our integrity and ethics. But when we're misusing corporate funds or engaging in questionable behavior while on a business trip, we need to remember that the sovereign, omnipresent eye of God is never shut. God does not abide by any privacy laws; He's always watching us.

Fortunately, God doesn't just see us when we do something wrong. He also notices when we make a right decision or do a good deed that goes unnoticed by everyone else. We may not get a promotion or a bonus for such acts, at least not in this lifetime. But that doesn't matter when we're living life for an audience of One. He sees, He recognizes, and He will be the One Who says, "Well done, thou good and faithful servant."

5

James

In Search of Authentic Religion

Introduction to James

Because of the literary style of the Epistle of James, we group this New Testament letter with the poetic books in the Scriptures. Located near the end of the Bible, this epistle is small—only five chapters, to be exact—but it packs a powerful punch.

Exactly which man named James wrote the letter is an interesting question. The name *James* is a rich biblical name. Although there were a number of men by that name in the New Testament, only two were prominent. One, the brother of John and a son of Zebedee, was one of Christ's twelve disciples (Acts 1:12–14). The other was the half brother of Jesus, another one of Mary's sons (Matthew 13:55). We believe that it was the latter of the two who penned this practical, hands-on, instructional book.

James apparently was not a believer during the time of Jesus' ministry (John 7:5). Imagine that. He grew up in the same household as Jesus yet chose not to believe. Somewhere along the way, however, James crossed over in his faith. In the Book of Acts, he appears as a part of a group of believers in the upper room (Acts 1:14). And then, toward the end of the New Testament (Galatians 2:9), Paul refers to James as a pillar of influence in the local church.

James's life is a profile of the development of a Christian leader. He began as a nonbeliever, full of doubt, questions, and skepticism. He became a member of the community of faith, then he arose as a leading member who ultimately became a pillar of faith. Charles Swindoll's teaching on the Book of James pinpoints a few reasons we can learn from James's life:

- We should never give up on God's ability to convert our skeptical families and friends.

- It takes time for us to progress into leadership, regardless of our family ties.

- One of the toughest battles we all have is fighting tradition and legalism. (This was a hard one for James, who mentions it frequently throughout his short letter.)

- Sometimes it is easier to serve God than it is to serve members of our own families.

Like the other biblical wisdom literature, the Book of James is a gold mine of insights into the world of work. It's not a book for casual believers, but serious followers of Christ will find in it much fodder for reflection and spiritual development.

A Slave of God

James, a servant of God and of the Lord Jesus Christ. JAMES 1:1

In New Testament times, slavery was widespread. As a matter of fact, the social structure and economy of the Roman Empire depended upon slave labor. Slaves performed a variety of tasks: from factory work and mining to medicine and secretarial work, from farming and business management to cooking and teaching. Because of its prevalence in biblical times, much spiritual meaning and application has been drawn from the concept of slavery.

The word for "servant" used in James 1:1 is the Greek word *doulos,* which means "slave" or "servant." Positioned inside the word *doulos* are a host of deep and meaningful concepts that add dimension to a believer's relationship to his Master and Lord, Jesus.

First, there is the concept of *aliens* (strangers) and *citizens* (John 15:16–20; 17:6–16; Philippians 3:20; Hebrews 11:13–16). Followers of Jesus are not simply a familiar group of folks who cluster on Sunday. We are an assembly of men and women who are only passing through this life. Our ultimate address is heaven.

The second concept is that of *adoption,* a procedure found in many legal systems through which a person leaves his natural family and enters another family. As believers in Jesus, we have been adopted into God's family with all the rights and privileges therein (Romans 9:4; Ephesians 1:5; Galatians 4:4–5).

The third concept has to do with *inheritance.* When a servant joins God's family, he or she is positioned for tremendous spiritual inheritance. The bounty and benefits that belong to Jesus are duly transferred to each of us (Ephesians 1:18–19).

The final concept is *redemption.* A servant belonged to his master but could be freed if someone purchased his freedom for him. According to Romans 6, we were born slaves to sin but Jesus purchased us with his life and death (1 Peter 1:18–19).

So when James opens his letter by calling himself a servant of God, he's not just giving himself a title that looks good on a business card. It is a rich label he has attached to himself as a follower of Jesus Christ. If you had written this book, would you have been able to give yourself the same title?

Why Me, Lord? (Part One)

Consider it pure joy, my brothers, whenever you face trials of many kinds, because you know that the testing of your faith develops perseverance. JAMES 1:2–3

It may be a blister on your finger—or an aneurysm in your artery. It may be that you've lost your wallet—or you've lost your business. It may that your plans for the day have been ruined—or your hopes for a lifetime have been crushed.

One thing is certain: Life delivers tough blows. Every day, every week, and every month we face the possibility of experiencing difficult circumstances and tough times. These are natural and inevitable elements of our lives. Simply being alive means we will face trials, be disappointed, and encounter hardship and hurdles.

It was family patriarch Joseph P. Kennedy who reportedly first said, "When the going gets tough, the tough get going." California pastor and author Robert Schuller added, "Tough times never last, but tough people do." However, centuries earlier, the apostle James revealed the best approach to the trials of life: When the going gets tough, the tough turn to God.

We who are followers of Jesus need to focus on that thought from James and incorporate it into our perspective on life. God uses difficult times to develop character in us. Even after we've learned that, we still ask, *Why me?* However, it's not just "me." It's every one of us. Pain and hardship are instruments God uses to shape us at our core. Knowing His purpose for tough times doesn't answer every cry or erase every pain, but it does help us grapple with the reality of hardship.

No matter how unfair and random our troubles may appear to be, God is not absent, removed, or disconnected from our pain. He is still tending to His universe at large—and to each individual in particular. When we hurt, God knows and feels. We are not alone.

So what do you do when the going gets tough?

Why Me, Lord? (Part Two)

Consider it pure joy, my brothers, whenever you face trials of many kinds, because you know that the testing of your faith develops perseverance. JAMES 1:2–3

Some days, toil and trouble come in spoonfuls. Other days, they come in a fleet of dump trucks. In the first few verses of the Epistle of James, the apostle describes certain aspects of trials that are essential to understanding and handling life's difficult days.

First, trials are *inevitable*. The word *whenever* signals the certain predictability of hard days and tough times. The question isn't *if* hard days and tough times will come; it's *when*.

Second, trials come in *many kinds*. To describe the various hardships that life delivers, James uses a word that translates as "diverse" or "many-kinded." The Greek word, in fact, is the same one used to describe the coat Jacob gave to his son Joseph, the Old Testament dreamer. Picture Joseph's colorful coat. It was diverse, "many-kinded," multicolored. So, too, are the trials of life. Some are big, and some are small. Some last an hour, and some last a lifetime. Some are chronic, and some are acute. Some pertain to the past, and some apply to the future. There are financial trials, relational trials, and health-related trials. Trials come in many kinds.

Third, trials are *purposeful*. The Old Testament details the story of the wandering people of Israel. Deuteronomy 8:2–3 recounts the story. What appeared to be a plight of aimless misdirection that seemingly made no sense is instead described in these verses as an intentional forty-year desert journey directed by God to build and fortify the character of the Israelites.

James tells us how to respond to trials so our character may likewise be built up and fortified: We are to approach each hardship with joy. James is not speaking here of dogged determination, an attitude that says, *I am going to make it through this.* Nor does he mean the hypocrisy of smiling on the outside and cursing on the inside. The joy he speaks of results from the subtle awareness that we are not alone. God's sovereign eye sees our pain, and if we simply acknowledge His tender care throughout our trials, He will bring peace and purpose to our most difficult days.

How do you respond when trials come into your life?

Maturity—God's Ultimate Goal

Perseverance must finish its work so that you may be mature and complete, not lacking anything. JAMES 1:4

God always has a purpose and agenda. He makes that clear in Jeremiah 29:11: "'For I know the plans I have for you,' declares the LORD, 'plans to prosper you and not to harm you, plans to give you hope and a future.'" But what specific plans does God have for us? Although He has a customized agenda for each individual, part of the plan is the same for all of us. That item on the agenda is captured in the word *maturity*.

James describes the concept of maturity in two distinct words and a final phrase. The first word is *teleios*. This is one of James's favorite words. *Teleios* means that everything has an intended purpose; when that purpose is fulfilled, *teleios* is achieved. Throughout the New Testament, *teleios* is often translated "mature." Maturity includes discovering and fulfilling our intended mission in life. That can include our work, but it is bigger than that.

The second word is *holos,* which means "whole" or "complete." James says the finished work of maturity is completeness or wholeness. Jesus expressed this thought when He said, "I have come that they may have life, and have it to the full" (John 10:10).

James adds one more phrase at the end of the verse—"not lacking anything." That literally means, "nothing has been left behind." No area of development has been overlooked or neglected. This is exactly the idea in Luke 2:52: "Jesus grew in wisdom and stature, and in favor with God and men." Jesus matured mentally, physically, spiritually, and socially.

God has a purpose and an agenda for every one of His children. Part of it is a mystery that each individual must investigate. But another part is crystal-clear, set down by James in his New Testament letter to the followers of Jesus. Maturity, he writes, is God's ultimate goal for each of us.

Coming up Short

If any of you lacks wisdom, he should ask God, who gives generously to all without finding fault, and it will be given to him. JAMES 1:5

When life's little quizzes or comprehensive exams hit, we often reach into our own souls for strength, peace, and perspective, only to find ourselves a few answers short. We are like a young boy who has been saving his quarters for a new baseball glove. He sits down, turns his piggy bank upside down, and counts every coin—but comes up short. He approaches his father and says, "Dad, will you help me? I don't have enough to buy a glove."

God has established the ultimate open-door policy with us. If we are short on answers and long on questions, His office is the place to go. If we don't know what to do, we can call on Him 24/7. If we are stranded at a fork in the road, we can ask for His guidance. When we are overwhelmed by complex problems, we can seek His help.

Navigating the waters of life successfully takes more than sheer knowledge; it also takes wisdom.

It's important to understand how knowledge and wisdom differ. Knowledge includes the analytical ability to take things apart. Wisdom provides the ability to put things back together. Knowledge is data and information and facts and ideas. Wisdom is the ability to see through to the other side of the clouds that blur our earthly vision. Wisdom is God's vantage point on our situation. Wisdom is seeing life through His eyes.

God looks ahead to the results of our decisions. He understands our motives. He grasps the consequences. He knows. He sees.

God is not a magic rock that we can rub or a genie in a bottle that we can manipulate or control. However, God never says to us, "Come back later. I'm busy." Never will He give us the raised-eyebrow, over-the-eyeglasses judgmental stare of a disapproving father. Never will we hear Him say, "You messed up again." When we have turned our self-sufficiency bank upside down, shaken out its contents, and still find that we're a few coins short, we can simply approach our heavenly Father for help.

God Who Is Able, God Who Is Willing

But when he asks, he must believe and not doubt. JAMES 1:6

We often think our problems are too big or too complex for God. At other times we think that our problems are too trivial for the God of the universe to be concerned about. No matter how enormous or how tiny a problem is, though, God is able to help.

Likewise, God is willing. Often in our minds and hearts, we want to ask God for help, but then we stop ourselves. Self-condemning questions and thoughts scroll across our minds: *Why should God help me? Why should He bail me out? After all, I've messed up so many times before. I don't deserve any help from God.*

But God doesn't keep a ledger. When our prayers come into His presence, God does not pull up the fact sheet on us to see if we are worth helping. We would do well to remember Jesus' words: "Which of you, if his son asks for bread, will give him a stone? Or if he asks for a fish, will give him a snake? If you, then, though you are evil, know how to give good gifts to your children, how much more will your Father in heaven give good gifts to those who ask him!" (Matthew 7:9–11).

In *The Pilgrim's Progress,* John Bunyan introduced a character named Mr. Two-tongues, a man of doubt and double-mindedness. But as followers of Jesus, we can't have it both ways. Once and for all, we need to clear up any confusion and erase any doubt.

The simple truth is this: God is able, and God is willing. He doesn't play games with us; His motives are good and pure. God is able to help us when we are desperately short of solutions, and God is willing to help us whenever we need help . . . again and again and again. He is a God Who is able, and He is a God Who is willing.

Fading with Influence

For the sun rises with scorching heat and withers the plant; its blossom falls and its beauty is destroyed. In the same way, the rich man will fade away even while he goes about his business. JAMES 1:11

A young plant bursts through the soil in early spring. As the noonday sun and gentle evening rains feed it, it begins to grow. Stems lengthen, leaves multiply, and flowers begin to appear. Throughout the summer, the plant stands upright in beauty and grace. Then the chill of fall and the first hard freeze of winter bring its growing season to an end. It withers and dies.

We, too, are born with the promise and excitement of growing up and growing old. Like the plant, we grow tall and become beautiful. The beautiful season is not the same length for all of us, nor do we all have the same garden presence. But for the most part, we all enjoy a season of full life. And then life, like a single plant, withers and draws to a close.

Today, our lives are full of work demands, family responsibilities, and many other things that tend to keep us from becoming too reflective about our mortality. But one day we will wake up and ask, *Where has life gone so fast? It seems like just yesterday I was doing* . . .

James encourages us to age with grace and beauty. That includes making sure we are enjoying life *now.* We must not be so attached to deadlines, demands, assignments, and obligations that our lives are reduced to something to be endured rather than to be enjoyed.

We also must be careful to spread positive influence before we enter the fall season of life. As we're standing tall in the sunlight, we must spread influence.

Look around your workplace and ask yourself the penetrating question, *Am I influencing my coworkers in a positive, healthy manner?*

The Crown of Life

Blessed is the man who perseveres under trial, because when he has stood the test, he will receive the crown of life. JAMES 1:12

An athlete rises a little earlier than other people so he can condition and train. He puts himself on a strict diet for months, denying himself sweets and snacks. Finally, the day of the race comes and all the runners line up. The gun sounds and the athletes take off. For what? They are competing for a medal, perhaps even for a crown.

Throughout history, the crown is a symbol of royalty, victory, and reward. In the New Testament, five crowns have special meaning. All five are worthy of our attention and desire.

The *imperishable crown* is for the man or woman who runs the race of life and exercises self-control in all things (1 Corinthians 9:24–25).

The *crown of joy* is for those who have declared the gospel to nonbelievers (Philippians 4:1; 1 Thessalonians 2:19–20).

The *crown of righteousness* is reserved for men and women who have lived for Christ's return. They have stayed focused, kept the faith, and finished the course of life (2 Timothy 4:7–8).

The *crown of life* is for those who have persevered under the trials and pressures of life (James 1:12).

The *crown of glory* is dedicated to leaders who shepherd God's flock willingly, sacrificially, and with integrity (1 Peter 5:1–4).

In a very real sense, every man or woman in the twenty-first-century marketplace should see him- or herself as a competitor for the crown of life. After all, the concept of reward is both biblical and effective.

Do you have your eye on the crown? Striving for the crown of life can motivate any of us on any given day at work.

Trial or Temptation?

When tempted, no one should say, "God is tempting me." For God cannot be tempted by evil, nor does he tempt anyone. JAMES 1:13

A trial can be a test of our character, a heavy burden intended to help us attain emotional and spiritual maturity. Maturity isn't always an automatic result of trials, but it is the original goal.

A temptation, however, is a snare designed to trick us, capture us, and drag us down. A snare is evil and treacherous.

We must never confuse a temptation with a trial. Although we may encounter both in a typical day at work, they are not the same—nor do they have the same outcome.

What exactly is temptation? Temptation is the urge and enticement to become involved in a good thing in a bad way. For example, sleep is a good thing, and it is normal. Laziness is a bad thing, and it is sin. Eating is a good thing, and it is normal. Gluttony is a bad thing, and it is sin. Sex in marriage is a good thing, and it is normal. Adultery is a bad thing, and it is sin.

Temptation is not sin; surrender to temptation is. Temptation becomes dangerous and harmful when, like an air-traffic controller, we provide clearance for sin to land in our lives. It is when we give that OK from the control tower that the real trouble begins.

But we do have a choice: We can turn the sin away, shut off the runway lights, and cease all communication from the tower. When we deny sin the permission to land in our hearts, we wisely follow the avenue of escape that God *always* provides (1 Corinthians 10:13).

Don't Take the Bait

[E]ach one is tempted when, by his own evil desire, he is dragged away and enticed. JAMES 1:14

Mark Antony was known as the silver-throated orator of Rome. He was a brilliant statesman who was magnificent in battle, courageous, and strong. He was handsome and endowed with many good qualities, but he had one fatal flaw—moral weakness. On one occasion his mentor shouted in his face, "Oh Marcus, oh colossal child, able to conquer the whole world but unable to resist a single temptation!" Temptation is an appetite that lurks deep in the heart of every person.

Today's workplace is full of temptations—the temptation to have an affair, to be rich, to wield power, or to acquire fame. There is even the temptation to strive for perfection, to shade the truth, or to cut corners.

Temptation can perhaps be best illustrated through the actions of a fisherman. He baits the hook and drops the line in place, hoping to lure an unsuspecting fish with the promise of fulfilled desire.

In James 1:14, James uses two terms that relate to the activity of a fisherman—"dragged away" and "enticed." Later in the New Testament, both terms are used to describe the wiles of a harlot (2 Peter 2:14, 18). You no doubt get the picture: The fish is enticed by a juicy worm dangling on a hook. Hunger and craving prompt the fish to take the bait, unaware of the fatal consequences. He was deceived, of course, and now he's caught. What he wanted for pleasure gave him nothing but pain.

Whenever we are confronted with an alluring temptation, we are free to choose whether to surrender to it. But we are not free to choose the consequences of the choice we make. Those were long ago determined by the eternal purposes of God.

Green Light, Yellow Light

Everyone should be quick to listen, slow to speak. JAMES 1:19

The Jewish rabbinic literature says it this way: "Silence is a fence for wisdom." The green "go" light is for listening. The yellow "caution" light is for speaking. Green light—listen. Yellow light—speak.

Proverbs 13:3 says it this way: "He who guards his lips guards his life, but he who speaks rashly will come to ruin." My (Steve's) mother said it this way, "God gave you two ears and one mouth. Use them accordingly and proportionately."

Quick to listen. Although James is referring to the way we receive instruction regarding truth, the phrase certainly has a much wider application. We all should be eager for learning. Would those who work next to you, over you, and under you say that you display a hearty appetite for instruction and learning? Would your listening skills be a valuable quality on your résumé? Would you say that you have gotten better or worse at listening during the last few months or years?

Slow to speak. This is a call for careful deliberation before we open our mouths and engage in dialogue. It's difficult to talk and listen at the same time. We all need to practice keeping the right balance between the activities of the ears and the activities of the mouth.

Once a young man came to the great philosopher Socrates to be instructed in speech. From the moment the young man was introduced, he talked incessantly. When Socrates finally managed to get a word in edgewise, he said, "Young man, I will have to charge you a double fee."

"Why is that?" the bewildered student asked.

"I will have to teach you two sciences," the philosopher replied. "First how to hold your tongue, then how to use it."

Green light—listen.

Yellow light—speak.

Yellow Light, Red Light

Everyone should be . . . slow to become angry. . . . get rid of all moral filth.
JAMES 1:19, 21

A yellow traffic light is a warning: Caution, slow down. Here, James instructs us to drive slowly into anger. Don't be a quick trigger or easily angered, he says.

What makes you mad? What causes you to be short on patience and long on temper? People who don't follow through with commitments? Circumstances that seem to create chaos and unpredictability? Losing control? Gossip? A boss who steals your good idea and never gives you the credit?

Anger might be a positive thing in some instances, but James clearly is guiding men and women of faith to be cautious of the dark side effects of anger.

So many followers of Jesus in today's culture look and act angry. Although they talk a language of salvation and forgiveness, they project an image of resentment and anger. Their faces and eyes reveal the anger in their hearts.

The word James uses for anger implies more than a passing irritation or displeasure. It refers to a strong and persistent feeling of indignation and active anger. It is an uncontrollable animosity that begins to build deep inside a person.

Yellow light—be slow to anger.

Red light—stop.

In some areas of life, it's not enough to just slow down. We need to stop. Take moral uncleanness, for example. That's an area we must get rid of completely. We need to throw it away, to put a stop to it immediately. Slowing down just isn't enough.

James advises followers of Jesus to put off bad behavior. The word picture is one of people stripping off garments. It is used elsewhere in Scripture to refer to divesting oneself of certain undesired qualities or deeds (Romans 13:12; Ephesians 4:22; Colossians 3:8; 1 Peter 2:1). God is never satisfied with partial purity, partial goodness, or partial righteousness. It starts with the word *no*.

Yellow light on anger.

Red light on moral filth.

The Danger of Empty Familiarity

Do not merely listen to the word, and so deceive yourselves. Do what it says.
JAMES 1:22

Empty familiarity doesn't describe a social handicap or a physical deformity; it's an innocuous-sounding phrase that describes a spiritual disaster. And it's rampant in our culture.

We all know that we live in an information-heavy society. We hear and read about everything—the good, the bad, and even the ugly. In fact, we take in so much information that we can become familiar with all the right facts and terminology but not really understand what we are talking about. For example, we can talk about the stock market, computers, or sports simply by picking up on the jargon used in those fields. We think we're engaging in intelligent conversation even as we mask our utter ignorance of the topic at hand.

This kind of pretense also applies to spiritual matters. We learn the language of the spiritual dimension, but we don't necessarily put it into practice. For example, we can learn the language of prayer and all the proper names for the different kinds of prayer—adoration, confession, thanksgiving, petition, intercession, etc.—but never actually get down on our knees to engage in prayer.

We can learn all about forgiveness—when to forgive, why to forgive, even how to forgive—but in the heat of a controversy we might hold a grudge, try to get even, and stubbornly refuse to forgive. That is empty familiarity. We know the language, but we fail to experience the reality.

James says we must apply truth to our daily lives. We must become "doers" of what we have learned. Perhaps this should become the standard for the authentic expression of faith in today's marketplace: not that we know the right spiritual jargon, but that we can deliver spiritual reality; not that we can weave God-talk into a conversation, but that we can inject the person of Jesus Christ into the busyness of the workday.

Empty Religion

[H]e deceives himself and his religion is worthless. JAMES 1:26

Each of us has a religion—a system of beliefs that pulls together our view of God, our understanding of ourselves, and our approach to living. A friend says that his religion is bass fishing. That sounds a bit strange, but anything is possible.

The question is not whether you have a religion, but, rather, what is that religion really made of? What is your view of God and where did you get it? Is it autobiographical? Is God simply a magnified image of yourself or someone you know? Is your understanding of God a compilation of movies, sermons, novels, and bedtime stories? Your view of God, your understanding and acceptance of yourself, and your approach to living are three threads that weave into the fabric of your religion.

Your religion will show up in the way you spend your time. It will evidence itself in the kind of decisions that you make at work, in the way you view and treat other people, in the way you handle money, in the way you treat people who wrong you, and in the way you maintain self-control. If your religion is based on truth, it will be revealed in the way you look for the best in others, the way you deal with authority figures, and the way you deliver excellence every day on the job, and the way you refrain from griping and complaining.

What is the core of your religion? Is it, as James puts it, "worthless"? Another translation of this word is "empty." Think of a nut, perhaps a pecan that, when it is cracked open, has nothing inside. The pecan was only an empty shell. It's the same way with a person whose religion is empty. All the external trappings are there, but there is no substance to his or her relationship with God. Strive to build and display a religion that is substantive and authentic.

Real Religion

If anyone considers himself religious and yet does not keep a tight rein on his tongue, he deceives himself and his religion is worthless. Religion that God our Father accepts as pure and faultless is this: to look after orphans and widows in their distress and to keep oneself from being polluted by the world. JAMES 1:26–27

What are the distinguishing traits of a person with real religion? Does he use a lot of God language? Does she vote for conservative candidates on Election Day? Does he listen to Christian music and not go to movies?

According to James, real religion is more than just external activities. It's more than a list of dos and don'ts. Rather, it is a relationship with Jesus that is developed from the inside out.

Real religion involves taming the tongue. This takes more than a handful of self-help steps at a therapy group. It requires the power of the Creator God coming alongside us in areas that we are not able to tame by ourselves. A person who can control her speech is a person who has tapped into a supernatural power. We might not need the power of God to attend a church, a Bible study, or a prayer group. We don't need a Higher Power to paste bumper stickers on our cars. But we do need strength from an external source—supernatural strength—to control our speech.

Real religion also demands that we help the helpless. James says that taking care of the disenfranchised and the less fortunate indicates that a person has a vital and ongoing connection with Jesus. To fulfill this mission, we must move outside ourselves to focus on someone in need.

In all likelihood, these people will never be able to pay us back. We will never receive an award or trophy for helping them. Perhaps that's exactly why it weighs in as real religion.

Spreading the Bounty

Religion that God our Father accepts as pure and faultless is this: to look after orphans and widows in their distress. JAMES 1:27

We live in a wealthy society. The rate and volume of wealth being produced in the modern world is staggering. The blessing and bounty trickles down to almost all of us, with a few notable exceptions. Two slices of our society continually struggle to make it day to day—widows and orphans. It was true two thousand years ago, and it is still true today.

The twenty-first-century business community is extremely wealthy; therefore, it has myriad opportunities to assist the less fortunate. The very soul of a business enterprise ought to include a desire to help, to reach outside itself and give back to those in need.

So how can a business give back? It can make quarterly disbursements to any community cause that focuses on orphans and widows. It can identify single parents and provide scholarships to send their children to schools, camps, and events. It can team up with a local church and provide assistance to the widows and orphans in the congregation. It can provide its products or services to widows and orphans at no charge.

However it's done, the business community has a responsibility to turn some of its profits back into these environments of need. It is payback time.

Perhaps a whole new benchmark for return could develop if businesses began this approach. Along with ROI (return on investment), ROA (return on assets), and ROE (return on employees), we could add KROI, or Kingdom Return on Investment. In other words, based on a company's investment, what kind of return is it getting in terms of shaping and delivering kingdom influence?

Taking care of the widows and orphans is not solely the church's responsibility. It is not just the responsibility of a few rich, elderly men or women. The business community must get into the game. Are you willing to get involved?

The Dangers of Favoritism

[A]s believers in our glorious Lord Jesus Christ, don't show favoritism. JAMES 2:1

As James continues his argument for real religion, he moves to another pillar of his discussion: favoritism. Real religion, he asserts, includes no trace of favoritism.

"Suppose a man comes into your meeting wearing a gold ring and fine clothes, and a poor man in shabby clothes also comes in," he writes. "If you show special attention to the man wearing fine clothes and say, 'Here's a good seat for you,' but say to the poor man, 'You stand there' or 'Sit on the floor by my feet,' have you not discriminated among yourselves and become judges with evil thoughts?" (James 2:2–4).

This occasion for showing favoritism was a church service, a meeting of a group of believers. *How could such an attitude ever manifest itself in the church?* you might wonder. *The church should be the one place where no distinction ever exists.* That's exactly right! There should not be a rich-over-here/poor-over-there mentality in the church. There should not be a famous-and-powerful section on one side and an average-and-unimportant section on the other side.

Unfortunately, however, that's exactly how it is sometimes, even at church.

Don't be hypnotized by the beautiful people and their nice clothes, expensive jewelry, and luxury cars. Look past their shine to their behavior, their lives, and their characters. After all, we all have feet of clay.

What about at work? Do we practice favoritism there? Sadly, the answer is yes. The same kind of preferential positioning and treatment that often goes on at church also happens in the workplace. Some people might call it politics, but most of the time it's just plain old favoritism.

So what is wrong with favoritism? At its core, it constitutes a breach of the law of love. God loves everyone unconditionally—no matter what a person's size, color, shape, income level, or social status. He loves all of us. He is not impressed with—or turned off by—our external packaging. He is focused on our hearts.

Faith without Works

What good is it, my brothers, if a man claims to have faith but has no deeds? Can such faith save him? JAMES 2:14

When the Bible speaks of faith, what exactly does it mean? The word *faith* could mean a body of belief or an adherence to a creed, or it could mean a warm personal trust toward God.

In James, the latter definition applies. That said, there's no doubt that figuring out the connection between belief and behavior has been a long and spirited debate. Sincere believers have been talking about this issue for thousands of years. Entire denominations have been formed and split as a result of these discussions.

James asks two questions as he introduces his opinion on this issue. First, he asks, What profit is there for someone who says he has faith but no good deeds to back up his plan to know God? Or, put another way, *What good are good works?* To drive home his point, James provides a compelling example: "Suppose a brother or sister is without clothes and daily food. If one of you says to him, 'Go, I wish you well; keep warm and well fed,' but does nothing about his physical needs, what good is it?" (James 2:15–16).

But James also wants to know something else: *Can good works save me?* Can a person present a long list of good deeds to God as the basis for an eternal relationship with Him? Will good conduct, benevolence, and philanthropy be enough to satisfy the demands of God and define a person's relationship to Him?

The apostle Paul steps in with the answer to that question—a hearty *no.* "For it is by grace you have been saved, through faith—and this not from yourselves, it is the gift of God—not by works, so that no one can boast" (Ephesians 2:8–9).

Have you been relying on your "good works" as a basis for your eternal relationship with God? If so, confess to Him right now that you would like to receive His gift of salvation, based not on your works, but on Jesus' once-for-all, completed sacrifice (Romans 6:23; Hebrews 10:10).

Faith versus Works

But someone will say, "You have faith; I have deeds." Show me your faith without deeds and I will show you my faith by what I do. JAMES 2:18

So what role do works play in the life of a follower of Jesus? If they cannot save us, are they of any value at all? Jesus talked about good deeds when He was leading His first coaching session with his twelve disciples.

"You are the salt of the earth," He said in Matthew 5:13–16. "But if the salt loses its saltiness, how can it be made salty again? It is no longer good for anything, except to be thrown out and trampled by men. You are the light of the world. A city on a hill cannot be hidden. Neither do people light a lamp and put it under a bowl. Instead they put it on its stand, and it gives light to everyone in the house. In the same way, let your light shine before men, that they may see your *good deeds* and praise your Father in heaven" (emphasis added).

One of the primary roles of good deeds is to positively and effectively convince a disbelieving world that a God exists Who can make a distinctive difference in someone's life. Many people will never go to church, open a Bible, or say a prayer. But all of humanity is in search for meaning and purpose. Most people don't doubt the existence of God; they simply are not certain of the relevance of God.

When other people see our good deeds—when they observe a pattern of ethical behavior and philanthropy in our lives—they question our motivation. What could possibly motivate such action? The answer, of course, is our faith—our warm personal trust in Jesus Christ. That is the reason for our good deeds—not to gain God's favor but to show that we already know Him.

What's the motivation behind your good deeds?

Faith That Works

As the body without the spirit is dead, so faith without deeds is dead. JAMES 2:26

Faith and works actually are two sides of the same coin. To best understand their synergistic connection, we must remember Paul's teachings connected to faith, as well as the truth that James outlines. For example, in Galatians 2:16, Paul writes, "Know that a man is not justified by observing the law, but by faith in Jesus Christ. So we, too, have put our faith in Christ Jesus that we may be justified by faith in Christ and not by observing the law, because by observing the law no one will be justified."

To best understand faith and works, they must be tied together, back to back. Paul calls attention to faith as the root; James looks at faith as the fruit. Paul looks at what happens at the moment of salvation, while James looks at what happens after salvation. Paul focuses on God's part, and James focuses on man's part. Paul deals with justification, and James deals with validation. Paul is against legalism, and James is against a lazy, presumptive lifestyle.

Following their collective example, we shouldn't try to cut faith and works apart. Instead, we should wrap them together.

The great theologian John Calvin once wrote, "It is faith alone that justifies, but faith that justifies can never be alone." James doesn't match faith against works. Rather, he states with confidence that biblical faith works. Together, faith and works comprise a harmonious blend of sound theology, and they should be a compatible combination in the life of every follower of Jesus.

Promotion with Caution

Not many of you should presume to be teachers, my brothers, because you know that we who teach will be judged more strictly. JAMES 3:1

The mature believer aspires to achieve his or her leadership goals cautiously because such roles of influence carry with them increasing levels of accountability to God. If you are applying for God to use you as an instructor, guide, mentor, tutor, coach, or trainer in someone else's spiritual life, be cautious. Don't impulsively volunteer your hand.

Remember that leading and teaching are not just formal positions. They include casual phone calls and conversations about life's big issues with people who trust and follow your opinion. They often include life-on-life mentoring of those around you. That's why, according to James, a desire for greater influence must be tempered with the reality that there will be stricter judgment for those who find themselves in leading roles.

James is not proposing that we do away with teachers, but he is calling for *mature* leaders and teachers. He is not saying that *no one* should teach, but rather that *everyone* shouldn't try to teach. He is not telling us not to lead at all, but rather to be careful and cautious if we desire to lead.

He offers these words of caution because he knows the human condition: "We all stumble in many ways," he writes in James 3:2. No, leaders and teachers aren't exempt.

James doesn't say that a person who stumbles is disqualified to teach. Nor does he imply that we have to become perfect before we can teach. What he is saying is this: Go ahead and start, but promote with caution. Take the lead with prudence. Be circumspect and attentive. Keep both eyes wide open.

The Tongue: Small Muscle, Big Force

[T]he tongue is a small part of the body, but it makes great boasts. JAMES 3:5

Nowhere in Scripture is there a more focused and magnified look at the tongue than in James 3. But although James frequently refers to the two-ounce muscle we know as the tongue, he's not engaging in an anatomical discourse. Rather, his emphasis is on self-control in the area of our speech.

James makes it clear that one single word can carry a lifelong, ever-expanding impact. He uses three scenes from nature to illustrate this: a small bit in a large horse's mouth, a small rudder anchored beneath a huge ship, and a small spark that ultimately inflames a whole forest. "When we put bits into the mouths of horses to make them obey us, we can turn the whole animal," he writes. "Or take ships as an example. Although they are so large and are driven by strong winds, they are steered by a very small rudder wherever the pilot wants to go. . . . Consider what a great forest is set on fire by a small spark" (James 3:3–5).

It is sobering and convicting to think that the words that roll off our tongues every day carry so much weight and influence. With words, we can encourage or destroy. We can praise or criticize. We can edify or intimidate.

Before you head off to work each day, commit your speech to God. Ask God to help you tell the truth and not to shade your speech with lies or half-truths. Ask Him to help you not to speak harshly, critically, impatiently, or unkindly; not to spread rumors and gossip; and to avoid the crude, immoral, irreverent words and jokes that might slip from your mouth. Consider carefully the power you carry around in your mouth, and ask God to strengthen your self-control.

Taming the Wildest of Beasts

All kinds of animals . . . have been tamed by man, but no man can tame the tongue. JAMES 3:7–8

So many things in God's creation lead us to curiosity, fascination, even awe. For example, have you ever been to Sea World, the circus, or a zoo? It is amazing to observe a huge whale escorting a trainer across the pool, a Siberian tiger jumping through hoops, or an enormous elephant walking on its back legs.

Our ability to tame and train wild animals is amazing. But there is one beast that none of us can train alone, no matter how hard we try. That beast is the tongue. "With the tongue we praise our Lord and Father, and with it we curse men, who have been made in God's likeness," James writes. "Out of the same mouth come praise and cursing. My brothers, this should not be" (James 3:9–10).

The tongue is the great betrayer. It relentlessly tells others what is going on inside of us. In Matthew 12:34, Jesus says, "[O]ut of the overflow of the heart the mouth speaks." In some ways, to tame the tongue is to tame the heart. A change of heart promises the possibility of a change of speech.

A friend once said, "Whatever is in us comes out when we are squeezed." If envy, anger, deception, or arrogance is in our hearts, it will come out when we are squeezed. On the other hand, if our hearts are full of love, joy, peace, patience, kindness, gentleness, faithfulness, and self-control, those, too, will come out when we're under pressure.

All real speech therapy must start with heart training. And heart training is best achieved under the guidance of the Master heart surgeon, Jesus. Concentrate on this prayer today: "May the words of my mouth and the meditation of my heart be pleasing in your sight, O LORD, my Rock and my Redeemer" (Psalm 19:14).

What comes out when you are squeezed by the trials and pressures you face at work?

The Power of Personal Ethic

Who is wise and understanding among you? Let him show it by his good life,
by deeds done in the humility that comes from wisdom. JAMES 3:13

The power of one good deed is hard to measure.

Jesus explored this idea in what we have come to know as the Sermon on the Mount. He urged his followers to spread their influence by serving as "salt" and "light" in a dark world. "In the same way," He told them, "let your light shine before men, that they may see your good deeds and praise your Father in heaven" (Matthew 5:16).

We must be careful not to misinterpret Jesus' words as "works theology" or a "social gospel." It is neither. He is discussing influence, not salvation; and He is making the point that the greatest instrument of influence to another individual is personal, ethical behavior.

In the Greek language, there are two words for *good*. *Agathos* denotes high quality, and *kalas* means that something is not only good in quality, but also is winsome, beautiful, and attractive. This goodness has a magnetic appeal to it. It invites people to participate. That is what a good life does.

All of us, no matter our age, spiritual maturity, or situation in life, continually stand at the intersection of right and wrong. Sometimes our decisions are private; sometimes they are public. But they are always individual choices. Choosing the right thing, over and over, results in the power of one—one individual demonstrating good deeds and personal ethic to a dark and questioning world.

The marketplace is an ideal place for followers of Christ to use their personal ethic to spread godly influence. When one employee continually makes ethically correct decisions at work, it isn't going to automatically triple the value of his company's stock, nor is it going to turn the workweek into a pleasure cruise. But over time, the practice of individual ethics will have an impact. It will make a difference. It will provide salt to create thirst in unbelievers and release light to a paralyzed, dark world. Doing the right thing is a raw demonstration of goodness.

The Wise and Otherwise (Part One)

Who is wise and understanding among you? JAMES 3:13

What is wisdom? Is it the ability to think on your feet, answer clever riddles, and handle hard questions? Is it being street-smart? Is it being able to read people easily? Is it raw intelligence or academic book knowledge? Is it the ability to roll Mark Twainlike proverbs off the tip of your tongue?

The answer, according to Scripture, is none of the above. In God's view, wisdom is relational. It's about relationships, not about intelligence.

James explains that wisdom can be either authentic or counterfeit. Like so many other godly traits, there is a counterfeit that often appears alongside the genuine article. The counterfeit of faith is presumption. The counterfeit of humility is false humility and self-deprecation. The counterfeit of confidence is self-driven pride. And the counterfeit of wisdom is envy and selfish ambition.

Read what James has to say about that: "But if you harbor bitter envy and selfish ambition in your hearts, do not boast about it or deny the truth. Such 'wisdom' does not come down from heaven but is earthly, unspiritual, of the devil. For where you have envy and selfish ambition, there you find disorder and every evil practice. But the wisdom that comes from heaven is first of all pure; then peace-loving, considerate, submissive, full of mercy and good fruit, impartial and sincere" (James 3:14–17).

Examine your heart. Does the wisdom you possess come from heaven, or is it counterfeit?

The Wise and Otherwise (Part Two)

Who is wise and understanding among you? JAMES 3:13

W*isdom* is a rich biblical word. One of its earliest references in Scripture is built around the personality and life of Solomon. We usually remember Solomon as the man with a thousand wives. But he also was an author, diplomat, engineer, financier, king, philanthropist, philosopher, poet, theologian, and writer of songs (and those are just a few highlights from his résumé).

Second Chronicles tells us that Solomon had one of the most unique opportunities that any human could ever have. God allowed him to ask for anything he wanted—and committed to providing it. And what did Solomon do? He asked for wisdom and knowledge so he could lead the people of Israel (2 Chronicles 1:10).

The wisdom Solomon asked for wasn't theoretical. It wasn't simply textbook knowledge, intellectual horsepower, or even a high IQ. It wasn't persuasion, logic, or rhetoric. What Solomon needed was practical insight into his life and into the lives of people who were within his circle and sphere of responsibility. We're not talking about a small team here. It is estimated that Solomon managed 160,000 people when he was overseeing the construction of the great Temple at Mount Moriah.

Solomon wanted to lead this large group of people effectively, so he asked God for wisdom. Why? He understood that true wisdom is a gift we receive from the Lord, not a capability we develop.

We all should follow Solomon's example in praying for the gift of wisdom. Parents should pray that their kids become wise. Employers should pray that they will be wise and that their employees will receive wisdom.

We may not have to manage 160,000 people every day, but, like Solomon, we do have people continually around us who require our leadership. Consequently, we also have a great need for wisdom. Here's an assignment. Get out a piece of paper and write the words *spouse, parents, kids, boss, coworkers,* and *friends* down the left side of the page. On the right side, write, *What must I do to demonstrate wisdom?* Then, prayerfully fill it out.

The Battle Inside

What causes fights and quarrels among you? Don't they come from your desires that battle within you? JAMES 4:1

Conflict is a fact of life. It comes in all sizes, shapes, and degrees of intensity. It occurs between siblings, between spouses, between workers, between companies, and between nations.

James connects all external conflict with a battle that is raging inside the hearts of men. Whether it's chronic hostility, a misunderstanding, a grudge, or a quarrel that will not go away, the source of the tension is within our own selves. This reminds us of when Jesus humorously pointed out that although we are so concerned about the speck of sawdust in our brother's eye, we should be more focused on the large planks in our own eyes (Matthew 7:3–5).

The battleground of conflict is within our own minds and hearts. Achieving victory in this area doesn't require an external arranging of life and circumstances; it involves coming to peace and settlement within our own hearts. Jesus warned us that we would have trouble in this world, but He also promised that we could still have peace in our hearts because He has already overcome the world (John 16:33).

When we rest in that promise, the desires that battle within us—those selfish attitudes and actions that draw us into conflict with our friends, family members, and coworkers—lose some of their attractiveness. They're still there, of course. But when we trust in Jesus and allow His desires to become our desires, we are less likely to engage in conflict. Peace, not strife, becomes our priority.

Check your heart. Is it full of envy, bitterness, tension, and all the other things that lead to conflict? Or is it brimming over with the peace that only God can bring?

Self-Centered Praying

When you ask, you do not receive, because you ask with wrong motives, that you may spend what you get on pleasures. JAMES 4:3

It has been said that God responds to our prayers with three different answers: "Yes," "No," and "You've got to be kidding." He affirms some prayers with a yes. He says no to others. But then there are those prayers that cause Him to smile and say, "Whom are you trying to fool?"

James makes the case that many times, although we utter words that sound like prayers, they actually are rooted in a self-centered agenda. Rather than being directed to God, they have a selfish ambition at their core. If you want a clue about the motivation behind such prayers, examine the personal pronouns used in James 4:3. The word *you* is used no fewer than five times. Instead of being centered on God, the prayers are all about us.

The debaters among us would step back and quote Matthew 7:7: "Ask and it will be given to you; seek and you will find; knock and the door will be opened to you." Certainly that promise is available to followers of Christ, but it is not an ironclad pledge that functions like a slot machine with God. We can't just plug our prayers in to God and expect Him to respond automatically and immediately.

Rather, we must attune our hearts to the heart of God. But that can be difficult. Ours is a culture of sophisticated and well-developed role-playing. We are so used to plastering smiles on our faces when we are anything but happy inside. Our culture has discouraged authenticity and transparency. This has had a detrimental effect on the way we pray. We think we can put on a façade before we come to God, but we forget that He knows what we want before we ask. We forget that He knows our innermost thoughts before we even think them.

Next time you pray, remember that God already knows your heart. So don't come to Him with a list of self-centered requests. Don't put the spotlight on yourself. Just talk to Him as if He were your loving Father. Because He is.

Returning to God (Part One)

Submit yourselves, then, to God . . . and he will lift you up. JAMES 4:7, 10

It may seem a bit odd for a follower of Christ to talk about *returning* to God. After all, aren't we supposed to be walking with Him on a daily basis?

Yes, but it's also a fact that most repentance occurs *after* Christian conversion, not at the time of our conversion. Even after we become believers in Jesus, it doesn't take much for us to move away from intimate lives with God. When that happens, we often respond by denying that the alienation has occurred. Or we put up a front and pretend that nothing is wrong. Occasionally we admit it and either try to change ourselves, or we just give up.

None of these responses will work. The only thing we can do when we lose our intimacy with God is admit it and return to Him. In other words, we must repent from whatever caused us to break fellowship with God in the first place.

The pathway back to God is not a complicated one, but it is one that demands a bending of the human will. In James 4:7–10, we find eight steps that help us in that process.

First, we must submit ourselves to God, which involves arranging of every area of our lives under His control (v. 7). This is not a subtle, casual drifting back to God. It is the decisive, urgent, clearly focused act of arranging our lives under God in every particular area.

Next, we must resist the devil (v. 7). This is literally the idea of standing in full battle array. We must come to fight. We must think back with vivid imagery to the experience that Jesus had in the desert. Satan *will* flee from us if we resist him.

We'll address the remaining six steps tomorrow. In the meantime, evaluate yourself in two areas: Are you intentionally focusing every aspect of your life—from your work to your thought life to your relationships—under God's control? And are you actively engaged in resisting the devil, no matter what kind of temptation he throws at you?

Returning to God (Part Two)

Submit yourselves, then, to God . . . and he will lift you up. JAMES 4:7, 10

As we learned yesterday, the first two steps we must take to return to God involve submitting to Him and resisting the devil. Neither is easy, but both are necessary. The same is true for the remaining six steps.

Third, we must focus on moving near to God (v. 8). We often have difficulty distinguishing between the conviction of the Holy Spirit and the condemnation of Satan. But with God's help, we *can* tell the difference. The conviction of the Holy Spirit is full of hope, whereas the condemnation of Satan is a downward pull of hopelessness. As James 4:8 reveals, God will move toward us when we focus on moving toward Him.

Next, we must cleanse our hands (v. 8). To cleanse our hands literally means to wash ourselves and become pure. This is an outward purging. We must eliminate any specific outward and external sins or sin patterns.

Fifth, we must purify our hearts, or make an inward examination of our attitudes (v. 8). This involves looking intently at ourselves and eradicating all the junk. Only by purifying our hearts will we be able to stand in the presence of God (Psalm 24:3–4).

Sixth, we must feel sorrowful for our sins (v. 9). James is calling for honest, vulnerable confrontation with sin. This is often overlooked. Many times, repentance is merely a mental assent that we did something wrong. But there's huge difference between repentance and remorse. Remorse is feeling sorry that we got caught; repentance is coming to grips with reality of our sins and expressing authentic sorrow over it.

Seventh, we must respond with visible signs of repentance (v. 9). We must grieve, to be sure, but we also must change our actions and our attitudes. If we say we're sorry yet continue to do wrong, we may as well have never said anything in the first place.

Finally, we must reverse our response to our circumstances and to God (v. 9). Rather than engage in shallow laughter when confronted with sin or wrongdoing, we must respond how God would respond, with mourning.

By walking through these steps, our actions show God what He already knows to be in our hearts: humility. And when we humble ourselves before the Lord, He will lift us up. When we return to Him, He welcomes us with open arms.

God's Business Credo (Part One)

Now listen, you who say, "Today or tomorrow we will go to this or that city, spend a year there, carry on business and make money." Why, you do not even know what will happen tomorrow. What is your life? You are a mist that appears for a little while and then vanishes. Instead, you ought to say, "If it is the Lord's will, we will live and do this or that." As it is, you boast and brag. All such boasting is evil. JAMES 4:13–16

A group of Hebrew businessmen are having an evening strategy session. Maps of the Roman Empire are spread out in front of them in the candlelit room. The atmosphere is similar to the electricity present when a twenty-first-century entrepreneur and his board of directors meet to discuss growth opportunities. One fellow leans over, points at the city of Philippi, and says, "I'll spend the next year here." Another puts his finger on another growth market and says, "I'm going to Ephesus tomorrow."

This mind-set, which apparently was just as real in New Testament times as it is in today's entrepreneurial, expanding marketplace, deeply concerned James. His warning is clear: God does not frown upon planning, but He does frown when He sees a man who considers himself to be secure without God.

James wasn't opposed to smart business strategy; he was opposed to cavalier boasting about the future. The businessmen in the candlelit room made presumptions about their time and their schedules. They presumed that there actually would be a tomorrow, when in reality, nobody can guarantee that tomorrow will ever come. They presumed about their ability and mobility when they said, "We *will* go." They presumed about their success of their work when they said, "This is what *will* happen; this is the guaranteed result and outcome."

What kind of presumptions are you making in your life? Do you have your whole future planned out, or are you willing to let God set the agenda for you?

God's Business Credo (Part Two)

Now listen, you who say, "Today or tomorrow we will go to this or that city, spend a year there, carry on business and make money." Why, you do not even know what will happen tomorrow. What is your life? You are a mist that appears for a little while and then vanishes. Instead, you ought to say, "If it is the Lord's will, we will live and do this or that." As it is, you boast and brag. All such boasting is evil. JAMES 4:13–16

There's nothing wrong with planning. Many Scripture passages speak of the necessity of counting the cost before you begin a construction project or of consulting wise counselors before embarking on a new venture.

In this passage in James, however, the businessmen made one fatal mistake: They failed to consult God about their plans. They neglected to follow the advice in Psalm 37:5—they forgot about committing their plans to the Lord. They didn't give God a second thought—their entire initiative was made as if He didn't even exist.

That is certainly not the approach we need to take if we want to do business God's way. At the beginning of each day, we must pause to recognize God's supremacy. Rather than make arrogant presumptions about the future, we must accept the reality of human frailty (James 4:14). We must acknowledge that despite all our planning and strategizing, we don't know what will happen tomorrow; we don't even know if there will be a tomorrow.

We must live as if we understand what life really is—a declining shadow (Psalm 102:11), a whiff of breath (Job 7:7), a vanishing cloud (Job 7:9), and a fleeting wildflower (Psalm 103:15).

In summary, God's business credo is this: Plan carefully and follow through on those plans, but never forget the presence of a sovereign God, the frailty of man, and the mysterious unpredictability of life.

Four Classes of Wealth

Now listen, you rich people . . . JAMES 5:1

When it comes to economic status, we tend to put people into two categories: the haves and the have-nots. But if we examine the Scriptures, we can actually find four categories of people when it comes to monetary and spiritual wealth.

The first category includes people who are *poor without and poor within.* They have none of the material goods this world has to offer, and they also are spiritually and morally bankrupt.

The second group includes people who are *rich without and rich within.* Abraham, Joseph, and Lydia are examples from this category—they had a great deal of monetary wealth, and they also were rich spiritually.

Third are those who are *poor without and rich within.* This includes people such as Mary and Joseph (Jesus' earthly parents) and the widow in Mark 12:42 who was commended by Jesus because she gave everything she had to the Temple treasury.

The fourth category includes people who are *rich without and poor within.* It is this group that James addresses in James 5. These people have large bank accounts and sizable stock portfolios, but they lack the moral and spiritual foundation that would allow them to handle their wealth properly. Rather than use their wealth to help those less fortunate and provide well-paying jobs for their employees, they use it to fund their luxurious lifestyles.

It's sometimes tempting to judge people based on their material wealth. In our minds, we elevate the people who belong to the country club and minimize the ones who are part of the "working class." But as these four categories show, some of the people who appear to be the wealthiest actually possess nothing of eternal value, and some of those who appear to be destitute actually possess great eternal wealth.

How do you evaluate the wealth of the people around you? Do you filter it through an eternal lens, or do you look at it from a strictly earthly perspective?

Two Warnings about Wealth

Now listen, you rich people, weep and wail because of the misery that is coming upon you. JAMES 5:1

James doesn't mince words when it comes to admonishing people who are rich monetarily and poor spiritually.

"Your wealth has rotted, and moths have eaten your clothes," he writes. "Your gold and silver are corroded. Their corrosion will testify against you and eat your flesh like fire. . . . Look! The wages you failed to pay the workmen who mowed your fields are crying out against you. The cries of the harvesters have reached the ears of the Lord Almighty. You have lived on earth in luxury and self-indulgence. . . . You have condemned and murdered innocent men, who were not opposing you" (James 5:2–6).

In this passage, James isn't condemning rich people, per se, but he does want to point out what can happen if wealth is elevated above God in a person's life. Two strong warnings seem to flow from these verses: First, that earthly wealth is only temporary; and second, that earthly wealth can produce self-centeredness. It can lead us to hoard our money and become miserly. It can make us mistreat our employees by not paying them decent wages. It can cause us to become so focused on ourselves and our own luxurious comforts that we forget all about other people and their needs.

So what application do these verses have for those of us who want to avoid those traps and handle our wealth in a Christlike manner? James reminds us that the affluent have the greatest responsibility to be stewards of what they have and that God also expects them to be more sensitive and responsive to human needs than those who don't have as much. As Luke 12:48 says, "From everyone who has been given much, much will be demanded; and from the one who has been entrusted with much, much more will be asked."

How are you doing with the amount of wealth—however big or small—that God has entrusted to you? Is it slowly turning you into a self-centered miser, or are you using it to enrich the lives of others?

The Power of Patience

Be patient, then, brothers, until the Lord's coming. JAMES 5:7

Patience is a virtue, or so the saying goes. Based on this passage, it appears that James is in complete agreement with that cliché. He instructs his readers to be patient, and then he illustrates what he means by offering three examples of patience.

First, he brings up the farmer. "See how the farmer waits for the land to yield its valuable crop and how patient he is for the autumn and spring rains," he says (v. 7). Without patience, any kind of agribusiness would be a miserable failure. The farmer does the necessary soil preparation, planting, and maintenance, but beyond that, all he can do is wait. He can't control the weather; he can't make the plants grow faster. And if he tried to hurry their progress, he would destroy them.

As an example of patience in the face of suffering, James uses the "prophets who spoke in the name of the Lord" (v. 10). Next time you feel like complaining because you have it rough at work or because nobody understands you, think about what Elijah, Jonah, or Jeremiah had to endure. Chances are, you've never been pursued by a wicked queen or swallowed by a large fish. And it's a safe bet that you haven't spent more than forty years in the same position without a single success story or convert. (If you want to know what that's like, read the Book of Jeremiah.)

Finally, James mentions Job as an example of someone who persevered and was blessed because of it (v. 11). Talk about a man who had to wait it out with no guarantee of a happy ending! And yet, throughout his sufferings, he refused to give up his belief that "the Lord is full of compassion and mercy" (James 5:11).

What are you waiting for? More important, what does the way you wait say about your faith?

Praying in Every Circumstance

Is any one of you in trouble? He should pray. . . . The prayer of a righteous man is powerful and effective. JAMES 5:13, 16

We have two options when we're faced with days of difficulty, distress, and trouble. We resort to complaining, doubting God, or talking behind His back (as if that were even possible); or we can pray.

No situation or circumstance in life is out of bounds when it comes to communication with God. No matter how bad the difficulty or how great the success, the correct response is to talk to Him about it.

There are no exceptions.

When we're in trouble, we should pray for deliverance (James 5:13). When we're happy, we should offer prayers of praise (v. 13). When we're sick, we should pray for healing (v. 14). When we sin, we should pray for forgiveness (v. 16).

Unfortunately, we sometimes forget to pray. It's easy to hold all our troubles within and think we can get through them on our own. But that only turns us into bitter people who eventually blow up at the slightest provocation. It's also easy to turn outward and dump all our problems on other people. But that can backfire, too. Our friends and coworkers may tire of hearing about all our difficulties, or they may give us bad advice about how to resolve them.

Again, the *only* correct response is to turn upward and respond in prayer and praise.

How do you handle difficult days at work? Do you attempt to carry the burdens all by yourself, or do you bring them to Jesus and ask Him to carry you through?

Just Like Us

Elijah was a man just like us. He prayed earnestly that it would not rain, and it did not rain on the land for three and a half years. Again he prayed, and the heavens gave rain, and the earth produced its crops. JAMES 5:17–18

After reading Old Testament accounts of Elijah's adventures, we might be tempted to elevate him to sainthood. But he was just like us.

Elijah lived out in an evil culture, not secluded in a sterile monastery. He struggled to obey God, just like we do. He encountered times of discouragement and disappointment. He dealt with pride, resentment, depression, and fear. He developed bad habits. He experienced intimidation, failure, and loneliness. He witnessed great miracles by God, but his life also was the inspiration for what we call the "Elijah complex"—the feeling that "I'm the only one left, the only one really serving God, the only one really worthy of God's blessing."

But despite all his struggles and insecurities, Elijah was a praying man. It was prayer that allowed this very ordinary man—a man who was "just like us"—to do extraordinary things. He prayed that it wouldn't rain, and God turned the faucet off. He prayed that it would rain again, and it did.

Elijah wasn't in control of the weather. He wasn't calling the shots for God. But by his prayers, he was letting God and everyone else know that he believed that God could do what he asked. As a result, God used him in a very powerful way to accomplish His purposes in Elijah's world.

Do you sometimes feel as if you are too ordinary, too common, for God to listen to your prayers? Do you ever think that He could never use you because of your internal struggles and insecurities? Remember Elijah. He was just like you, and he accomplished great things for God.

Retrieving the Wandering Brother

My brothers, if one of you should wander from the truth and someone should bring him back, remember this: Whoever turns a sinner from the error of his way will save him from death and cover over a multitude of sins. JAMES 5:19–20

Anyone can wander from the truth. It can happen to the best of us. It can happen to the worst of us.

The word *wander* literally means to float aimlessly in space or to be caught in a pattern off-center. People wander from the truth and from a vibrant relationship with Jesus for many reasons. They might wander because they were hurt by someone who had spiritual authority over them. They might wander because they put their faith in a religious person who disappointed them. They might wander because they are deceived by a teacher who twists the Scriptures to suit her own agenda. They might wander because they have no one to disciple them. They wander because they enjoy their sin too much to give it up.

It's very hard for someone who wanders to pull himself back into line with truth and behavior. That's why Scripture outlines a method of rescue that involves another person coming alongside the wandering believer and literally retrieving him from the wayward path he's on. According to James, the rescuer accomplishes a significant ministry when he does this.

The apostle Paul refers to a similar process in Galatians 6:1: "[I]f someone is caught in a sin," he writes, "you who are spiritual should restore him gently." In this passage, outside help also was necessary to restore the fallen brother. The idea presented here is that such restoration must be done gently.

In either case, God enlists other believers to serve on His rescue team. We must be sensitive to His call and willing to do the difficult work of retrieval. It's not a pleasant task, but it brings with it great eternal rewards.

Is there someone in your life who has wandered from the truth and needs to be "retrieved"? Have you made any rescue attempts? If not, perhaps you should start today.

Vacation Appendix

Well, here it is, time for another few days of rest and relaxation away from the hustle and bustle of the job. Nothing to do but kick back and catch up on your sleep and reading.

If this describes you, just pitch this book into the stack and make sure you take the time to reflect on some of the following questions over the next few days and weeks. Unless, of course, you are a "pack-it-all-in-from-sunup-to-sundown" person. In that case, be very intentional about scheduling time to read through this section. It will help you to assess where you are, where you've been, and where you are headed.

Vacation time is a great time to spend with friends or family—a time to have fun, a time to rest, and also a time to reflect. This section is broken down into seven different daily activities. If your vacation is shorter, then pick and choose a few to focus on, or stretch it into your daily devotional routine once you are back at work. If your vacation is longer, pace yourself and take more time for reflection and prayer.

Whatever the case, make sure you approach this time with an open heart, an open mind, an open journal, and an open Bible. Allow the Lord to speak to you. He will gently and lovingly encourage, correct, and direct you in new ways.

DAY ONE: UNWIND

If you are like most people, it takes twenty-four to forty-eight hours to purge work from the forefront of your mind. Perhaps this activity will help.

Do a massive brain dump in your journal. Write down all the issues that are pressing you at work. List everything: personal conflicts, disappointments, phone calls you forgot to make, ideas that came to you on your travels, a memo you need to send. Don't hold back, get it all down on paper. When it seems to have dried up, just wait a while longer. There's always more.

When you have really finished getting it all on paper, spend time with the Lord, praying over the items you are having a hard time releasing. Ask Him to intervene in these situations, and ask Him to allow you to disconnect from work and plug into Him and your time of rest fully.

DAY TWO: REFLECT

During the next two days, you will have a chance to look back over the past year and do a personal inventory of what has transpired. We will hit a number of categories so spend time where you need to.

- *Spiritual.* How would you describe your walk with Jesus? What about your devotional life? Fellowship with other believers? Prayer and worship life? Other disciplines? Service and care for others? Tithing?

- *Emotional.* Do you feel emotionally healthy? What is your mood most days? How is your temper? When is the last time you cried? What about? How often do you laugh?

- *Mental.* What is the last book you read? What did you learn this year? How much time did you take to think? What new things were you exposed to? What new experts did you meet?

- *Volitional.* How disciplined were you this year? What about your habits— both good and bad? Were they a problem? What commitments did you follow through on? Which ones did you let slip?

- *Physical.* How is your health this year? How often were you sick? Did any serious issues arise this year? When was the last time you had a physical? Visited the dentist? How often did you exercise this year? How was your diet?

Day Three: More Reflection

- *Home.* How has your family life been? How is your relationship with your spouse (if you have one)? Your children (if you have them)? Your siblings and parents (if they are living)? What conflicts exist that need to be worked through? What great moments did you share together?

- *Colleagues.* How are your work relationships? How many new people have you met, either in your field or in your office? Whom have you added to your Rolodex? What conferences did you attend? How are your relationships with customers and vendors?

- *Friends.* What did you do with your close friends this year? What special trips, events, or activities did you enjoy together? What conflicts did you work through? What did you learn about your friends?

Day Four: Here and Now

Take some time to assess what you think and feel about the past year. Read back over your answers to the previous questions. What do you think? How would you grade the past year? What would you change if you could? What are you proud of? How do you feel about it in general? What specific instances elicit a strong response (good or bad) from you? Why?

Day Five: Look Ahead

Today, think creatively and strategically about the upcoming year. It will be an opportunity to address issues that have surfaced in the past three days and also a time to dream and set goals.

- *Issues.* Look back through the above categories, as well as any that you added. List critical issues that surfaced. Leave space to write beneath each issue. Now below each issue begin to think (and pray) creatively about how you would like to see those issues change. Don't write ways to change them; instead, write what new outcome you would like to see come to pass.

- *Dreams.* Now look back through each category again and write down two or three things you would like to accomplish in the coming year in each one. Be creative. Have fun. Dream big.

Day Six: More Looking Ahead

Today is a time to devise action plans for the strategies you developed yesterday. This is a time to be very specific—name names and write in dates. Don't worry about getting it perfect; you can alter it when you get back into your routine. But now is the time to get an action plan for your commitments.

- *Issues.* For each issue outcome, write down your intended method for seeing this outcome come to pass. Then write down target completion dates. Don't get paralyzed by exact dates; just get the month down.

- *Dreams.* Now repeat the same exercise for your dreams. Feel free to edit or list new items you may have thought of since yesterday.

Day Seven: The Word

Today is the day to determine your Scripture reading plan for the year. If you typically read through the Old, New, or both Testaments each year, then you may consider a more thorough examination of a few books—and vice versa. No matter what you've done in the past, today is a new day. Spend this time with the Lord asking Him to renew your love of His Word and to show you where in the Word He would like you to spend your time this year. This is a critical element in your spiritual journey.

After you've completed all these stops, you should be refreshed, reenergized, refocused, and ready to go back to work!

Notes

1. H. A. Ironside, *Studies on Book One of the Psalms* (Neptune, N.J.: Loizeaux Brothers Inc., 1952), 3.
2. Ibid.
3. Ibid, 4.
4. Stewart J. J. Perowne, *The Book of Psalms. 2 Volumes Complete in One* (Grand Rapids, Mich.: Zondervan, 1976), 20–21.
5. John H. Hayes, *Understanding the Psalms* (Valley Forge, Pa.: Judson Press, 1976), 5–11.
6. Charles R. Swindoll, *Active Spirituality* (Dallas: Word, 1994), 3.
7. Ibid.
8. Charles R. Swindoll, ed., *The Living Insights Study Bible* (Grand Rapids, Mich.: Zondervan, 1996), 632.
9. Robert Alden, *Proverbs* (Grand Rapids, Mich.: Baker, 1983), 15.
10. Charles Bridges, revised by George Santa, *A Modern Study in the Book of Proverbs* (Milford, Mich.: Mott Media, 1978), 270.
11. Alden, *Proverbs,* 136.
12. Ibid., 139.
13. Ibid., 147.
14. Swindoll, ed., *The Living Insights Study Bible*, 653.
15. William Arnot, *Studies in Proverbs.* (Grand Rapids, Mich.: Kregel, 1978), 513.
16. Alden, *Proverbs*, 184.
17. Ibid., 202.
18. Ibid., 44.

THREE WAYS TO

LIFE@WORK JOURNAL

The *Life@Work Journal* blends biblical wisdom
and marketplace excellence to help you enjoy a more
fulfilling and successful life at work.

To subscribe, call 1-877-543-9675 or visit www.lifeatwork.com.

IMPROVE YOUR

THE BUILDING BLOCK SERIES:
Ethical Anchors
The Mentoring Blue Print
Framing Your Ambition
The Hard Work of Rest
Cornerstones For Calling
The workplace is certainly one of the scariest testing grounds for personal faith and conviction. Here are five key areas of work where Christians can apply God's truth. Each book is built around sixteen timeless principles.

**THE CORNERSTONES
FOR LIFE AT WORK SERIES:**
A Case for Calling
A Case for Serving
A Case for Skill
A Case for Character
In these four books,
Dr. Thomas Addington
and Dr. Stephen Graves
examine the core issues
of a godly work ethic and
how they become the
cornerstones for Christians
in the workplace.

The Fourth Frontier
Men and women of faith can discover how to have tremendous kingdom influence in and through the new world of work, which is the "Fourth Frontier."

The Life@Work Book
Sixteen respected leaders talk about combining biblical wisdom and marketplace excellence.

Women, Faith, and Work
How ten successful professionals blend belief and business.

LIFE@WORK BOOKS

To find workplace books, check with your local
Christian bookstore or call 1-800-739-7863.

Life@Work
RESOURCES

LIFE AT WORK

LIFE@WORK GATHERINGS

It's been nearly two years since the Life@Work staff began to hear stories about readers who were getting together to discuss articles and to share their experiences in the marketplace. As such reports became more frequent, we dubbed these groups Life@Work Gatherings. The idea has caught on — people want to connect with others. They want to touch base and interact with folks who understand the successes and pressures they face on a daily basis.

To start a Gathering, go to www.lifeatwork.com where you can access discussion questions and special product deals.

Life@Work
RESOURCES